IMAGES
of America
WARNER HOT SPRINGS

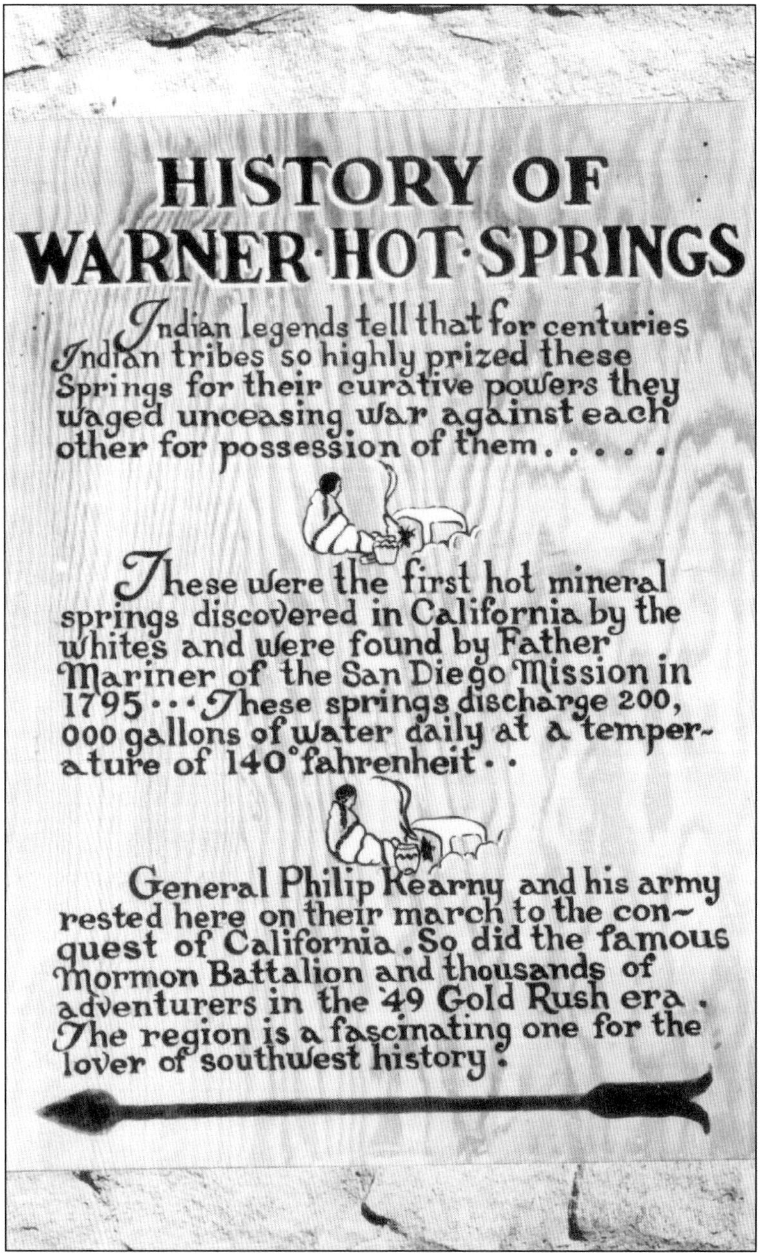

This sign, posted at the hot springs with a brief history of the area, was read by thousands of visitors over many years. (Courtesy Warner Springs Historical Society.)

On the Cover: Three tourists in the 1930s look into the miraculous bubbling mineral waters of Warner Hot Springs. The sulfur waters were sacred to the natives of the area since ancient times and were enjoyed by succeeding generations of travelers and visitors for their healing qualities. (Courtesy Warner Springs Historical Society.)

IMAGES
of America

WARNER HOT SPRINGS

Kathryn Lee Fletcher and
Warner Springs Historical Society

ARCADIA
PUBLISHING

Copyright © 2016 by Kathryn Lee Fletcher and Warner Springs Historical Society
ISBN 978-1-4671-1676-3

Published by Arcadia Publishing
Charleston, South Carolina

Printed in the United States of America

Library of Congress Control Number: 2016941984

For all general information, please contact Arcadia Publishing:
Telephone 843-853-2070
Fax 843-853-0044
E-mail sales@arcadiapublishing.com
For customer service and orders:
Toll-Free 1-888-313-2665

Visit us on the Internet at www.arcadiapublishing.com

To all past, present, and future lovers of Warner Hot Springs, including five generations of my family who have cherished this special place on earth

Contents

ACKNOWLEDGMENTS

Many people have been guardians of Warner Hot Springs history and deserve thanks. Thanks go to Terry Chambers, founder of the Warner Springs Ranch Historical Committee in 1990 and historian at the Sherman Foundation Library; committee members Bill Kettenburg, Lee Bibb, Paul Newell, Steve Monfort, Joe Copp, Griff Henshaw, the late Skip Starkey, Marion Kennedy, and Spike Webb; and especially Betty Rayfield, president of the committee for many years before entrusting it to me. Thanks go to historian Phil Brigandi for his oral interviews, research, and speaker programs throughout the years. Save Our Heritage Organisation of San Diego restored the St. Francis Chapel, Santa Ysabel Store, and, along with the Vista Irrigation Water District, the Warner Carrillo Ranch House. Many families provided photographs, letters, memoirs, and oral histories, especially those of William Henshaw, Sam Taylor, Col. Ed Fletcher, Sidney Furze, and Henry Dart Greene. The short booklet *Old Timers of Southeastern California* by Lester Reed gives a picture of local cowboy life. Bill Schairer, grandson of John Treanor, who founded Mataguay Ranch and had the *History of Warner Springs Ranch and Its Environs* written by Joseph J. Hill and privately published in 1927. Most photographs came from the Warner Springs Historical Society, some obtained in the 1990s from the San Diego Historical Society (now Center), but many are from the private collections of the visitors who enjoyed Warner Springs Ranch for decades. Thank you, Lisa Polanski, Judy Jarvis, and my sister Jane Fletcher for encouragement, and my acquisitions editor Jesse Darland. Unless otherwise noted, all images appear courtesy of the Warner Springs Historical Society.

Additional Arcadia books about this area include *Native Americans of San Diego County*, *Ranchos of San Diego County*, and *Stage Routes of San Diego County*.

INTRODUCTION

The charm of Warner Hot Springs is that of a freer bygone day, a bit of Old California tucked away among the mountains of San Diego County, remaining much as it was when the mission fathers first saw it. From among the oak, pine, and cedar trees at the peak of Hot Springs Mountain, you see a gigantic panorama. To the west are green valleys, the purple slopes of Mount Palomar, and the far-off blue Pacific Ocean. To the east lies the dun waste of the great Anza Borrego Desert, enlivened only by the sapphire jewel of the Salton Sea. The historic Anza Trail crosses the valley, as does the Pacific Crest Trail on its way from Mexico to Canada. There is a delightful four-season climate, and nowhere else are there such health-giving springs within such a spacious and beautiful countryside. The nearest town of any size is more than 30 miles away.

Native Americans occupied San Diego County for a period in excess of 10,000 years, including the Cupeño and Cahuilla tribes at Warner Hot Springs, known in ancient days as Cupa. Later thousands of visitors from all over the world would come, but the Indians in the area had been living around and bathing in the therapeutic waters for generations.

In 1776, Capt. Juan Bautista de Anza marched through on his way to San Francisco. In 1795, a Spanish expedition let by Fray Juan Mariner visited, and the adventurers were struck by a remarkable phenomenon, the gushing hot mineral waters. The first record of ownership of the rancho was in 1834 by Silvestre de la Portilla, but he abandoned the ranch, and in 1840, Jose Antonio Pico made a formal application for the ranch and springs he called Agua Caliente.

In 1830, twenty-three-year-old John Warner ventured from his native Connecticut to St. Louis and joined a trading expedition of Jedediah Smith. Smith died in Santa Fe, but the expedition ventured farther west, passing through the beautiful Valle de San Jose. In Los Angeles, Warner met and married Anita Gale, who had been raised as a ward of the widowed mother of Pio Pico, later the last governor of California under Mexican rule. Warner became a naturalized Mexican citizen and in 1844 applied for the Rancho San Jose del Valle land grant, claiming it was unoccupied. The grant to Warner was approved by the legislature on May 21, 1845, and he was awarded ownership of the 47,000-acre Valle de San Jose. He officially changed his name to Juan Jose Warner and the name of the region to Warner's Ranch. Lt. William Emory, chief of the Corps of Topographical Engineers for the Army of the West and an early visitor to the springs, wrote in 1846: "A day will come no doubt, when the invalid and pleasure seeking portion of the white race, will assemble here to drink and bathe in these waters, ramble over the hills which surround it on all sides, and sit under the shade of the great live oaks that grow in the valley."

The Indians were not disturbed in their possession of the springs but should have presented their claims of ownership to protect their interests. Warner built a ranch house a few miles from the springs where he lived with his wife and three children and established a trading post. Gen. Stephen Kearny's army and the Mormon Battalion, bound for the conquest of California, rested in the green meadows from their fearful march across the desert before they fought the Battle of San Pasqual. In 1851, Antonia Garra, a Cupeño residing at the springs, led a resistance of various tribes against the white man, killing some at the springs. Warner's ranch house was burned and his livestock stolen, and he left, never to return. The revolt failed, and Garra was found guilty of treason, murder, and theft and executed in January 1852. Warner, later elected to the California State Senate, diligently fought for Indians' rights and protection despite his experience. He became a newspaper publisher and served as the first president of the Southern California Historical Society.

In 1856, Warner sold the land to Henry Hancock. Vicenta Carrillo, a prominent Californio woman rancher, and her husband, Ramon, purchased a portion of the grant and built an adobe ranch house beside the immigrant trail in 1857. In 1858, John Butterfield established the first transcontinental stagecoach line from St. Louis to San Francisco, carrying passengers and mail in an average of 23 days. The Carrillo Ranch House became a regular stop for the Butterfield Stage and thousands of people migrating westward. The Valle de San Jose was the first glimpse of the promised land for many after crossing the great southwestern deserts. The house is now fully restored as the Warner-Carillo Ranch House, part of the National Historic Landmark known as the Warner's Ranch. Operated as a museum by Save Our Heritage Organisation and owned by the Vista Irrigation District, the museum tells the story of stagecoach riders, cattlemen, vaqueros, pioneers, and settlers who spent time at this home, stage stop, and trading post.

In 1880, Gov. John G. Downey became sole owner of the Warner Ranch. During this time, the question of ejecting the Indians without a fight was a problem, and the Indians had nothing but the right of possession.

The Indians from Cupa attempted to maintain possession of their lands near the springs, but it was the policy of the government officials at that time not to give Indians their rights but to dispossess them. Downey's heir J. Downey Harvey brought suit in the 1890s to eject the Indians. They lost in San Diego courts and took their fight to the Supreme Court, where they again lost their rights in 1901. In 1903, they were forcibly transported by 100 fully armed soldiers and teams 30 miles west to the Pala Reservation in a "Trail of Tears" and settled among a distinctly different Luiseno people, with whom they eventually became integrated. Some Cupeños took to the hills and live today along with Cahuilla Indians on the nearby Los Coyotes and other reservations. The original Cupa village underwent the first of many renovations, and the adobes were remodeled as guest casitas.

In 1911, William G. Henshaw, who built Lake Henshaw in 1922, purchased the Warner Ranch. Many improvements were made under his long ownership as the Warner Resort Company. There were stables for horseback riding, a tennis court, hunting, a school, and a trading post. During World War I, the resort was a rehabilitation center, and during World War II, pilots practiced landings at the airport. Modern pools were built, and even with wartime gas rationing, the resort was popular and within reach. In 1945, a par-3 nine-hole golf course, a dining room, a lodge, and a dance hall were added, along with more cabins and a new trading post. It was a popular film location and retreat of Hollywood stars and everyday families from San Diego, Orange, and Los Angeles Counties, especially in the 1950s, 1960s, and 1970s. In the 1960s, an 18-hole golf course was added.

The Henshaw Warner Resort Company sold in 1975, and several owners have come and gone since, but Warner Hot Springs has retained its idyllic beauty and fame as a scenic and nature-blessed place of wonder. Generations of families have returned year after year, and nowhere else in Southern California is there a resort similar to it, with such health-giving springs and beautiful countryside. There is only one Warner Hot Springs.

One

CUPA

Fifty earthquake faults run through the Valle de San Jose from the Gulf of California to Lake Elsinore. When normal seepage is blocked off by a slippage or fracture along a fault line, hot water bubbles up from the depths. There is little record of recent seismic activity around Warner Hot Springs, and the flow and temperature seem to have remained fairly constant through recorded history.

Archeologists have established prehistoric occupation around Warner Hot Springs for 6,000 years. Indian tribes congregated where they found water and other natural resources. The hot springs area known as Palatingua was used in times of little rain by many tribes with differing language derivations. Among them were the Diguenos, who called the hot springs Jajopin, and the Cahuillas, who called the place Ko-Pa or Kupa, thus becoming Cupeños in Spanish records. Cupeño Indians, a very small tribe, are primarily located on the nearby Los Coyotes and Pala Indian Reservations in San Diego County. The Cahuilla Indians are primarily located on Los Coyotes and in Riverside County.

The Cupeño Indians were not nomadic and occupied what was called under Spanish rule the Rancheria Jocopin and the Agua Caliente area before the year 1700, with temporary shelters close to both warmth and fresh water and farming as the need arose. The valley had been their ancestral tribal grounds from time immemorial, and some lived at Mataguay, Puerto de la Cruz, and near the present-day Lake Henshaw dam. They attached great religious value to the hot springs, which they used for leaching their acorns, washing their clothes, and bathing.

The original Indian village at the springs, of combustible homes, was burned after the Garra Raid in 1851, the last resistance to the complete domination by those who moved in and took over the land they thought was theirs. They rebuilt their rancheria with a street of adobe homes, which they learned to make from the missionaries. It still exists today along the banks of the hot springs.

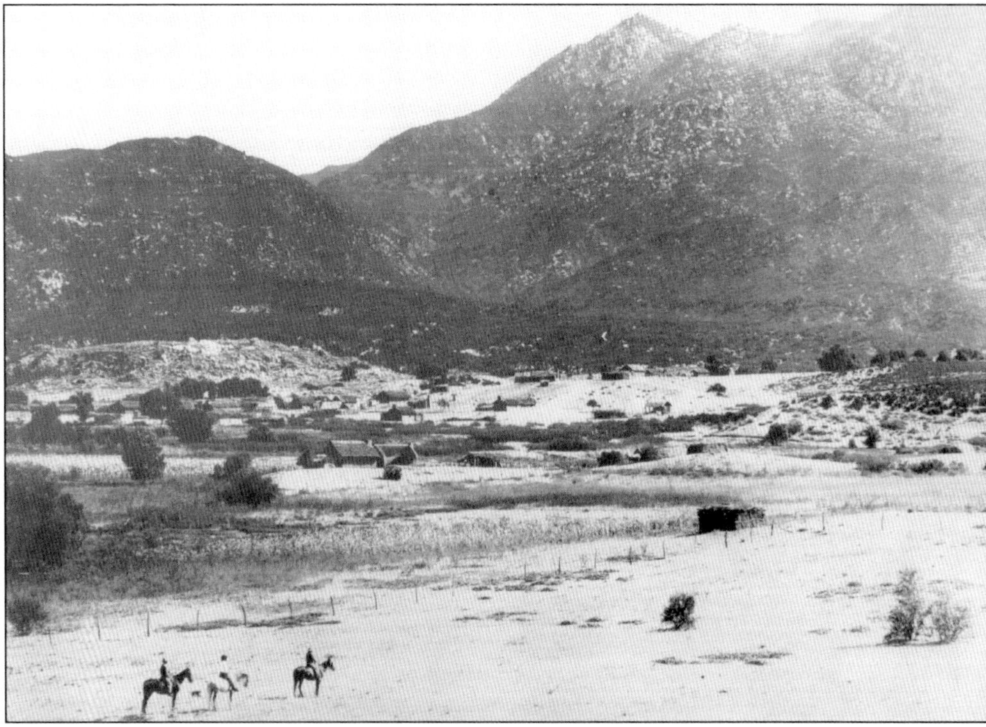

A photograph from 1908 shows a snowy valley and the original village of Cupa in a view looking east towards the 6,500-foot peak of Hot Springs Mountain. The valley ranges from 2,800 to 3,500 feet in elevation. It is no uncommon thing to see snow during the winter months and small ponds and lakes in the valley in years of heavy rain.

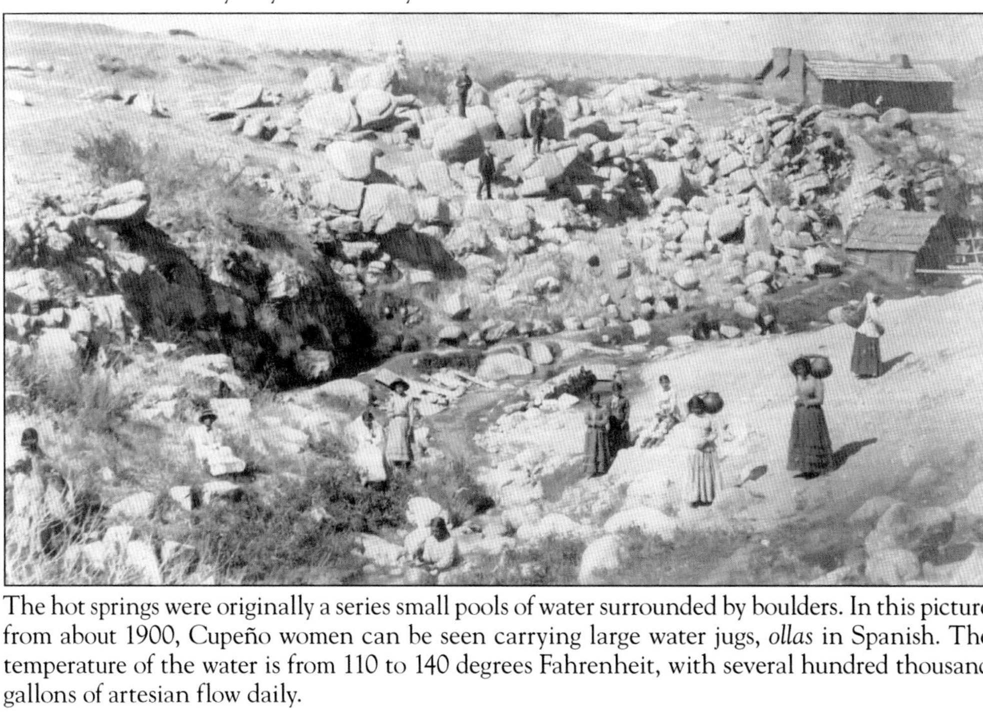

The hot springs were originally a series small pools of water surrounded by boulders. In this picture from about 1900, Cupeño women can be seen carrying large water jugs, *ollas* in Spanish. The temperature of the water is from 110 to 140 degrees Fahrenheit, with several hundred thousand gallons of artesian flow daily.

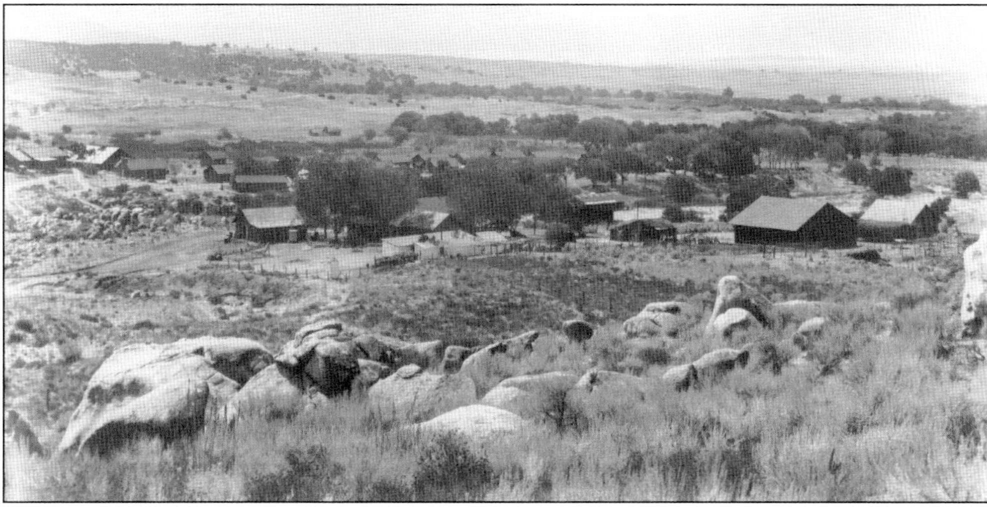

This early panorama looking southeast shows the village after the removal of the Cupa in 1903. Note that the original thatched roofs have been replaced with shake roofs in this photograph. The size of the original beams in the adobes was determined by the size of trees used for them. When they were remodeled, new beams made the adobes larger and taller.

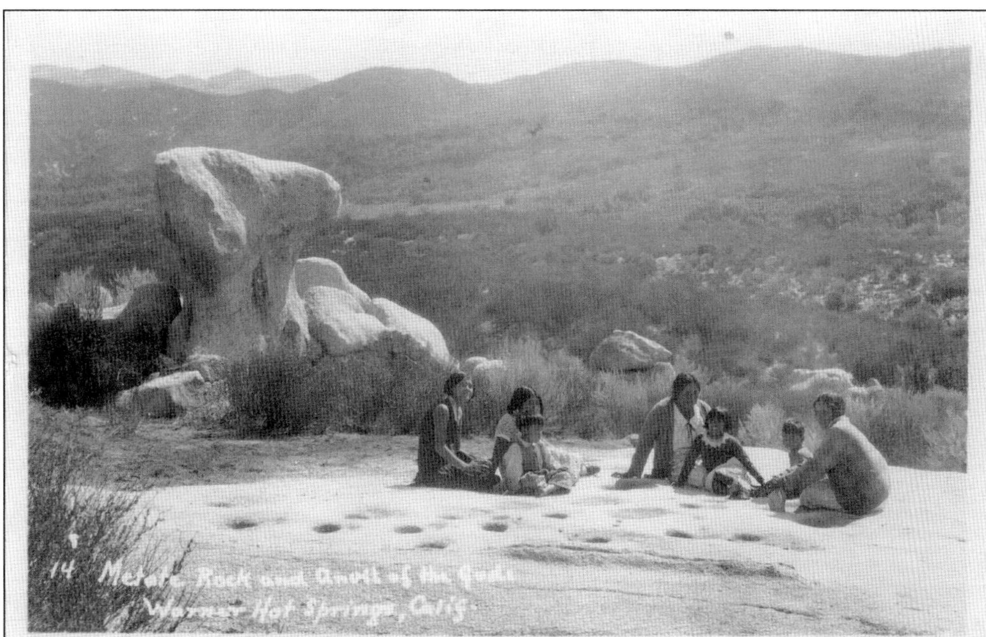

Metate Rock, above the hot springs, has over 50 grinding holes or *morteros* in the immediate area, some of the deeper ones worn down to 10 to 12 inches. Shown in this picture are Martha, Lucille, and Elizabeth Ortega, Felicita Hyde, Stanley Maxey, Roscinda Nolasquez, and Joe Blacktooth. Descendants of some of these families are still in the area.

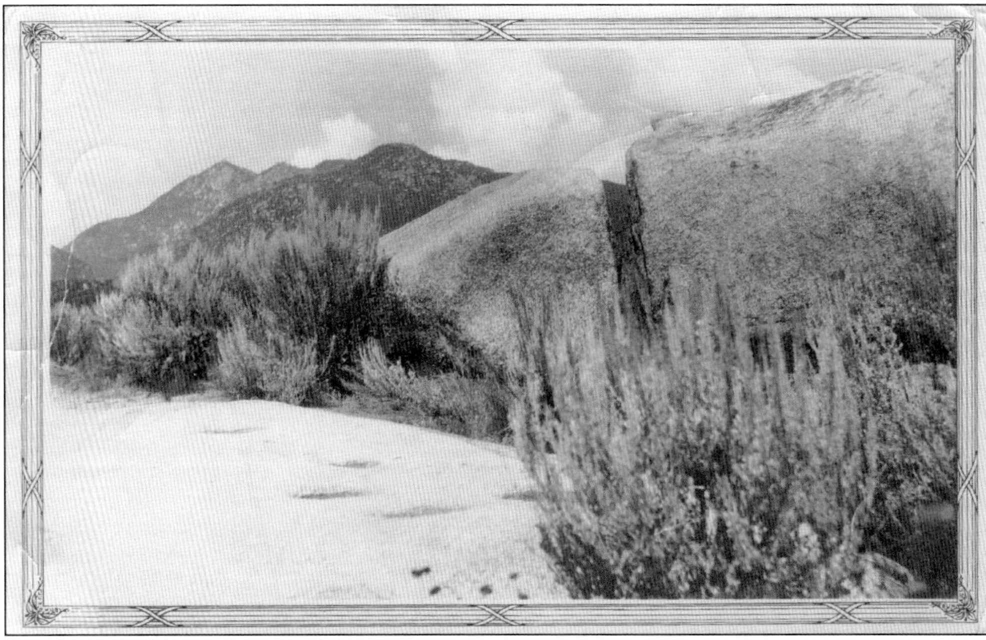

Another picture shows Metate Rock. A senior state geologist estimated that it would take 300 years of daily use to wear down the granite rock. Other morteros can be found upstream in the cultural preserve and in the surrounding residential area of Los Tules, previously a farm of Adolfo Moro.

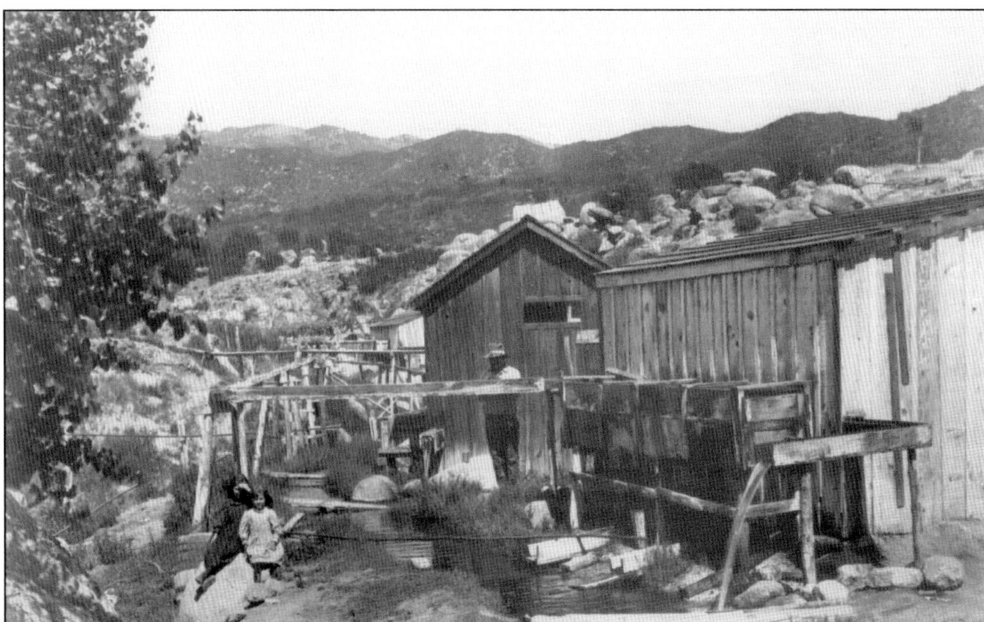

This picture from the late 1800s shows the wooden bathhouse built by the Indians. A quarter-mile-long wooden trough carried hot water from the springs. A soak cost 25¢. In 1903, Alejandro Barber and Cinon Moro were the last hereditary owners of the Indian bathhouses at the springs. In 1908, they were torn down and replaced by a 16-room bathhouse.

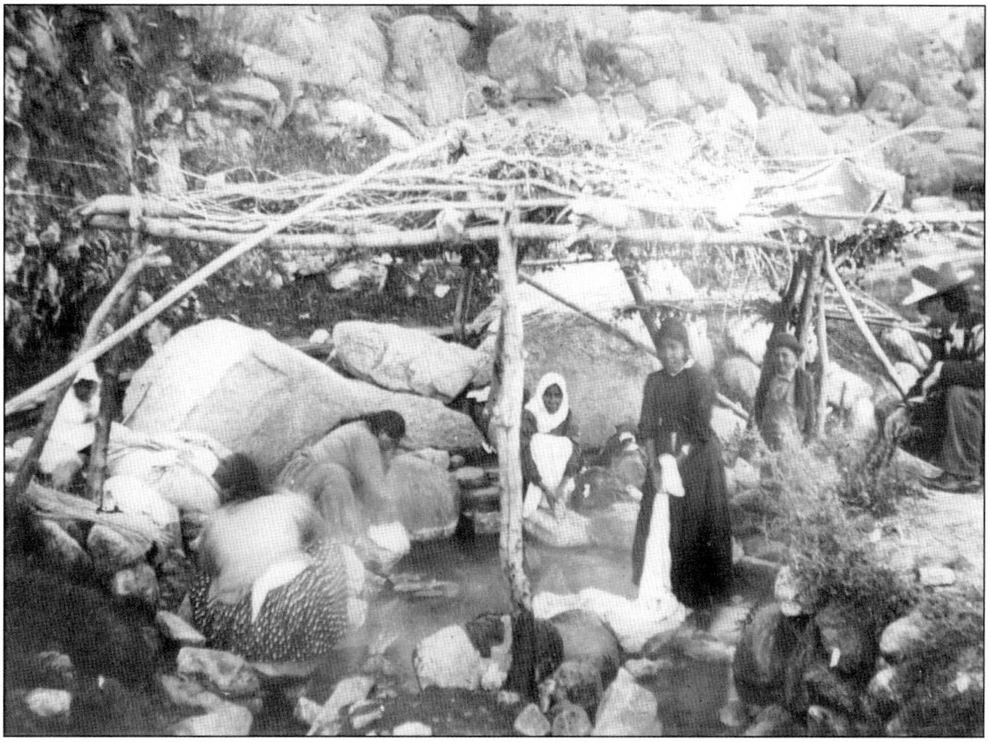

Indian women under a ramada shade structure at the springs do laundry not only for themselves but also for visitors. The Cupeños were also known as the "Blacktooth Clan" as a result of exposure to the waters of the spring since birth, which gave them their characteristic black teeth from the charged sodium sulfide waters.

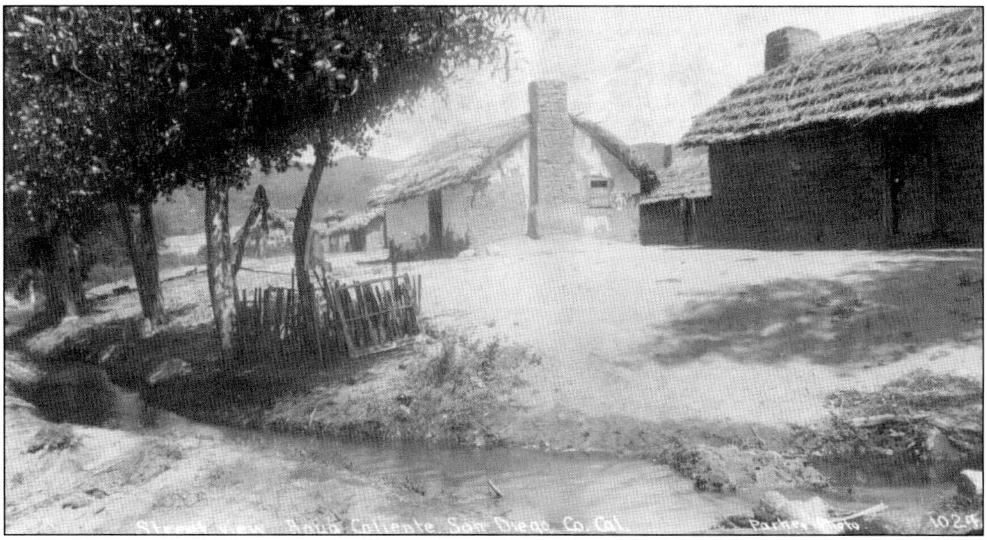

Early photographs of the original village show roofs made of thatch and a stream bringing water from the springs near the homes. The mingling of the hot springs with the cold spring nearby made the waters soft and pleasant for bathing. Benjamin Hayes, in his diary crossing the continent in 1849, tells of how at night, with snow on the ground, the Indians bathed in the water all night to keep warm.

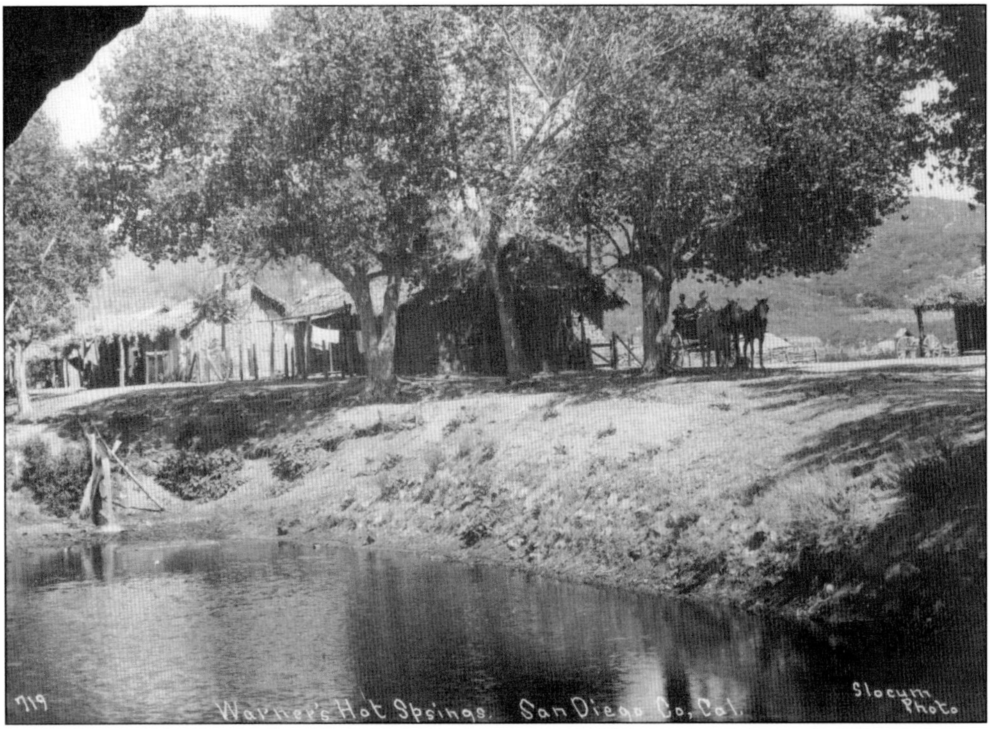

Native cottonwood trees surround the homes and a pond, giving much-needed shade during the hotter months. There were many more cottonwoods and willows in the valley, but drought conditions and the pumping of the giant aquifer beneath have caused many to die. Pines and oaks have also been damaged by pine beetle and golden oak borer and sadly lost.

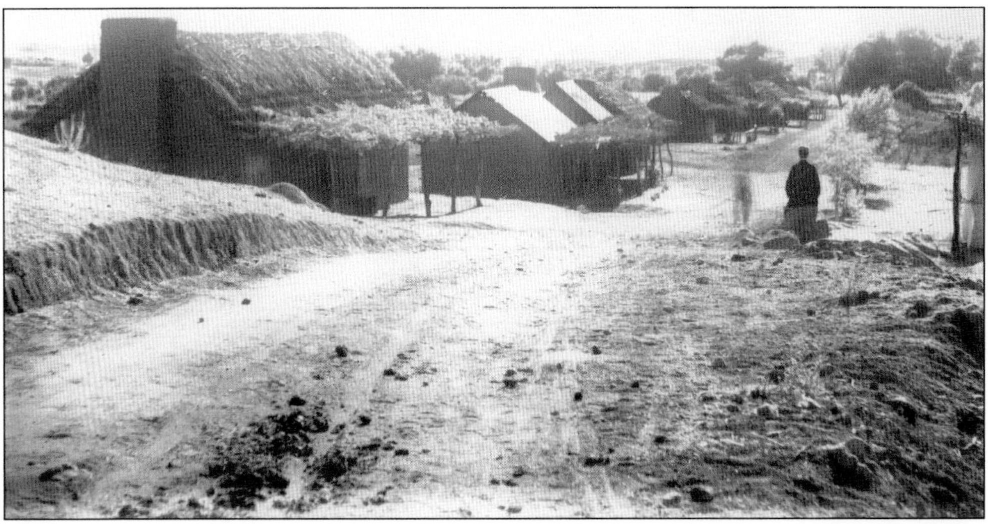

This is the main street of Cupa in a view looking west. The inhabitants and names of the original village homes were identified by Roscinda Nolasquez, the last living Cupeño from the 1903 removal, in an interview with historian Phil Brigandi in 1983. A copy of the handwritten map and her descriptions is included at the end of the book. On the fateful night before their removal, the Indians called on their god Chungichnish and placed a curse on all white men who supplanted them at the springs.

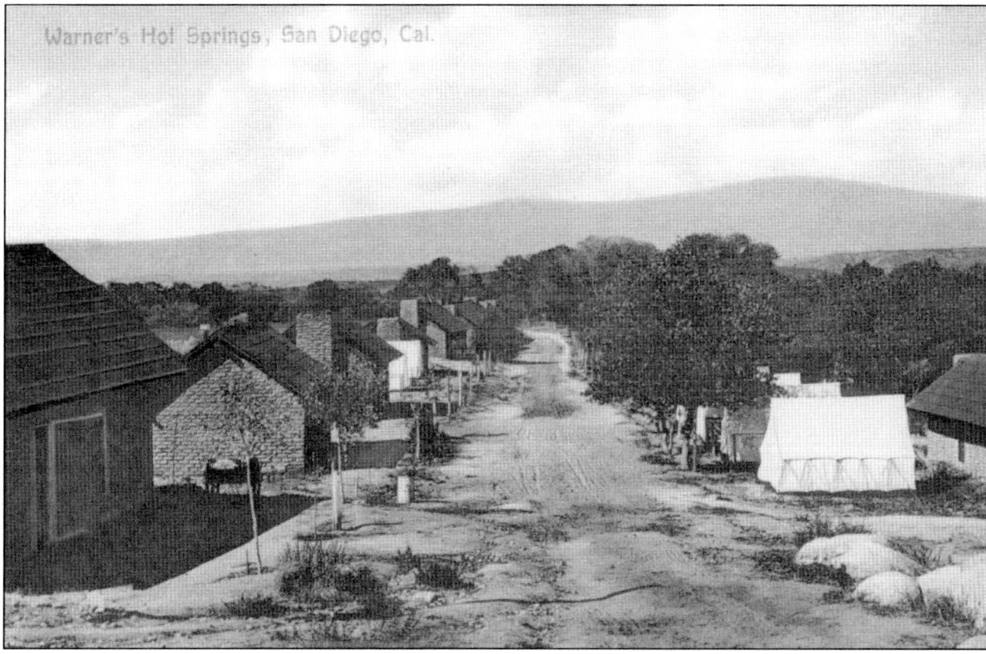

A view of the main street in 1915 shows the remodeled adobes and tent cabins. In 1908, manager F.S. Sanderford had accommodations for 100 to 125 people in 50 rooms in the adobe houses and 25 tents. An ice plant stored 1,000 pounds a day, and a complete water system costing $2,000 brought water from the springs to the casitas, a vegetable garden, and a dairy herd of 12 Jersey cows.

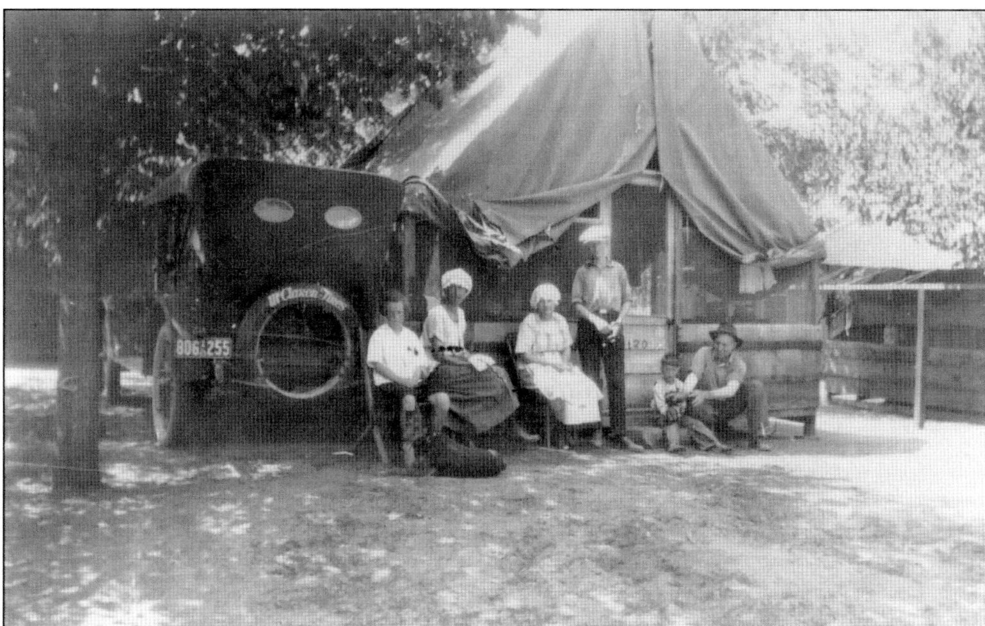

This photograph from 1923 shows a family in a wooden tent cabin. By this date, there was an early dining hall and the first of two concrete Olympic-sized pools built by William Henshaw, who bought the ranch in 1911. He also planted 360 shade trees, including cork elms, black locusts, and white maples.

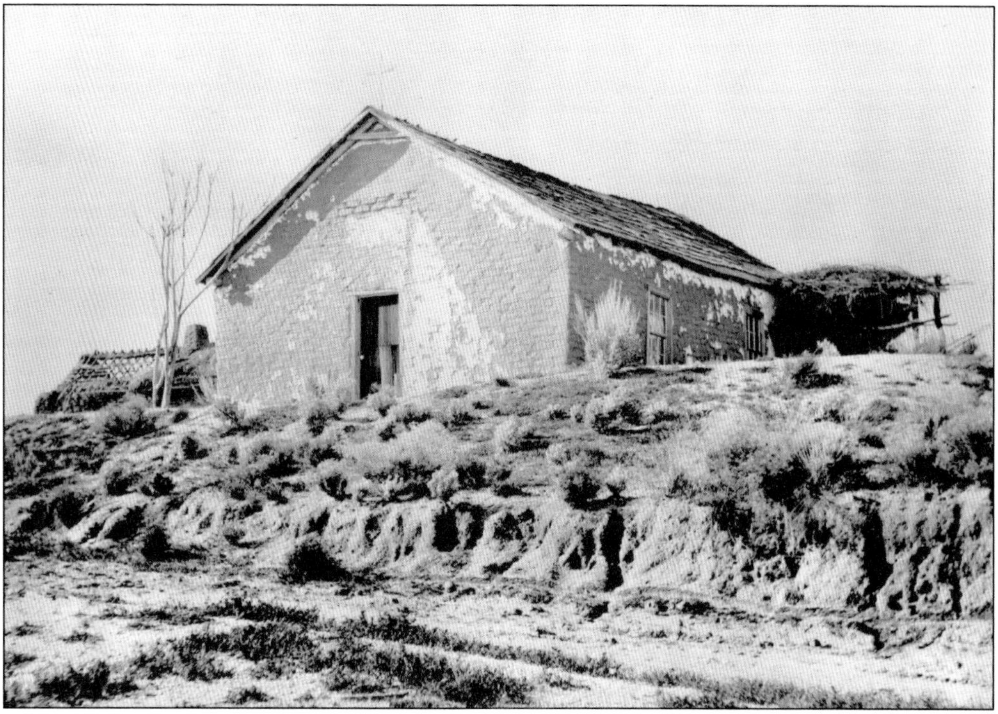

In this 1908 photograph, the Chapel of St. Francis is shown in disrepair. Reported to have been built in 1830, it may have originally been used as a barn or granary. The original *asistencia*, which no longer exists, is seen in the background. The photograph below shows the chapel as it is today. Col. Ed Fletcher, who negotiated the purchase of the ranch by William Henshaw from the Downey heirs, and his brother-in-law ranch manager E.C. Batchelder were sympathetic to the Indians, allowing them to use the old bathhouse for their ailments and bury their dead in the old graveyard.

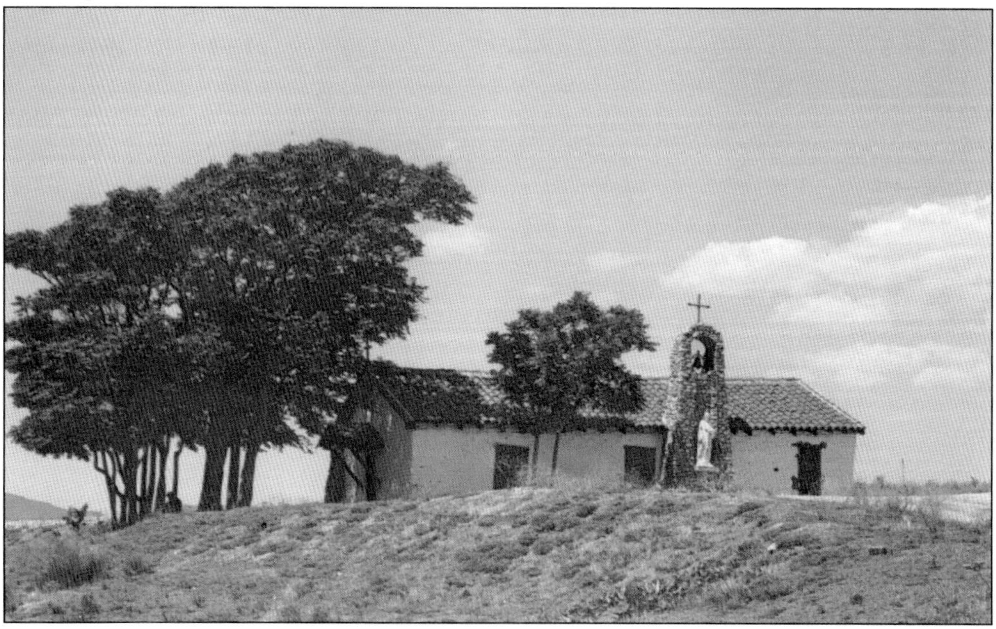

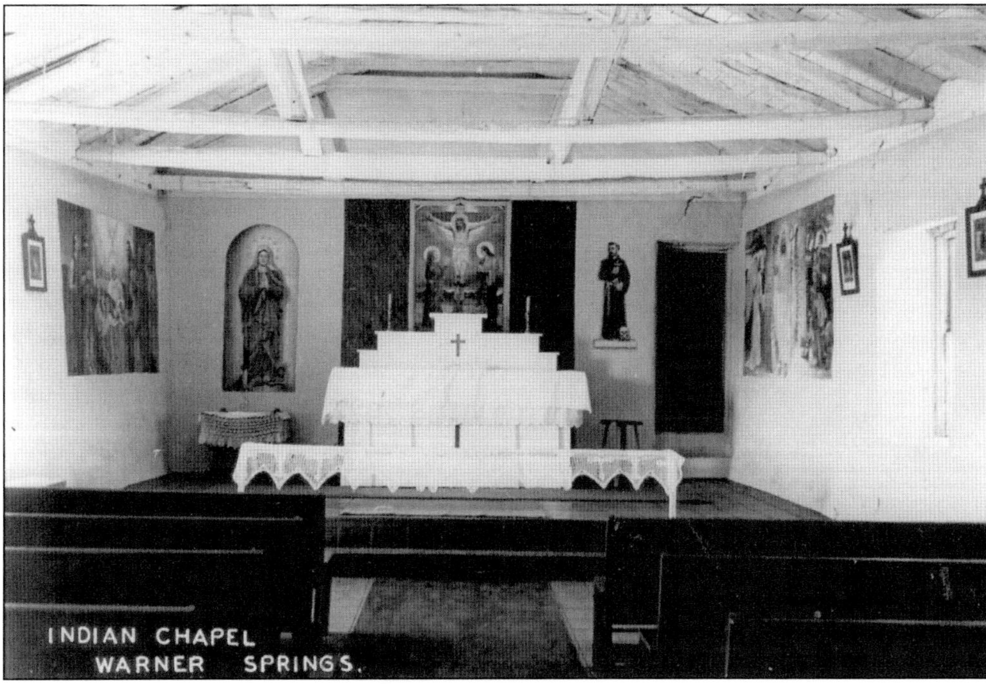

Fletcher and Batchelder, along with masseur Ben Hayward and help from Henshaw, raised enough money to restore the chapel in 1928 and turn it over to the Catholic Church for use. The Indians held their first fiesta in 24 years. Thousands gathered, and the Indians, encouraged by Fr. Edmund La Pointe, held another religious ceremony and removed the curse in appreciation. Shown is the interior of the church as it remains today.

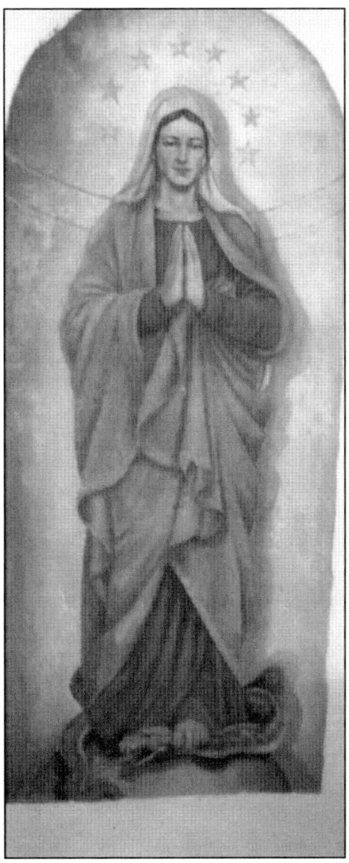

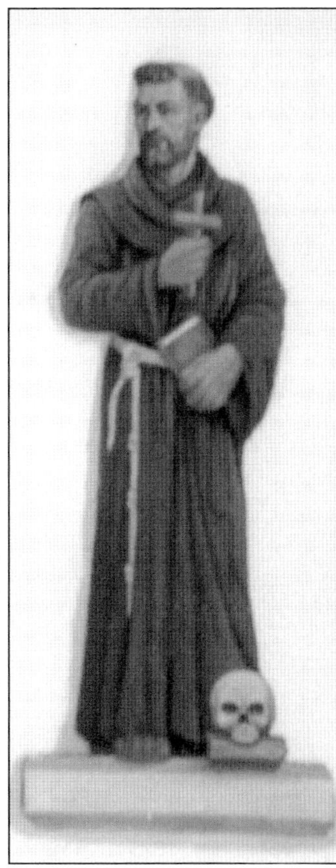

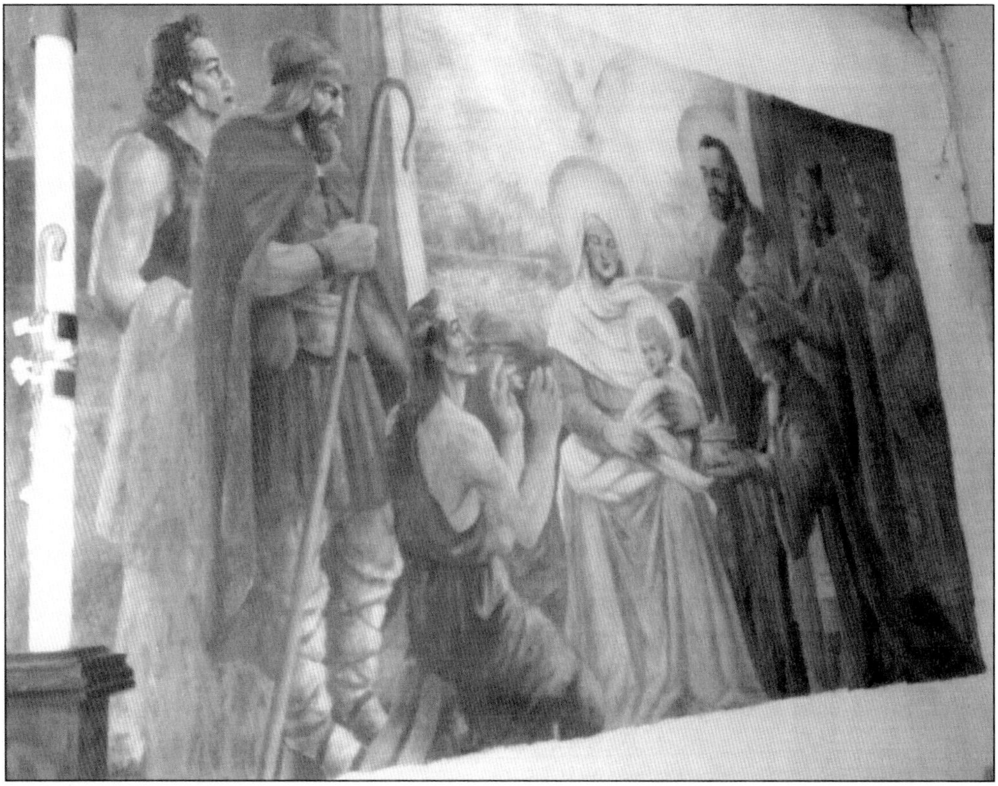

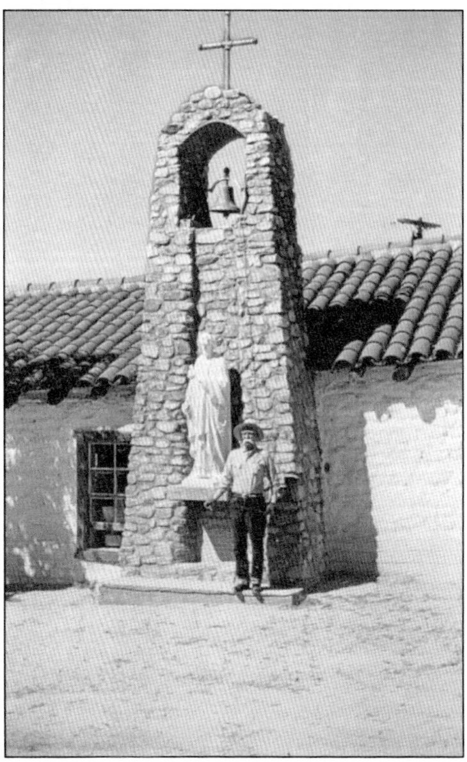

This large mural and those of the Virgin Mary and St. Francis were painted by Paul Matthews, a dishwasher and artist at Warner Hot Springs who later became an artist for Disney Studios. The chapel is always open, and mass is held every Sunday at 11:45 a.m. as it has been for many years, with the priest coming from the Mission Santa Ysabel after mass there.

Julio Ortega is shown next to the bell tower, which was added in 1945 so that parishioners could be called to mass. Atop the tower is the *Ramona* bell from an old ferryboat of the same name that ran between San Diego and Coronado; it was found by Ortega's friend Jose Galvin in a junkyard.

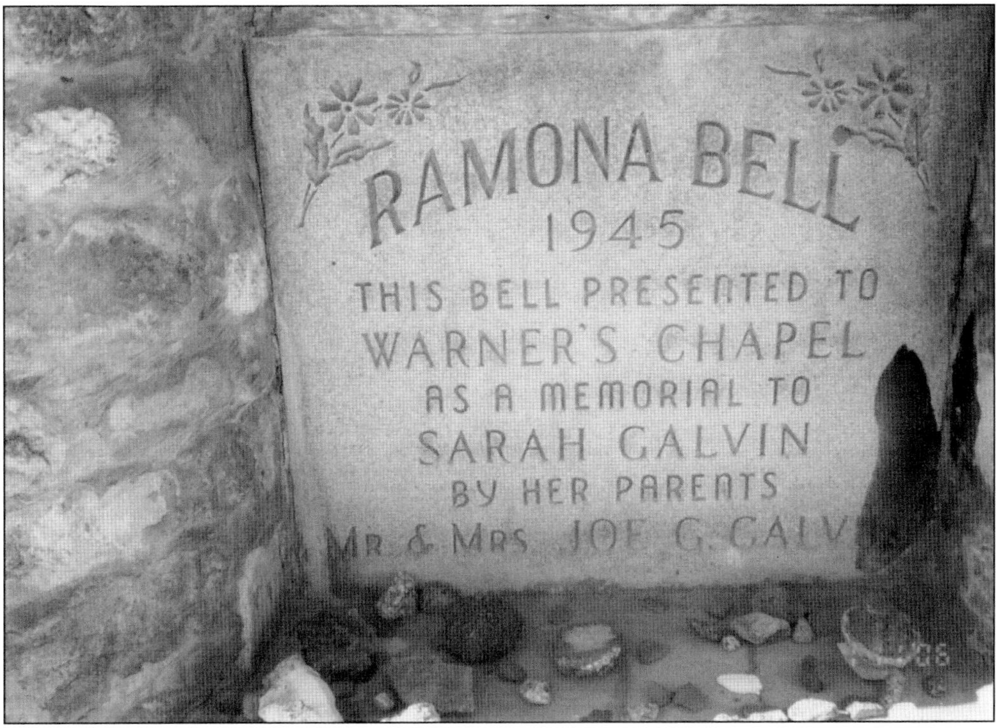

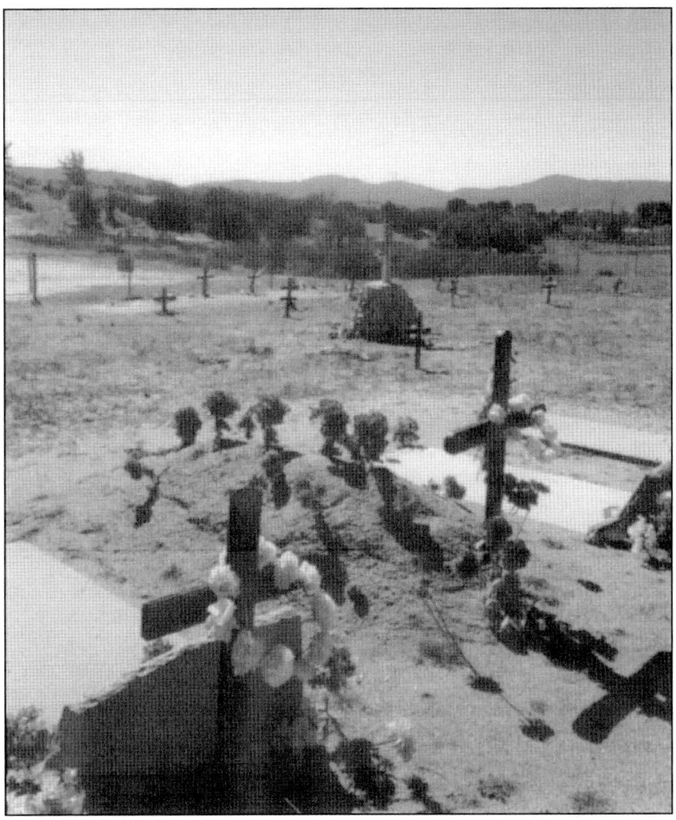

The plaque shown states that the bell was given to the chapel in memory of Sarah Galvin by her parents. Sarah was a pretty Indian girl from Warner Springs who had worked hard during World War II and gone to school but who had died before the war was over.

A short walk over the hill behind the chapel is the graveyard where many area residents have been buried for centuries. Most have simple wooden crosses, but others have headstones, like members of the well-known Taylor family. Often, when a loved one died, the Indians would simply say "they went west."

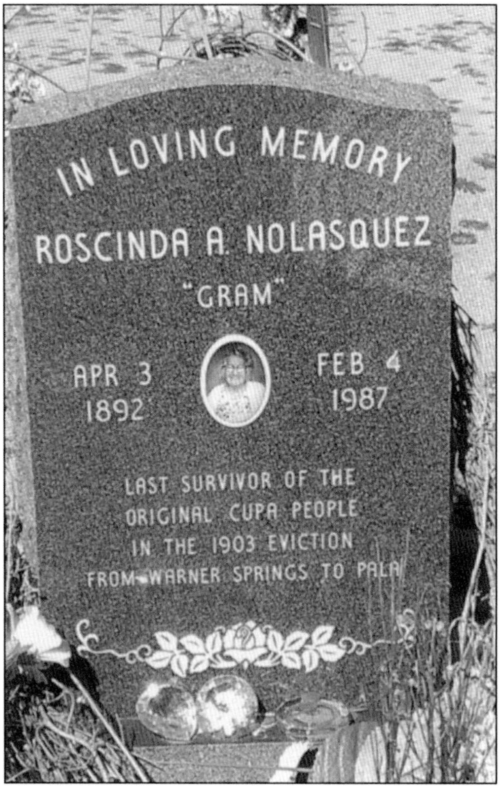

Pictured is the headstone of Roscinda Nolasquez, 1892–1987, the last survivor of the original Cupa people who were evicted in 1903 to Pala. As a small child, she witnessed the placing of the curse by Capt. Juan Cibemoat, who stamped his foot three times and spat the traditional three times on the ground and said, "No white man will ever make a profit from the Agua Caliente; let them eat sand."

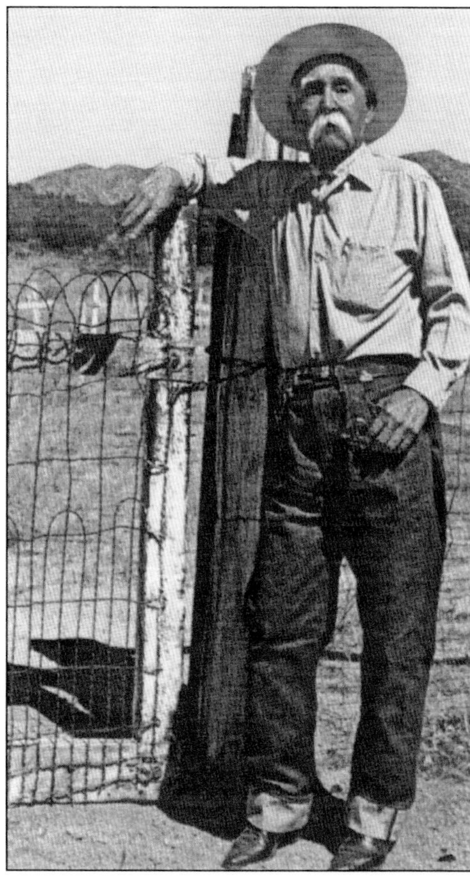

Julio Ortega, longtime wrangler, guide, and storyteller at Warner Springs Ranch, is pictured at the gate to the graveyard. He is buried in the graveyard on the Mesa Grande Indian Reservation. Other longtime inhabitants are buried at the Santa Ysabel graveyard.

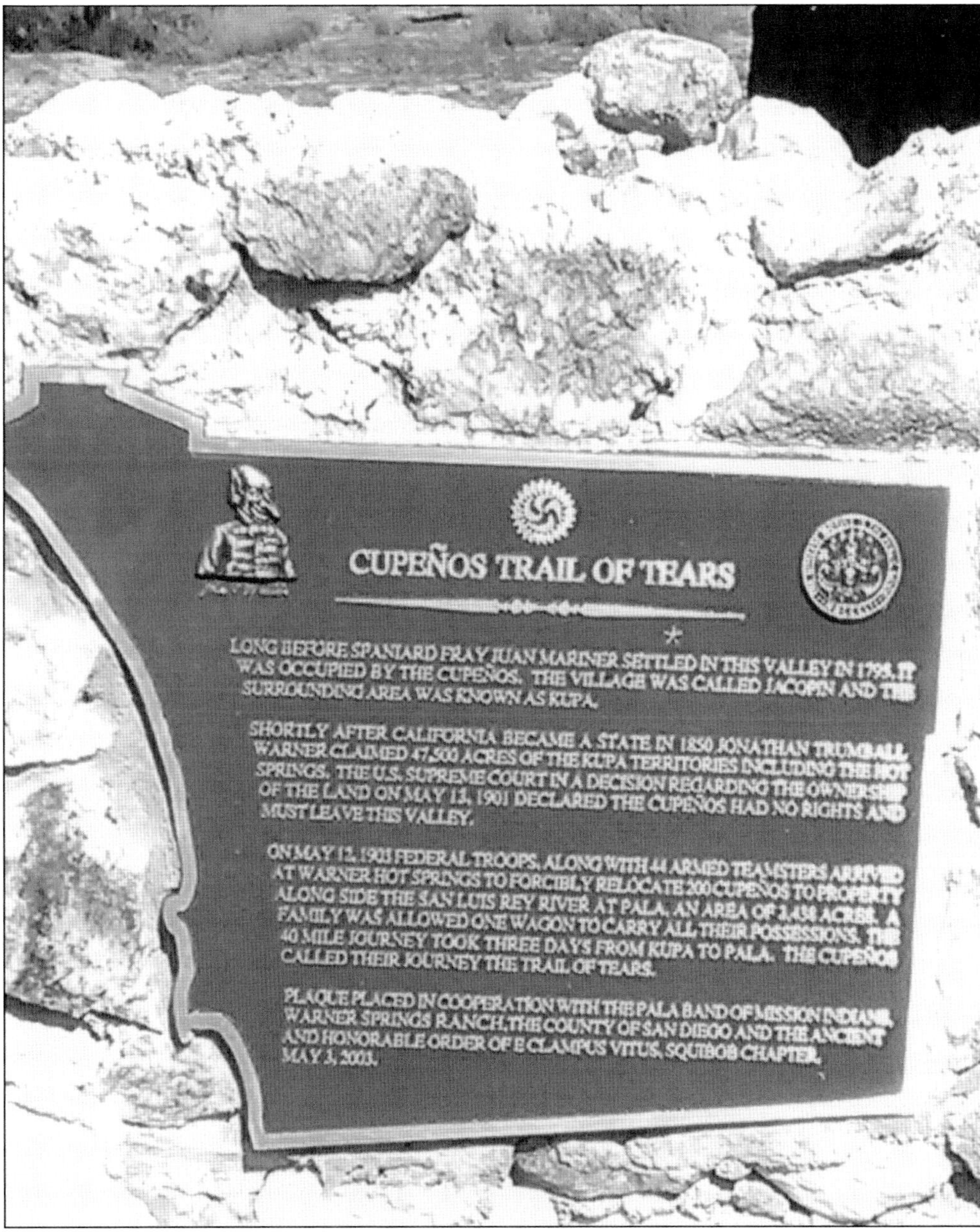

This plaque under the big oak tree near the graveyard commemorates the Cupeños Trail of Tears. It was erected in 2003 by the Pala Band of Mission Indians in cooperation with the Warner Springs Ranch Owners Association and the County of San Diego.

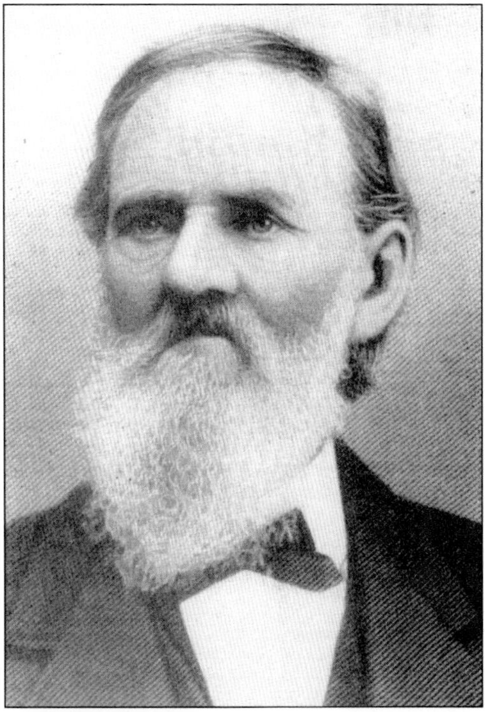

John Trumball Warner, who came to California in 1834, filed a petition for both the land grants of the Valle de San Jose and San Jose del Valle in their entirety in 1844, an area of 48,030 acres. He became a Catholic and dropped his American citizenship to become a Mexican citizen in his adopted land. The valley then became known as the Warner Valley.

Warner, also known as Juan Largo because of his six-foot, three-inch height, is pictured with a group of Cupeño vaqueros. Though Warner often complained of the Indians' raids on his herds, he permitted the Cupeños to remain in their long-established rancherias during his ownership. Their presence was tolerated because their labor was needed on the huge rancho. Later, as a state senator, he would testify in court against their removal from their homeland.

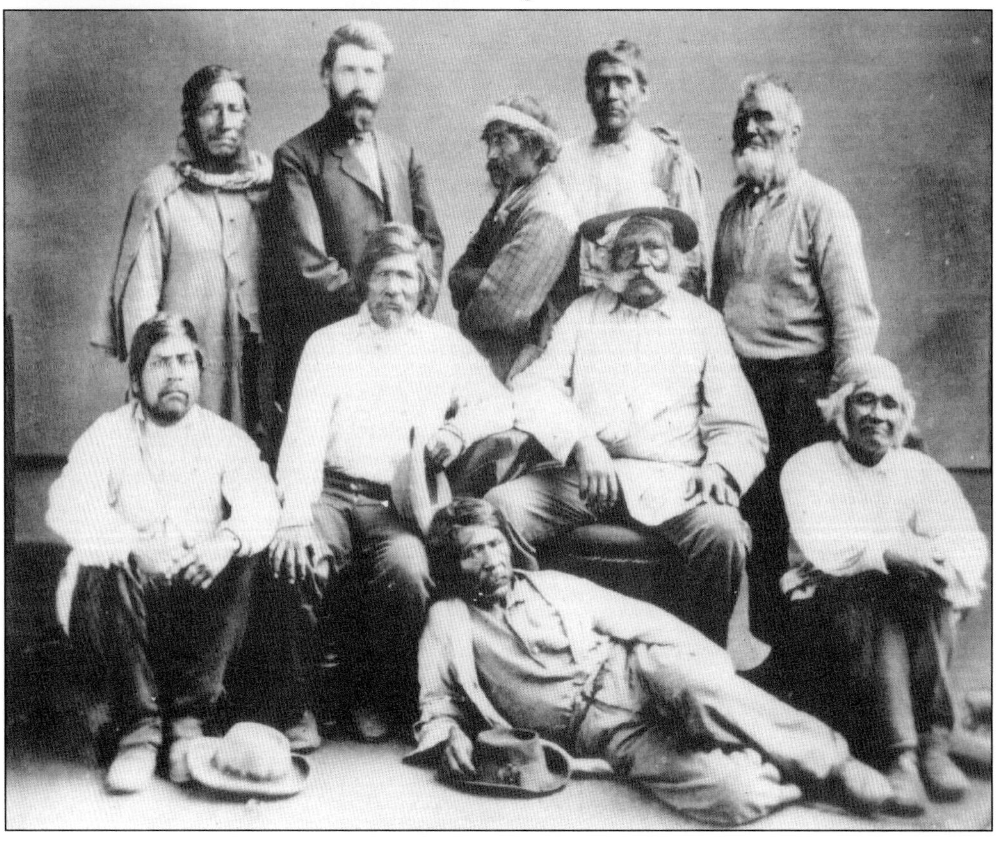

Two

The Way West

The war with Mexico ended in 1848 with the signing of the Treaty of Guadalupe-Hidalgo, and California became a part of the United States. Land grants made to citizens of Mexico like Warner began a complex process of challenge and proof of ownership. San Diego, the first county in the new state in 1850, levied taxes, including upon the Indians, setting the stage for open revolt among a coalition of varying tribes under Chief Garra. This was the last resistance to the complete domination by immigrants and settlers.

The southern route west became key, and the Warner Ranch, astride this trail, was the first green oasis and resting point for travelers making the trek over the desert. During 1847 and 1848, Warner lived at the springs, but it was only natural that he built a ranch house and store four and a half miles south on the immigrant trail. Gen. Stephen Kearny's army rested here en route to San Diego under the guidance of scout Kit Carson. The Mormon Battalion also passed this way, and over time, so did 250,000 people, 80,000 alone after the discovery of gold at Sutter's Mill in 1849. After being burned out in 1851 in the Garra raid, Warner never returned, but the valley retained his name.

Another famous period in the history of Warner Hot Springs was from 1858 to 1861, when the Butterfield Stage carried passengers, gold, and mail on the Southern Immigrant Trail from Tipton, Missouri, to San Francisco in an average of 23 days and nights. In 1857, Vincenta and Ramon Carrillo acquired 14,000 acres of the valley and built their ranch house west of the creek near Warner's original house north of the creek. In 1858, it became a favorite stage spot for the Butterfield Company. Just off what is now San Felipe Road, or Highway S-2, and about a half mile from Highway 79, the restored Warner-Carrillo Ranch House has been a National Historic Landmark since 1961 and is now a museum operated by Save Our Heritage Organisation of San Diego; it is open to visitors on weekends.

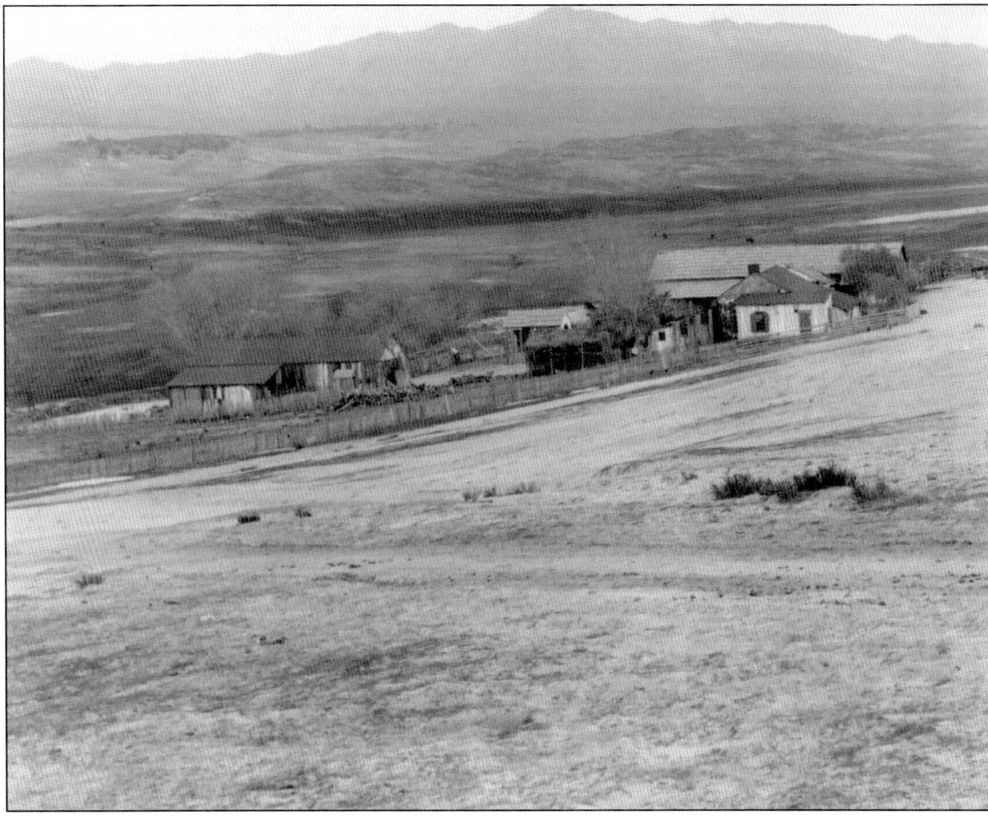

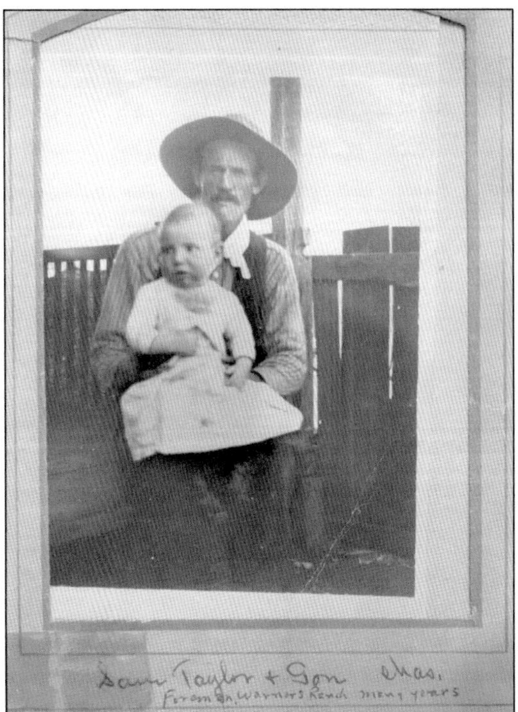

The Warner Carrillo Ranch House is shown with Hot Springs Mountain in the background. In 1859, Ramon Carrillo was appointed postmaster, but he could not write. No wonder the mail was slow. Ramon was reportedly murdered not long after. His stepson Jose Yorba, a graduate of Boston College, then assisted his now twice-widowed mother Vincenta in running the ranch. Later, the post office was moved to Warner Hot Springs.

The longest occupants of the ranch house were Sam B. Taylor, cowboy and foreman for both the Vail and Sawday Cattle Companies, his wife, Mary Helm, and their eight children, who lived there from 1894 to 1910. Sam was a significant person in the history of the area, becoming a trustee of the school board and justice of the peace. Many Taylor descendants still live in the Warner Valley.

This portrait is of John Butterfield, who won the contract from the US government to establish the Butterfield Overland Stage Route. The Civil War put an end to the Butterfield Stage Line, as most of the states and territories it passed through either became part of the Confederacy or were heavily sympathetic to the Confederate cause.

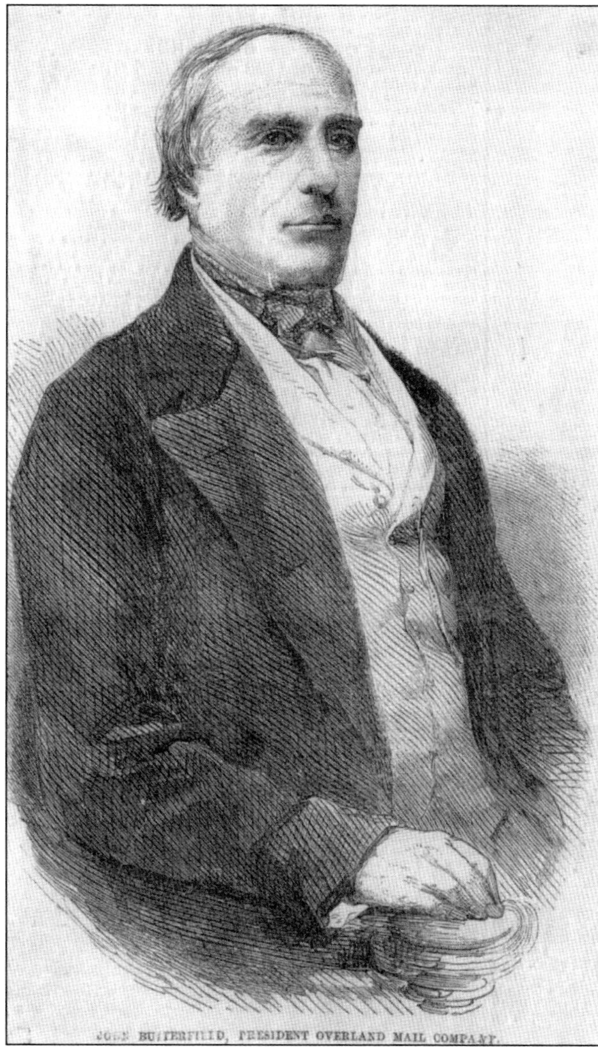

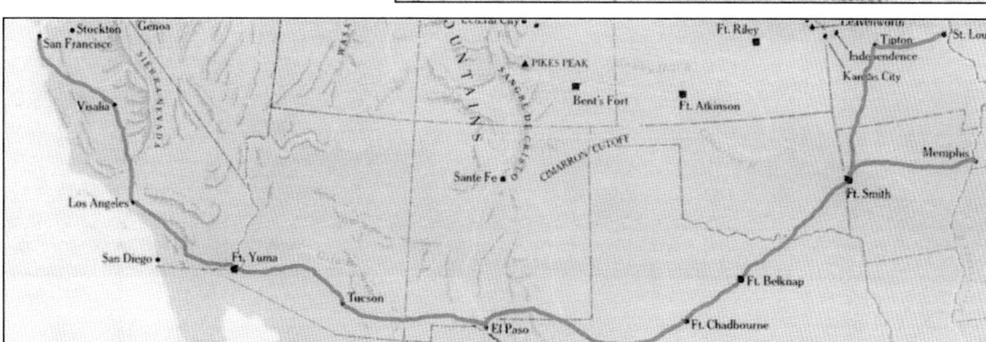

This map shows the Butterfield stage route from Missouri to California. Before this, many travelers to California took a treacherous and expensive sea voyage around South America that lasted three months. The cost for the stage was about $150. Stops along the way were just long enough to change a horse team and gulp down a cup of coffee and meager meal at a "swing station" like Warner's Ranch.

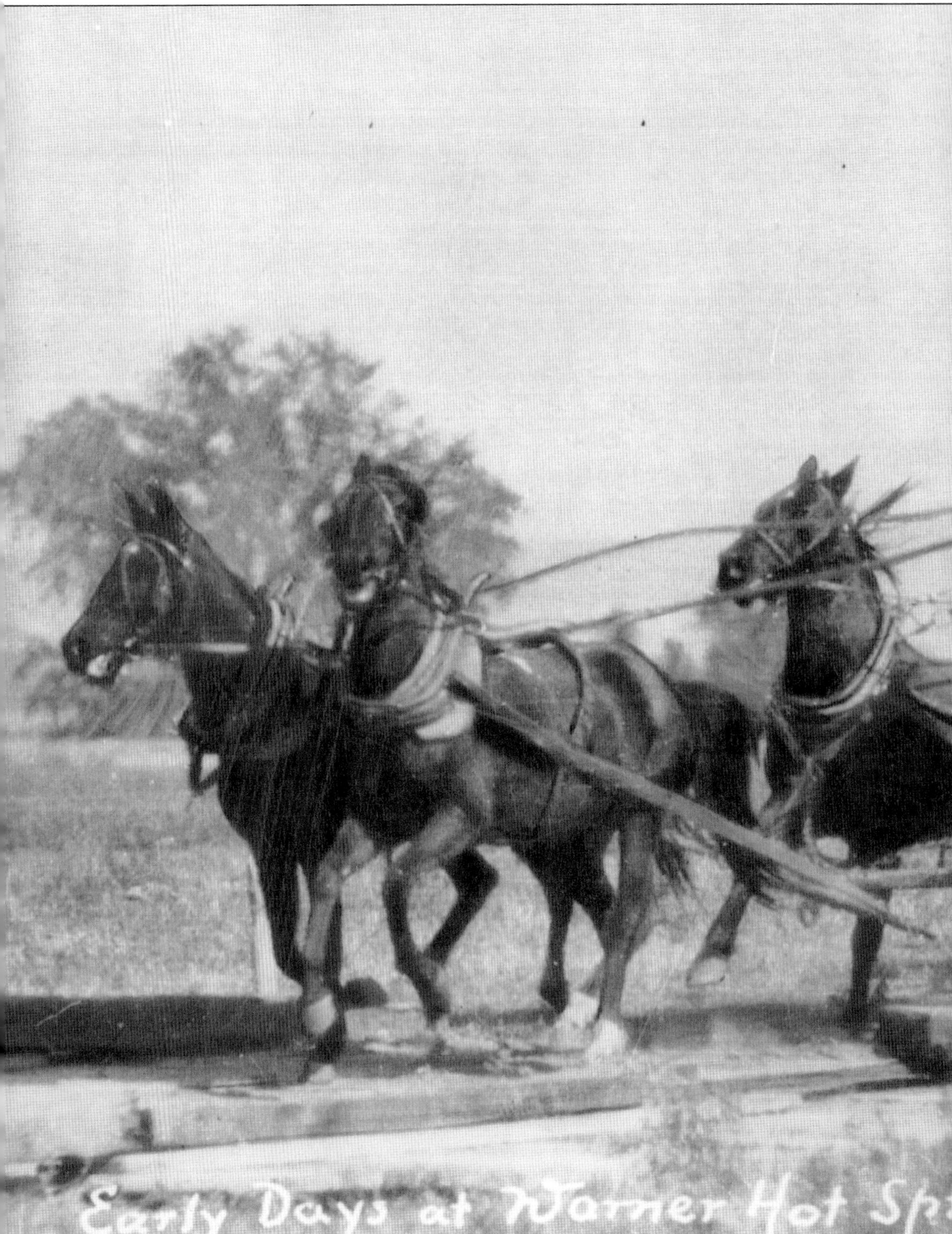

A promotional photograph shows a six-horse Concord coach thundering across the plains in the early days of Warner Hot Springs. The horse-drawn—and in rougher areas, mule-drawn—vehicle

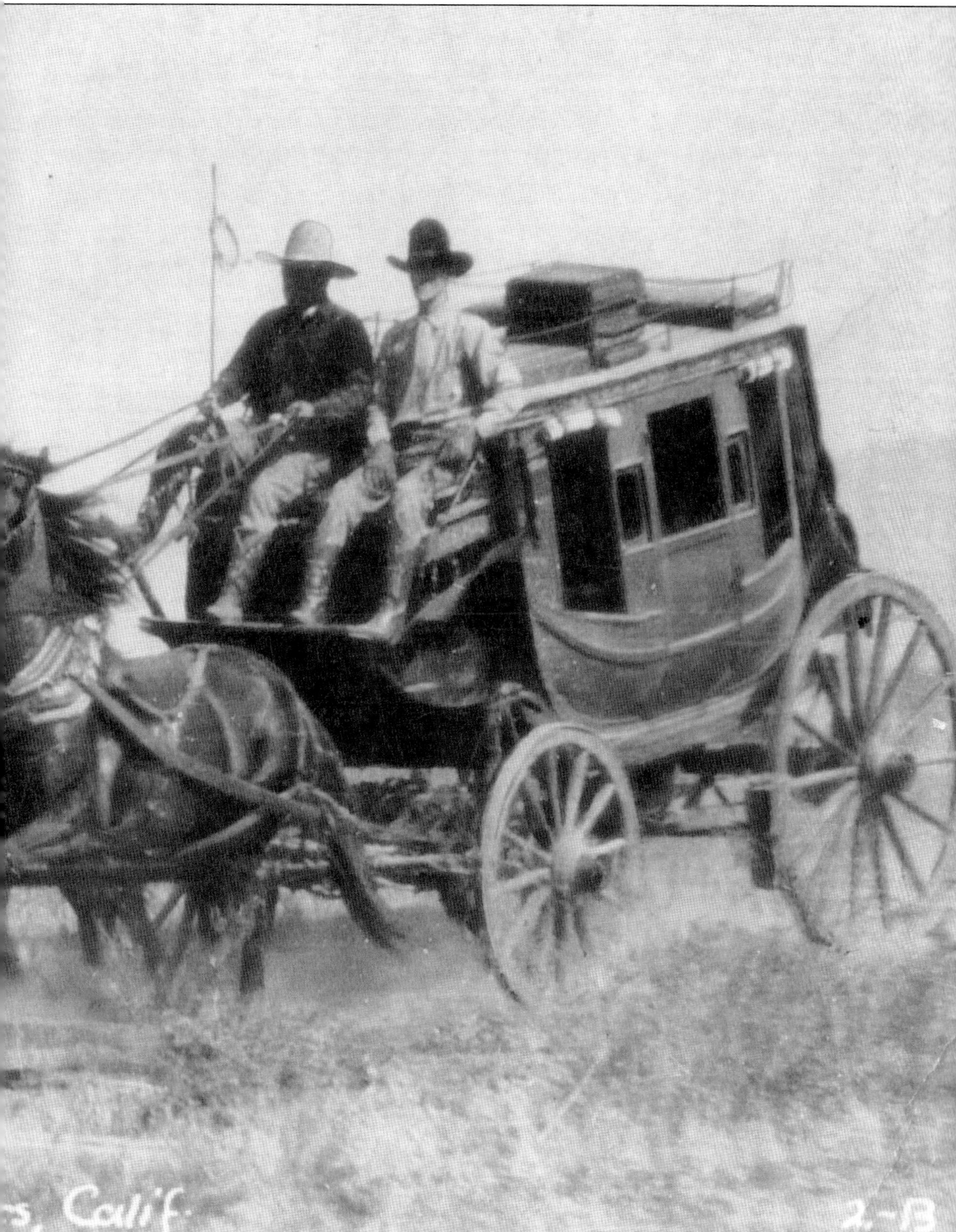

ran across wild open territory, offering rapid and reliable delivery despite sometimes hostile Indians and robbers. The twice-a-week runs traveled at 6 to 12 miles per hour.

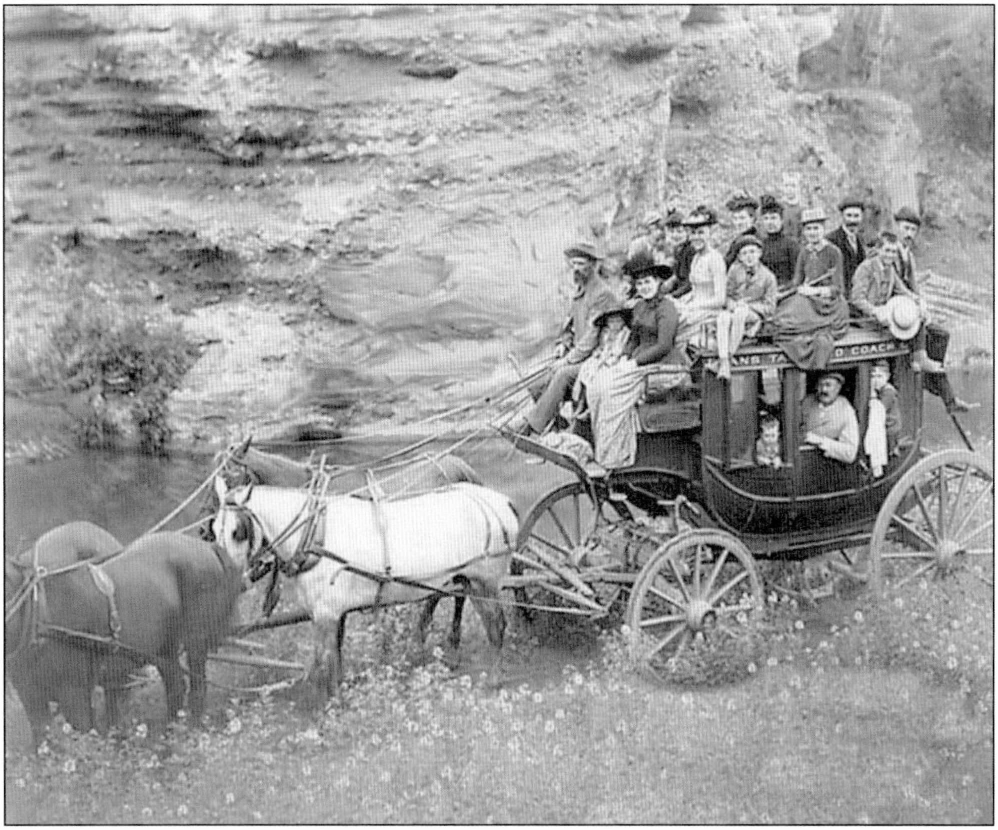

According to one passenger, the 19th-century coach was more than a little rough: "Fifteen inches of seat, with a fat man on one side, a poor widow on the other, a screaming baby in your lap, a bandbox over your head, and three or four more persons immediately in front leaning against your knees."

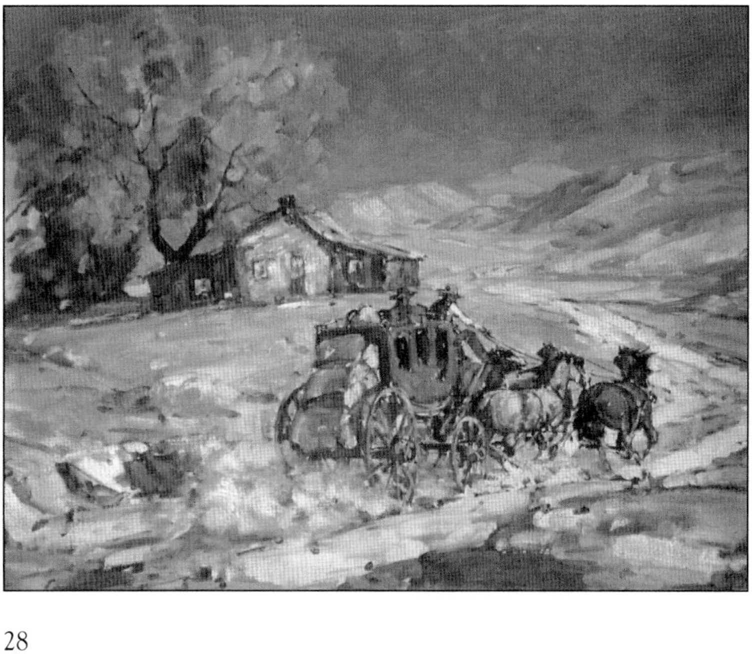

Part of a series by famed artist Marjorie Reed, this painting depicts the Warner Ranch Stage Stop as a coach arrives at night. Coaches were often called "sleeping hotels," as they ran all day and all night. Reed lived at many of the stops and in nearby Julian, and she died at the Campbell Ranch at the bottom of the San Felipe Grade.

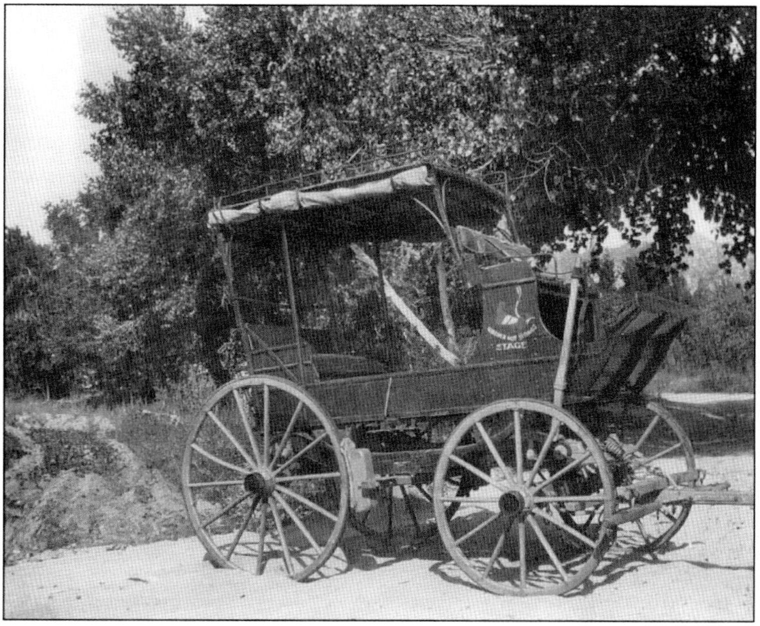

This type of coach was known as a "light stage" and was used to transport passengers across sandy deserts and difficult terrain where a Concord stage would be too heavy. Having been on display at Warner Hot Springs for many years, it belongs to the Warner Springs Historical Society and is now at the Warner Carrillo Ranch House awaiting restoration.

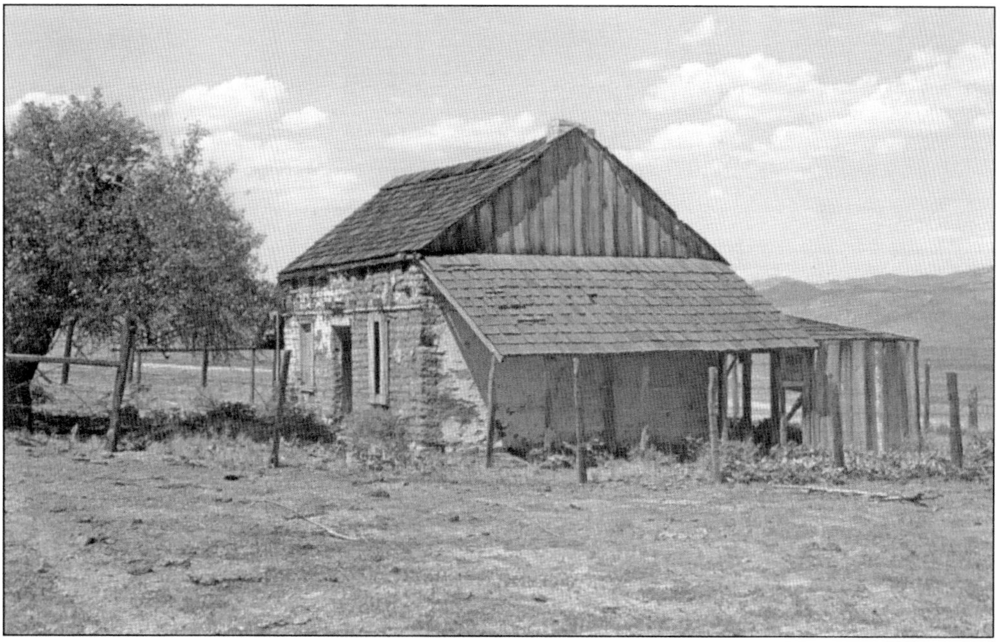

An old mercantile store and saloon known as the Wilson Kimball Store, awaiting restoration a mile and a half south of the Warner Carrillo, is erroneously identified as a stage stop but did not exist until five years after the discontinuance of the Butterfield Stage over the southern route. Operated by Henry Wilson from 1875 until 1908, it also served as a rural schoolhouse and living quarters.

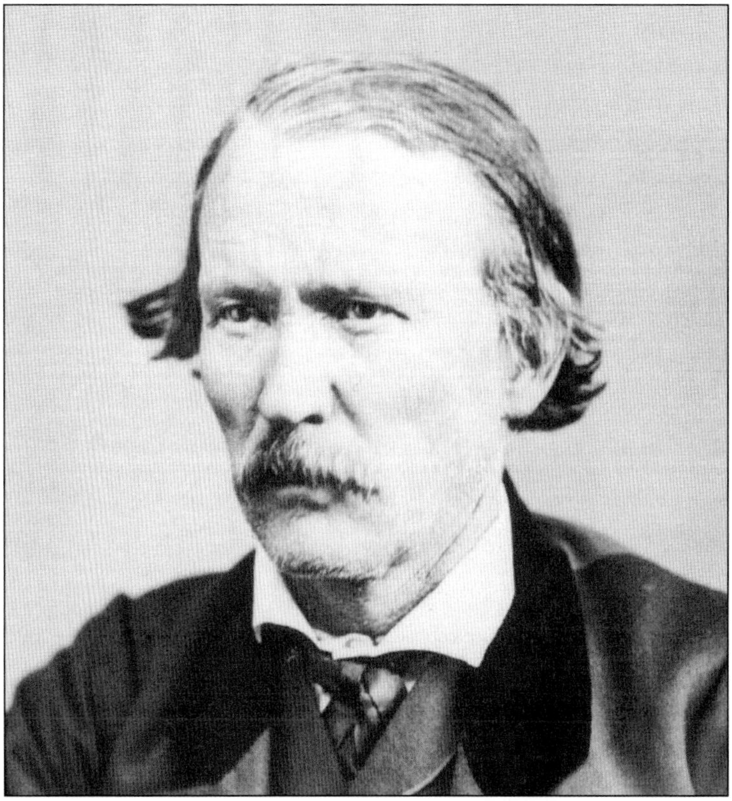

Famous scout Kit Carson (pictured) was asked in 1842 by John C. Frémont to guide the first of three expeditions mapping the West over a four-year period. They participated in the Bear Flag Revolt of 1846, and both were reported to have stayed in the adobes of the Indians at Warner Hot Springs. One south of the springs has been called the Carson Adobe and one north the Fremont House.

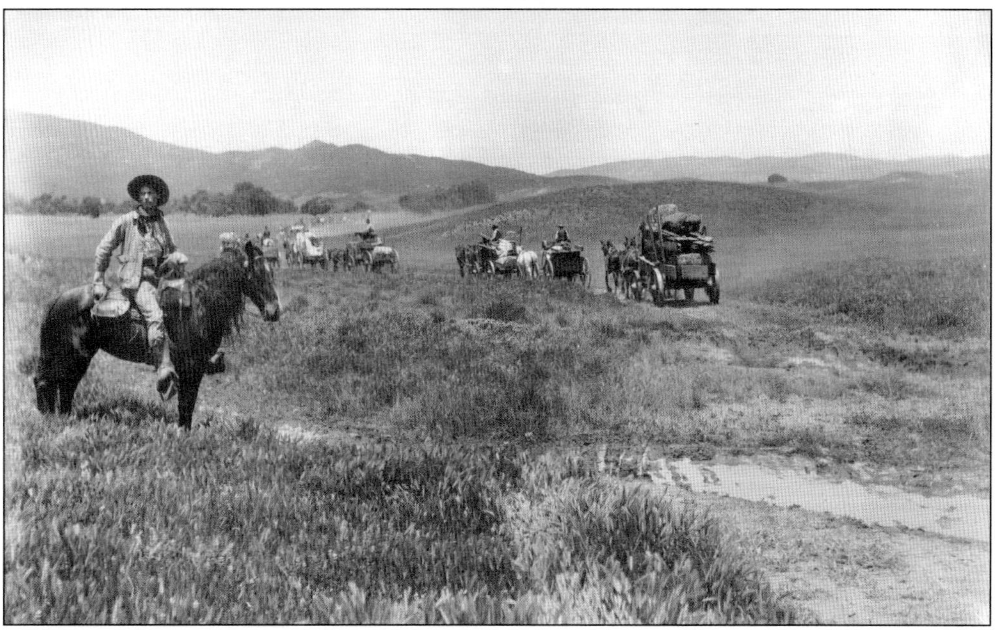

On May 11, 1903, teamsters and 41 teams from surrounding ranches, as pictured here, loaded 98 Cupeños and their possessions in wagons. Some fled to the hills. The grade southwest down to Pauma Valley was too steep, so they traveled north, stopping at Pauba Ranch near Temecula for the night then moving onward south to Pala. A new era had begun.

Three

A Legendary Resort Is Born

Senator Warner in 1859 helped to elect John Downey lieutenant governor. Three months later, Downey became governor after the resignation of Gov. Milton Latham. Later, the ex-governor Downey, skilled in forceful land acquisitions, reassembled the entire 47,000 acres once held by his friend John Warner. By 1875, the various parts of the ranch, some from beleaguered sources, were under his ownership with Louis Phillips. In 1890, Walter Vail and C.W. Gates leased the valley and had 6,000 sheep and 3,000 cattle there.

The resort area was leased to a series of operators, and the *Julian Sentinel* noted in 1890 that Alejandro Barker expected to install a new bathhouse at the springs. John Downey filed a complaint in 1893 seeking the eviction of the Indians living on Ranch Valle de San Jose. He died in 1894, and his nephew J. Downey Harvey was named in the eviction suit. He declined to sell a portion of the ranch to the federal commissioners appointed by Pres. Theodore Roosevelt for a reservation, feeling it was unworkable to accommodate the Indians' desire to remain at the springs. By 1894, pamphlets were being published advertising "the waters that cure when others won't."

About 1900, the first cabins were built and some existing adobes previously owned by Indians remodeled. By 1908, F.S. Sanderford was the lessee operating the resort, and Daniel Cunningham was the foreman of the ranch. An adobe assembly hall measuring 65 by 40 feet was built, and a larger adobe was used as a store and post office. The old schoolhouse was remodeled, a garage and stable erected, and a new bathhouse built.

By January 1910, William Griffith Henshaw acquired all the interests and power rights to the entire Warner Ranch to ensure the riparian rights for downstream properties along the San Luis Rey River. In following years, he successfully developed a series of dams to provide water for the County of San Diego. By 1911, Henshaw began improving and developing the resort area as Warner Hot Springs, and a legendary resort was born.

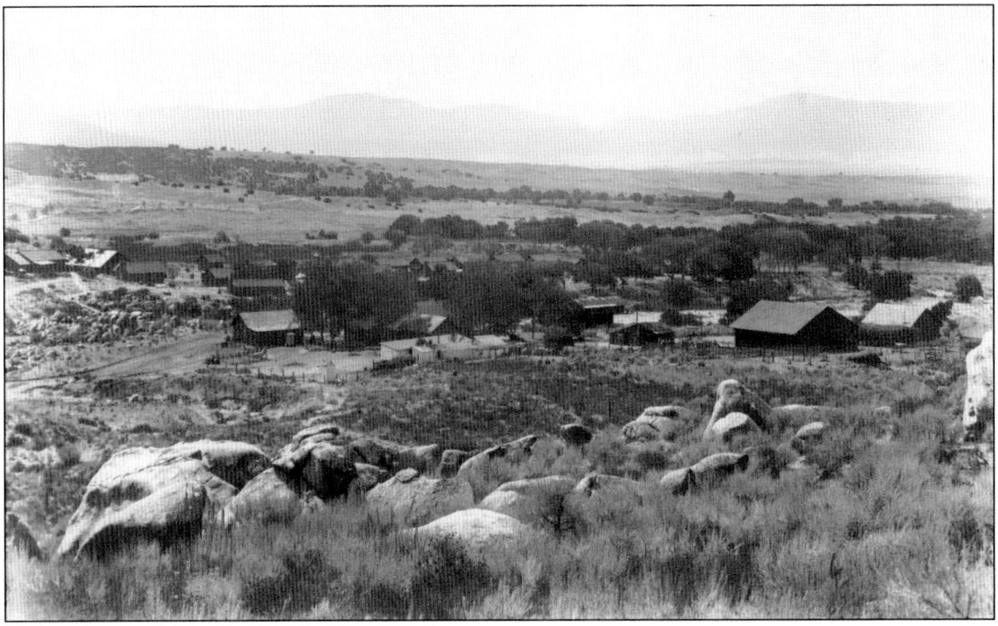

This picture, taken from Metate Rock with a view looking west over the valley towards Mount Palomar, shows the resort as it takes shape, with the adobe homes now showing new roofs instead of thatch.

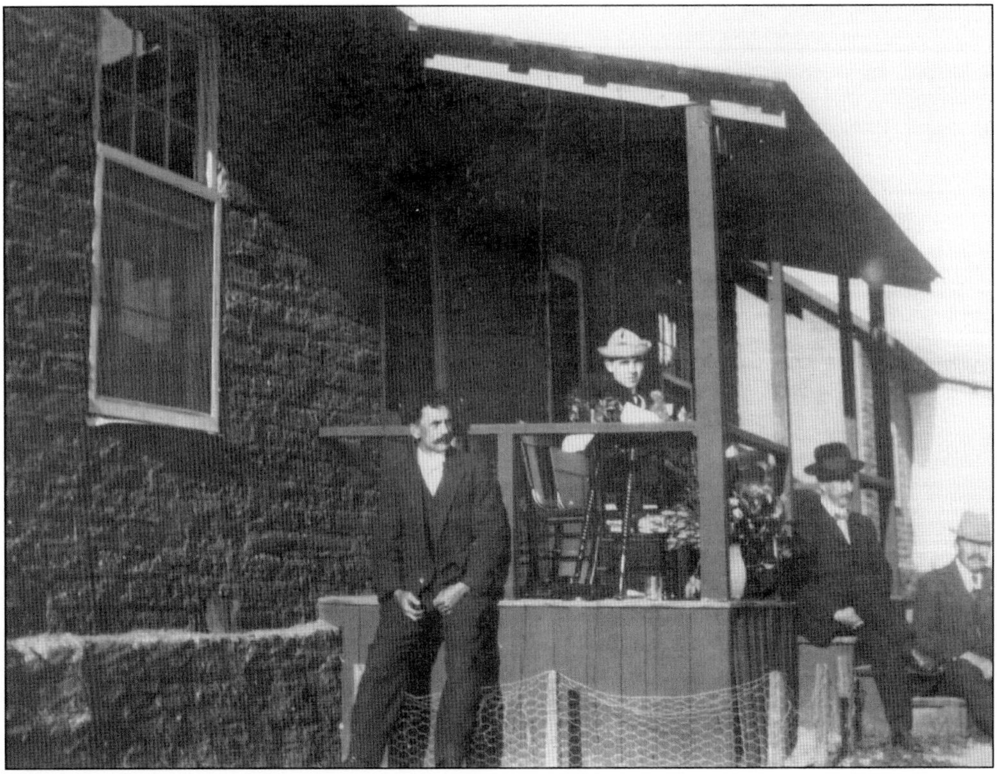

Early visitors sit on the porch of the original reception building and store south of hot springs on the hill. This building is still standing and has been remodeled many times for many different uses.

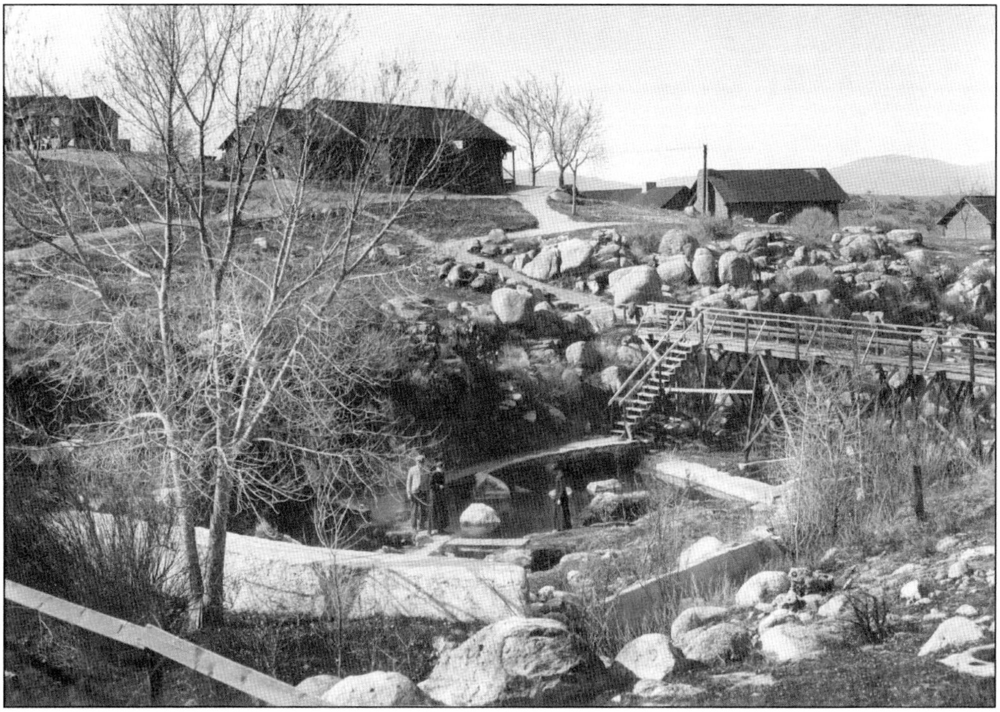

The reception building is shown in the back in this picture of the hot springs. The pools are taking shape, and the old wooden bridge led to the school and barn. (Courtesy Ed Fletcher Papers, University of California at San Diego Library Archives.)

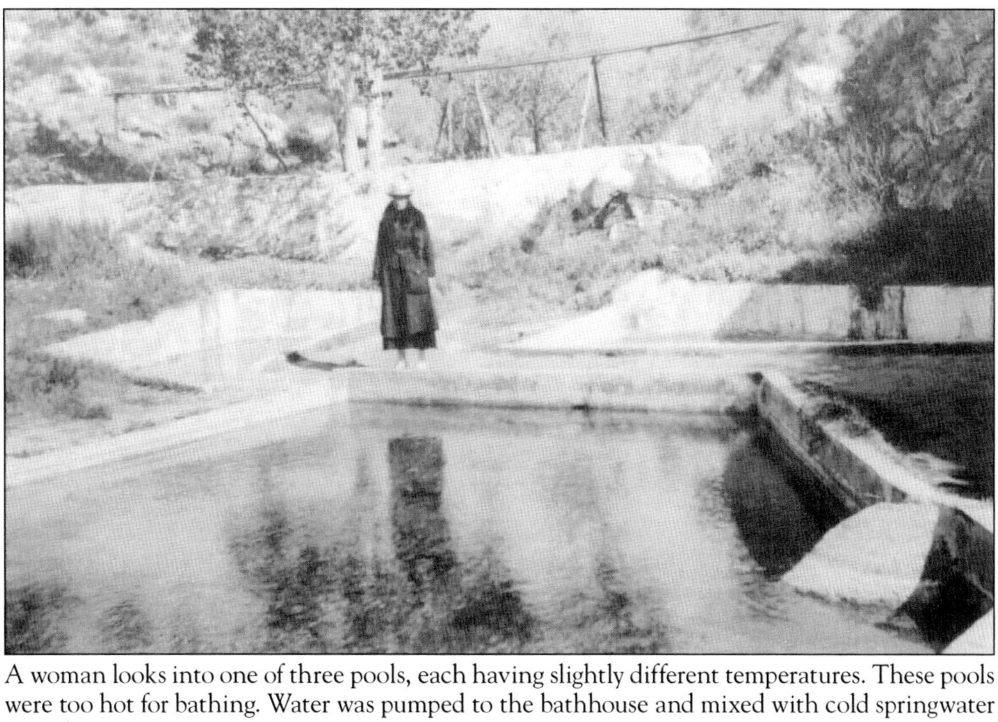

A woman looks into one of three pools, each having slightly different temperatures. These pools were too hot for bathing. Water was pumped to the bathhouse and mixed with cold springwater to make it more temperate.

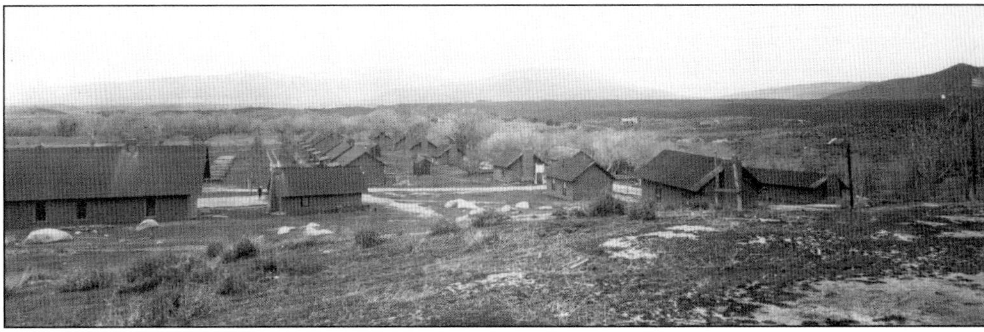

The Assembly Room, later called the Ortega Room, is shown on the far left. The single-room duplex units were built during the Downey ownership. This area was later called Broadway. The trees, barely visible in the photograph, are now mature and provide heavy shade and coolness during the hotter months.

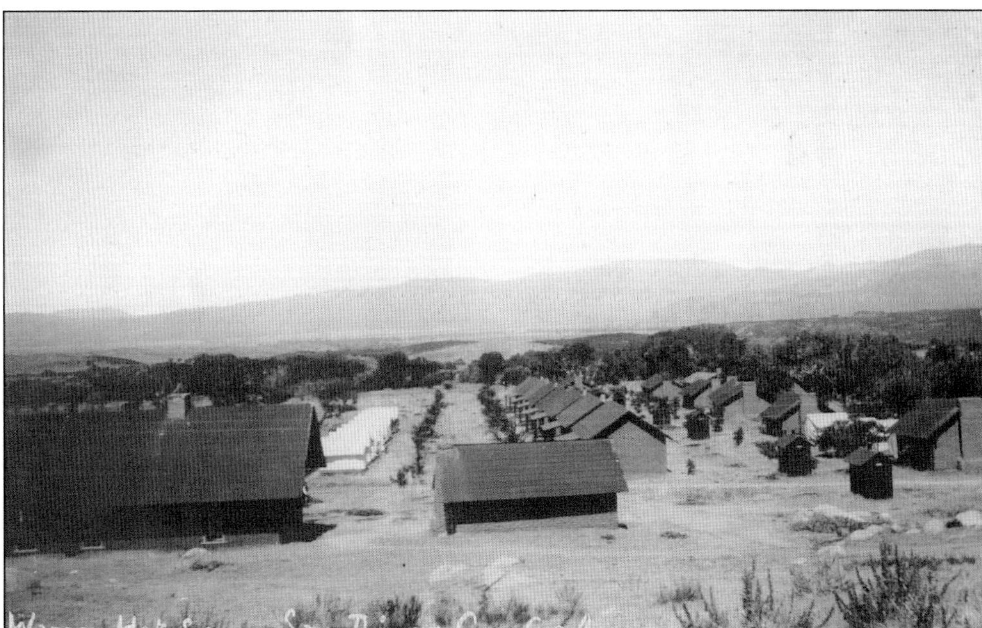

This photograph, taken from a slightly different angle, shows the reroofed original Indian adobes on the far right, Broadway cabins, growing trees, and the tents favored by many vacationers in the early 20th century. The walkway was called the Anza Walk. Note the outhouses between the adobes on the right and the newer cabins.

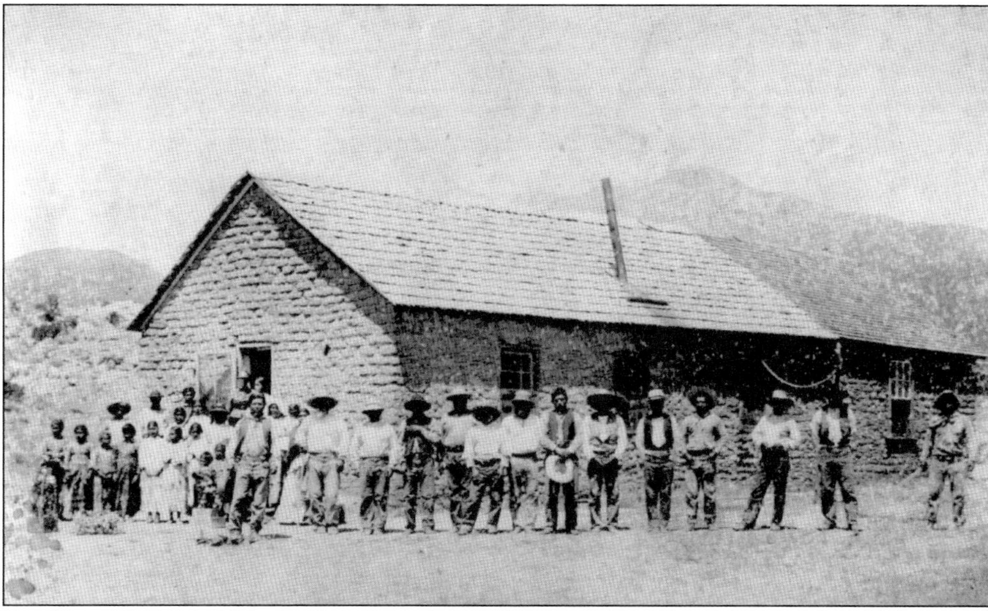

Pictured in front of this adobe structure are many Indians, ranchers, and children. This building was used as a health center. Many of the children went to school at the ranch.

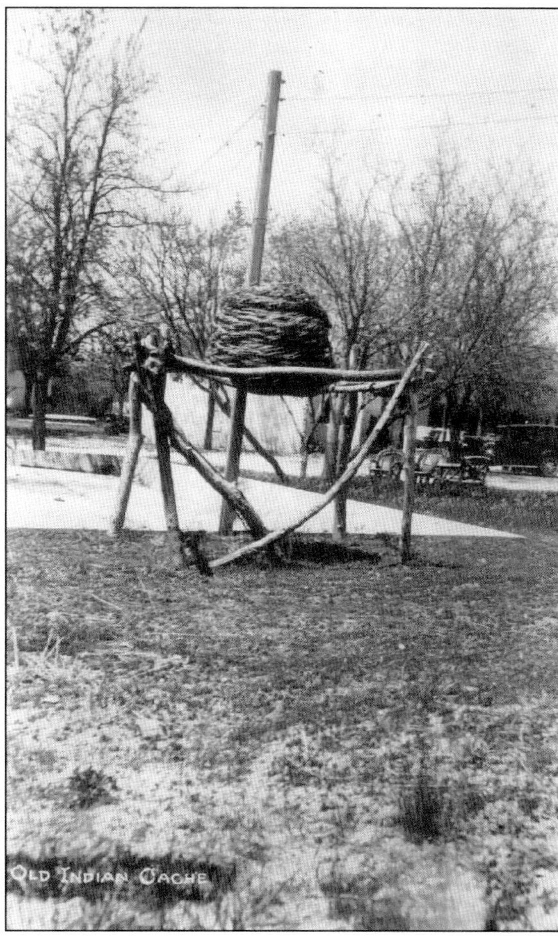

Behind an old "Indian cache," an electric pole shows that electricity has finally reached Warner Hot Springs in the 1930s. Before, there was a lack of refrigeration, and electricity was supplied by two unreliable Kohler generators producing only six kilowatts. California at that time had a 15-to-1 standard, meaning a power line would be installed if the projected 15-year usage would pay for it.

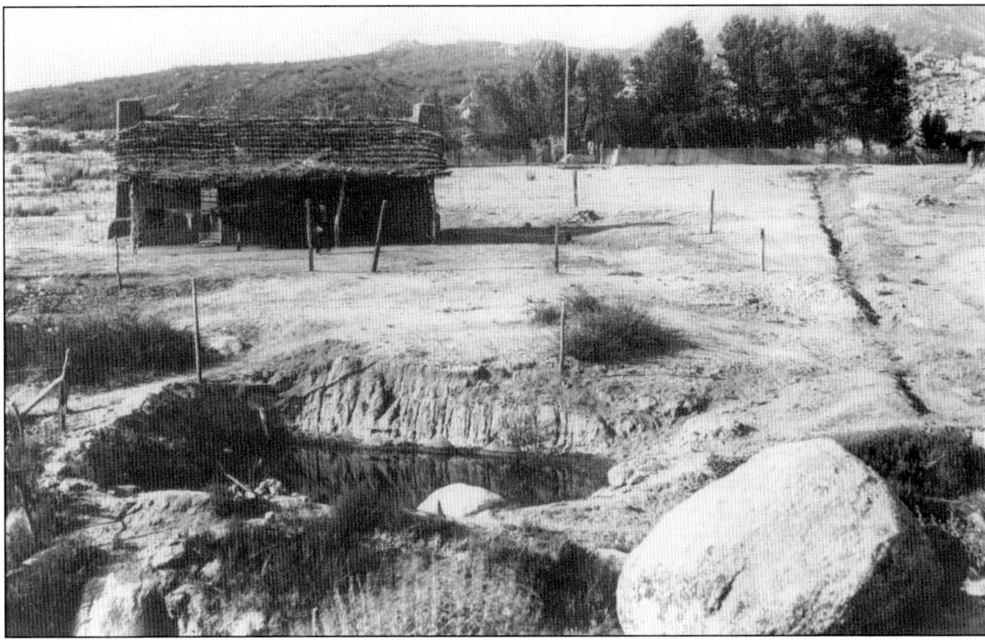

North of the springs lies the Fremont House with its two chimneys. Behind a flagpole in the distance was a red wooden one-room schoolhouse with eight grades. In a memoir, Dr. Robert Long writes that he was the principal and teacher of four schools, including Warner, Oak Grove, San Felipe, and Volcan Mountain, for a salary of $1,215 a year plus $15 for cooking the noon meal and custodial duties.

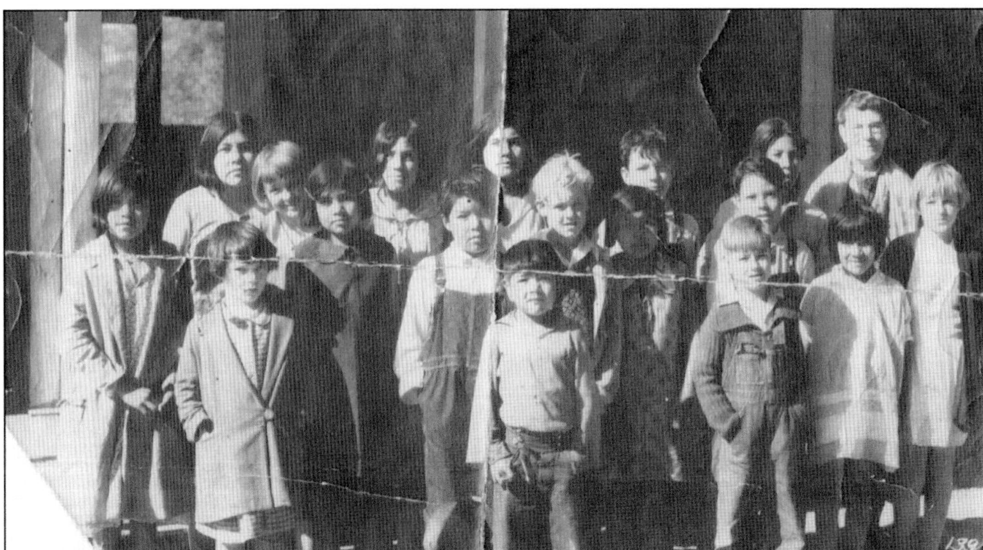

This school picture shows, among others, Chet Taylor (second from the right in front), Marie Segunda, Verla Sharp, Martha Ortega, Betty Howe, Pauline, Theodore, and Gloria Chutnicut, Mary Matay, Billy Segundo, Clarence Means, and Frank Urban. When the first school burned down, a barracks building was relocated from the Civilian Conservation Corps (CCC) camp near Puerta de la Cruz, as were two more when San Felipe and Oak Grove students and two teachers joined them.

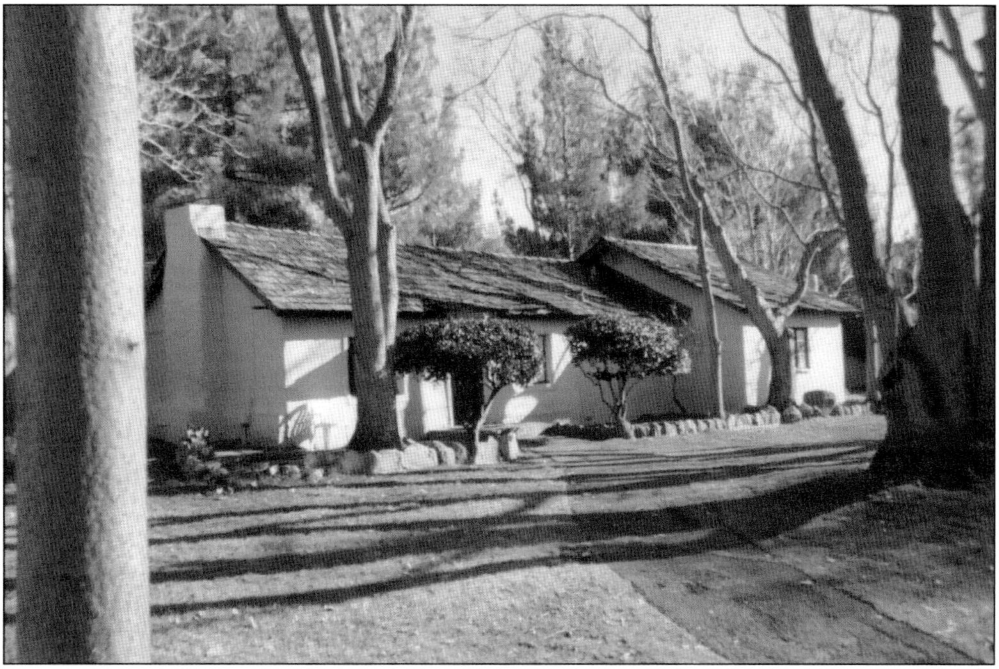

The Los Coyotes Adobe, southeast of the lodge, was the original school before the red schoolhouse, then remodeled as living quarters by Dr. Long. Playing fields were constructed through the generosity of John Wayne and others. Ed Norte was hired as bus driver and lived at the end of the line, so he gathered the children on the Los Coyotes Reservation on the way down and dropped them off on the way back.

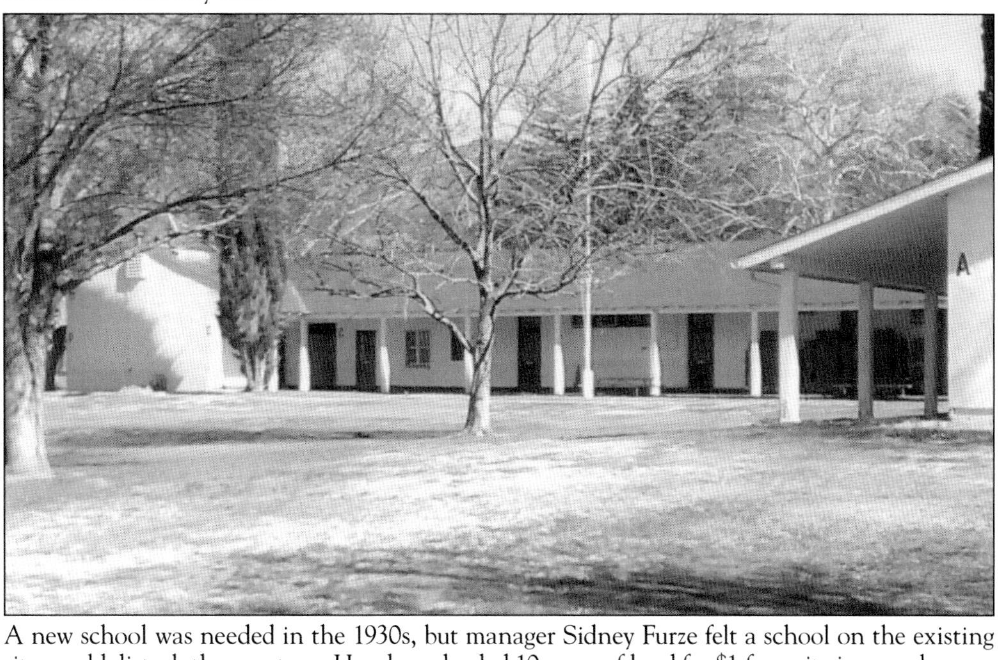

A new school was needed in the 1930s, but manager Sidney Furze felt a school on the existing site would disturb the guests, so Henshaw deeded 10 acres of land for $1 for a site in an oak grove on Highway 79. The Works Progress Administration pledged $20,000, Congress $10,000, and the school board floated a $60,000 bond for the school, which opened on January 19, 1939.

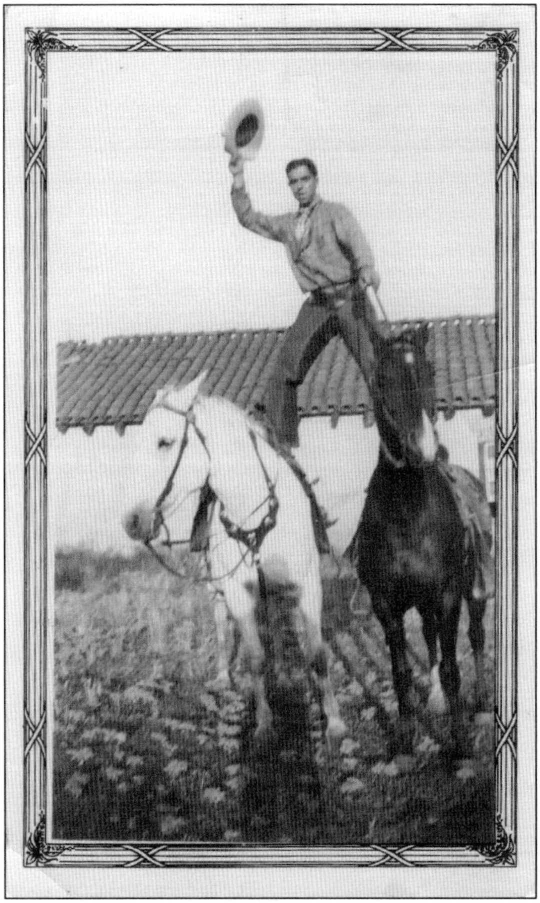

"Fritz the cowboy on Whitey" is the caption on the back of these photographs taken in front of the St. Francis Chapel. He was one of the many professional cowboys who worked for the cattle barons in the valley. The Vail and Gates and the Sawday cattle companies leased the land for many years. Some cowboys became wranglers and trail guides for Warner Hot Springs Resort.

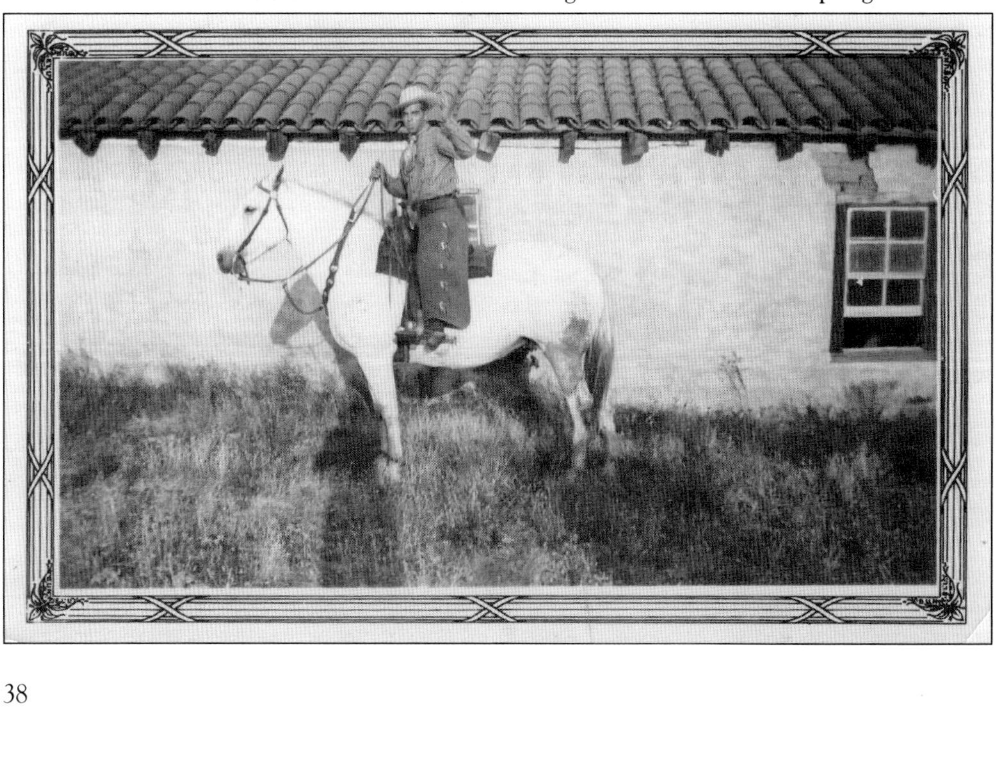

Four

Happy Trails

The Warner Valley fed thousands of sheep and cows over the years, and cowboys like Sam Taylor were needed. Born in 1861 in Grass Valley, he came south and met and married Mary Helm, whose family were early settlers. They moved to the Warner Carrillo Ranch House when Walter Vail and C.W. Gates became owners of a quarter interest in the ranch in the 1890s. "Cattle King Vail" owned the Empire Ranch in Arizona and the Pauba Ranch in Temecula. When a 25 percent freight increase from the railroad threatened profits, cowboys herded cattle 300 miles from Arizona, often 30 miles or more between water, as detailed in Ed Vail's diary. Eight-inch-tall grass, water, and the hot springs awaited them at Warner's, where they rested before going to Temecula and the railway.

Writer Lester Reed fondly describes cattle drives, rodeos, hayrides, and dances with fellow cowboys Hank Smith, Charlie Ponchetti, Charley McGarey, Ralph Jasper, Domingo Cuero, Cleve Helm, and Gib Reed. Famous cattleman George Sawday, born in Julian in 1876, retained the grazing rights from 1913 until 1960, his herd reaching 5,000 at times. Ed Grand, born in Ranchita in 1891, was foreman for Sawday and lived at the Warner ranch house until 1935 with a multitude of cowboys.

The Cupeño curse continued. J. Downey Harvey would die bankrupt. Walter Vail nearly lost his life being thrown from a horse at the springs, then in Arizona he shot a Gila monster and tied it to his saddle, but it was still alive and bit him. Finally, he was killed by a streetcar in Los Angeles while crossing the street. Gates, hunting with Col. Ed Fletcher at the springs, died of a heart attack. Fletcher came to the ranch in 1896 on a bicycle, then in 1902 ascended Hot Springs Mountain by horseback, finding a homestead owned by A.M. Keyes. Falling in love with the "rocky, jagged hills surrounded with marvelous timber and meadows" he bought it for $50 down and $25 a month. He built a home there that was much loved by his family for generations.

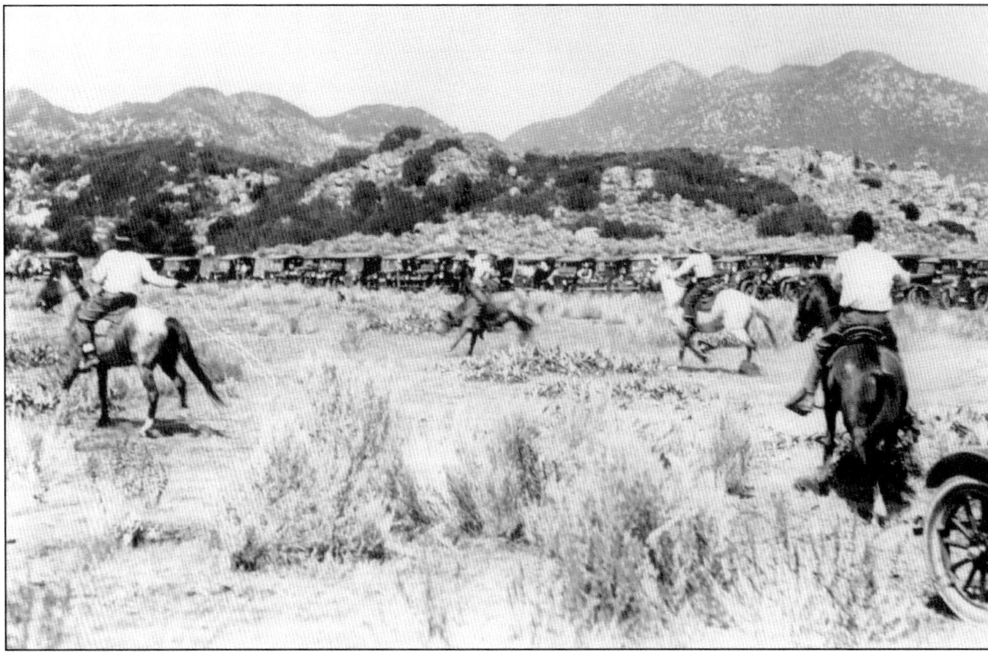

This photograph shows automobiles lined up for a rodeo with 6,500-foot Hot Springs Mountain in the background. Chet Taylor recalled an Indian game where a live chicken would be partially buried and then the vaqueros would compete on horseback to pull it free.

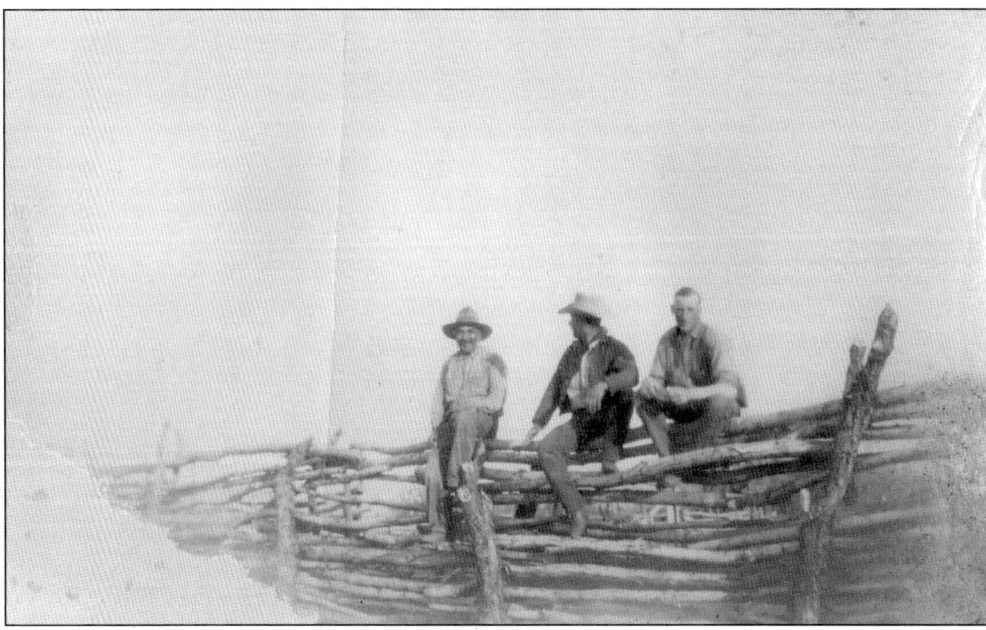

These cowboys are sitting on one of the many split-rail fence corrals on the ranch. Corrals were also made of adobe like the one near the Rincon and were used for gathering and branding cattle. This picture and others were found under the floorboards in the old Warner Carrillo Ranch House in a wallet that belonged to Charlie Ponchetti.

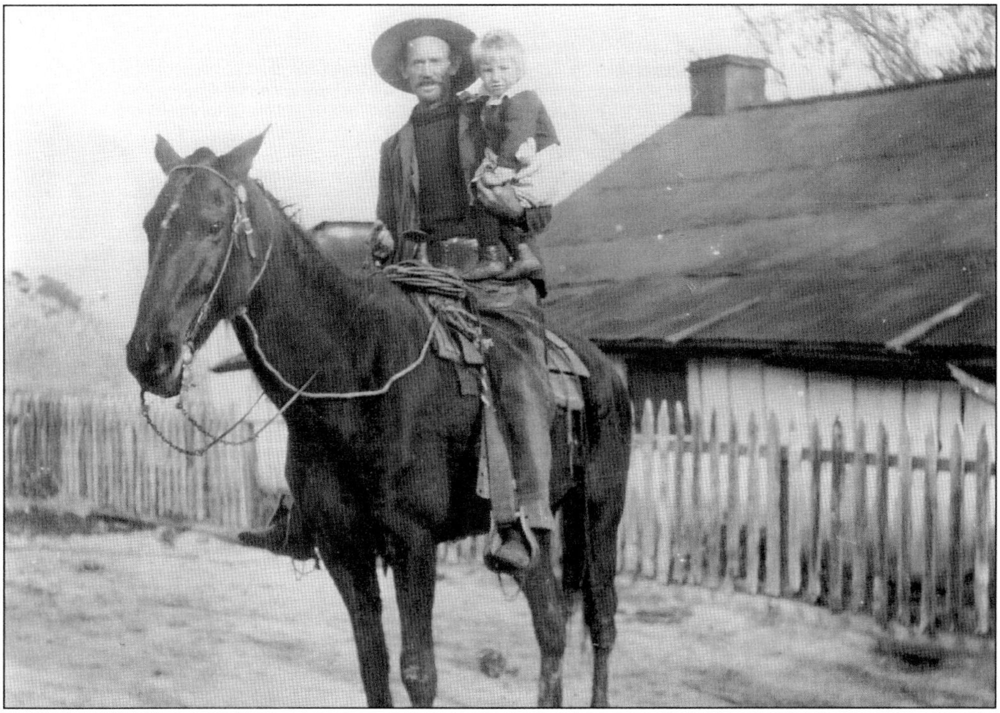

This photograph is of cowboy Sam Taylor and his son Charles in front of the Warner Carrillo Ranch House. In addition to his duties as foreman for the Vail and Sawday cattle companies, he was an experienced guide, taking riders to Hot Springs Mountain and Lost Valley. (Courtesy Chet Taylor.)

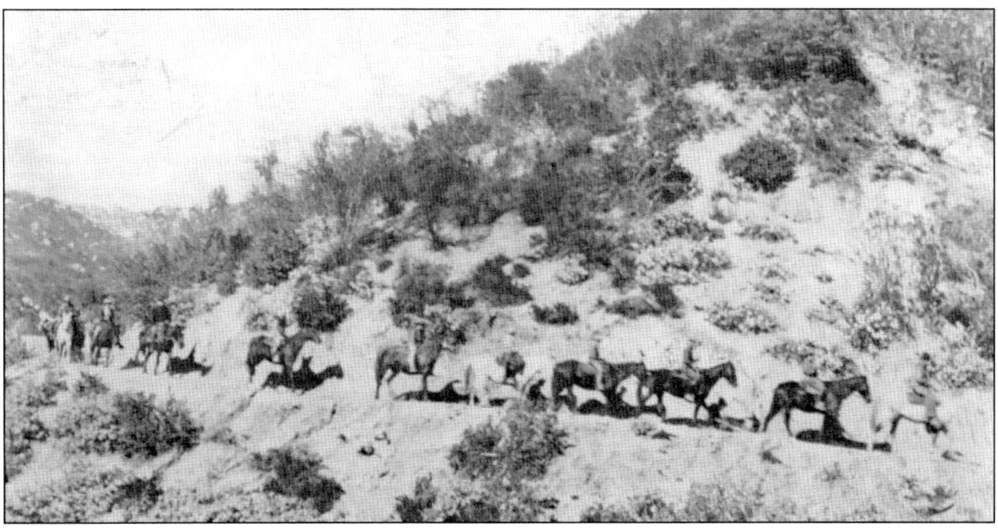

A favorite ride for visitors was a guided trail ride up Hot Springs Mountain and back in one day. The hotel would pack box lunches for the riders, who left early in the morning for the peak. They would enjoy their lunch and water the horses at Ed Fletcher's Eagle's Nest Ranch before climbing the summit single file and returning by sundown.

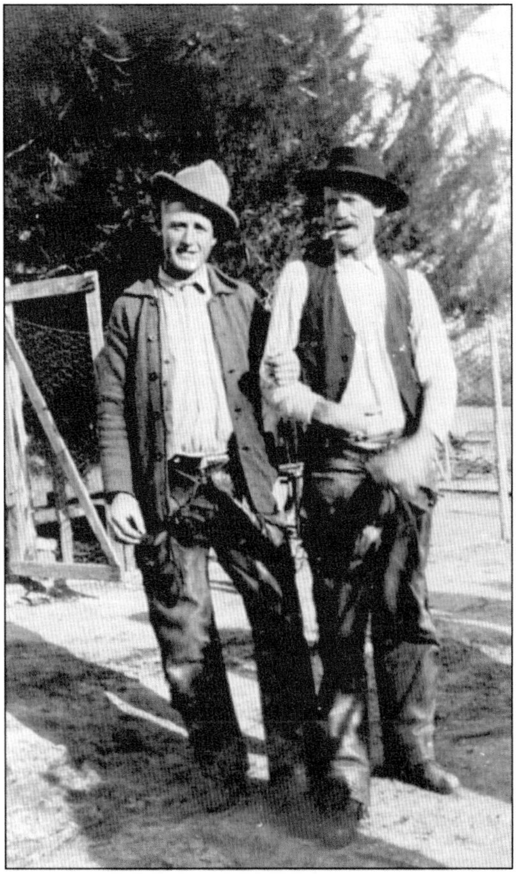

At Eagle's Nest, Fletcher built a dam and created a small lake, which he stocked with trout. Sam Taylor, shown here on the right with Ed Vail, had the difficult task of bringing gravel and sand up the mountain, where he, Fletcher, and others mixed the mortar by hand and poured the dam in sections. (Courtesy Chet Taylor.)

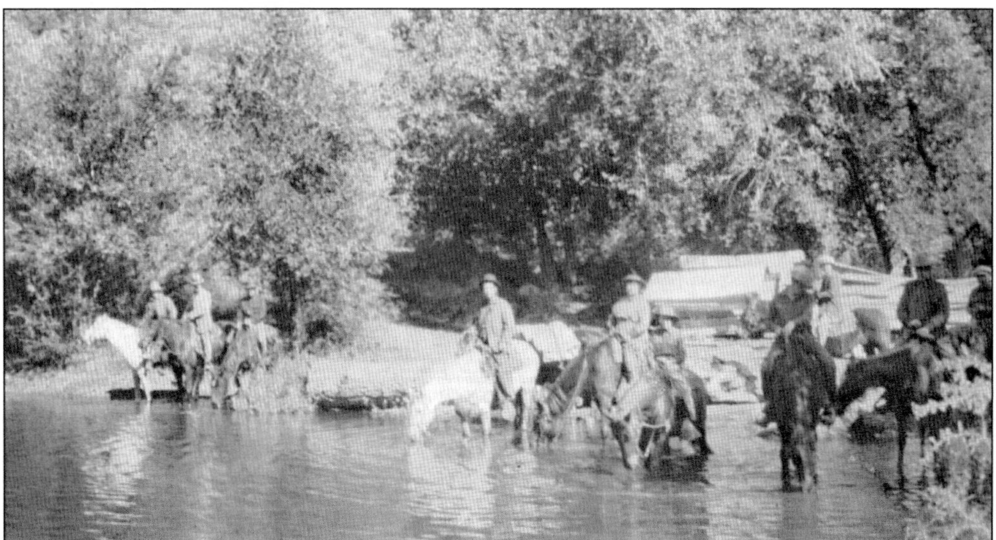

Trail riders are pictured watering their horses at Eagle's Nest. Ed Fletcher was heard once in the dining room, when told fresh trout was the catch of the day, to exclaim "that's my damn trout from my damn lake." The Indian legend about Eagle's Nest was that a small babe lying on a blanket near the springs was picked up by an eagle who flew to the mountains.

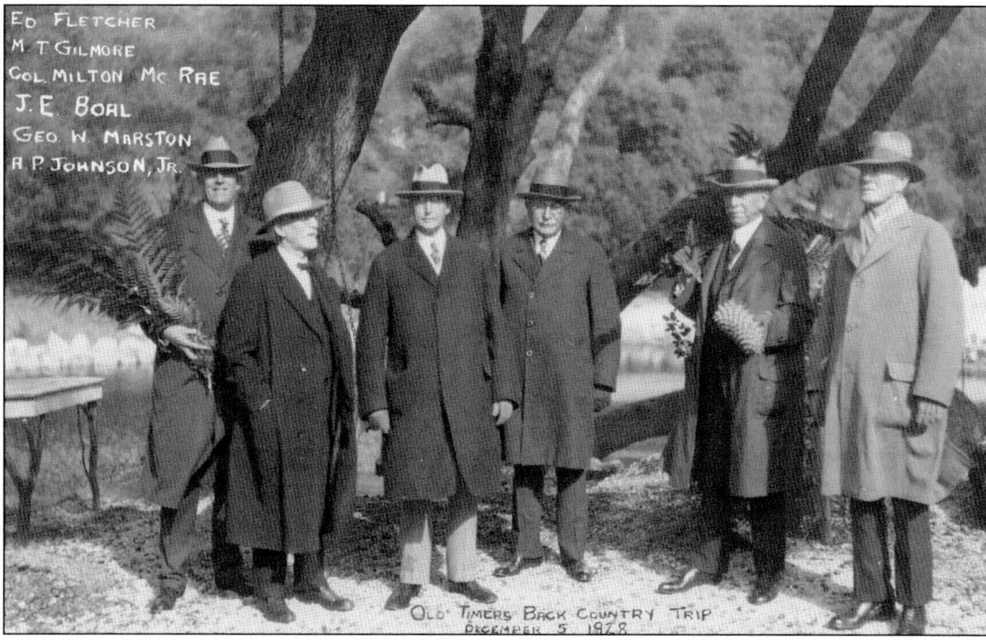

Ed Fletcher (left) is pictured with other San Diego founding fathers at Eagle's Nest. He was one of the most significant people in the development of San Diego County. Others, from left to right, are M.T. Gilmore, Col. Milton McRae, J.E. Boal, George Marston, and A.P. Johnson Jr. (Courtesy Ed Fletcher Papers, University of California at San Diego Library Archives.)

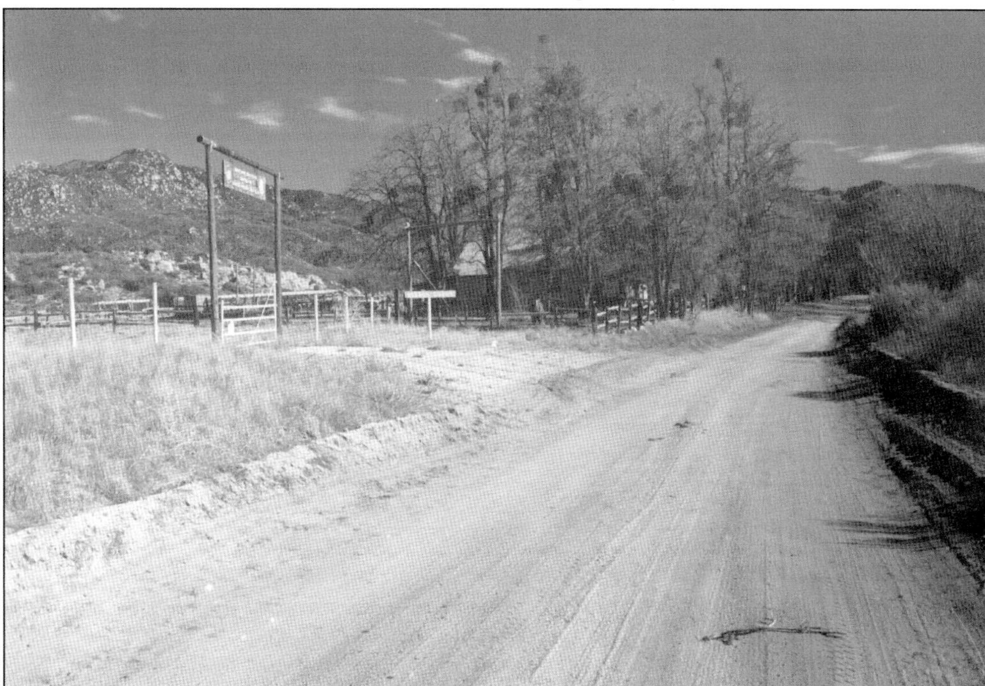
This photograph shows the original dirt road that led from the main highway up to the stables, around the springs, behind the lodge, and south through present-day Los Tules. When the highway was realigned in 1936, several hairpin turns were eliminated.

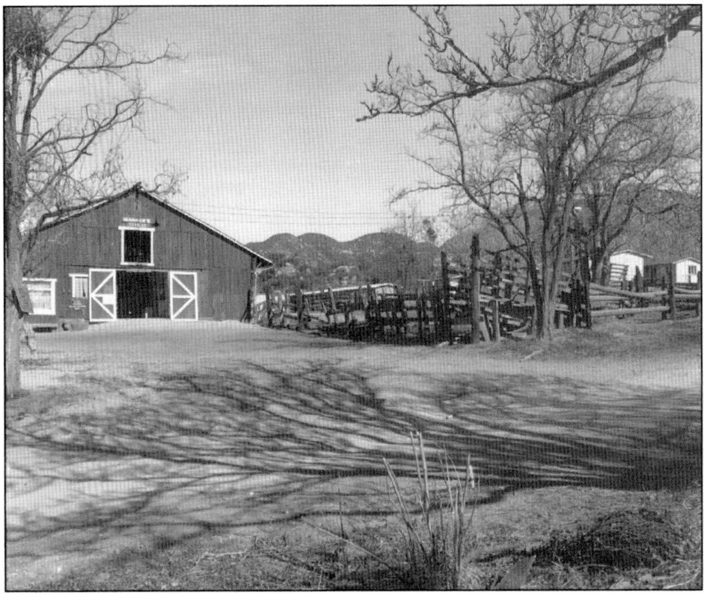

This old red barn was built in 1910 by Hank Smith and lasted until the 1980s, when it was torn down by the Rossi ownership and replaced by a modern equestrian facility. Mrs. Smith was always called "Ladle" or "Ma," the former having something to do with all the meals she cooked. Seasonal employee housing, as seen in the background, consisted of rooms and shared baths for teenage wranglers and hotel staff, especially during the busy summer months.

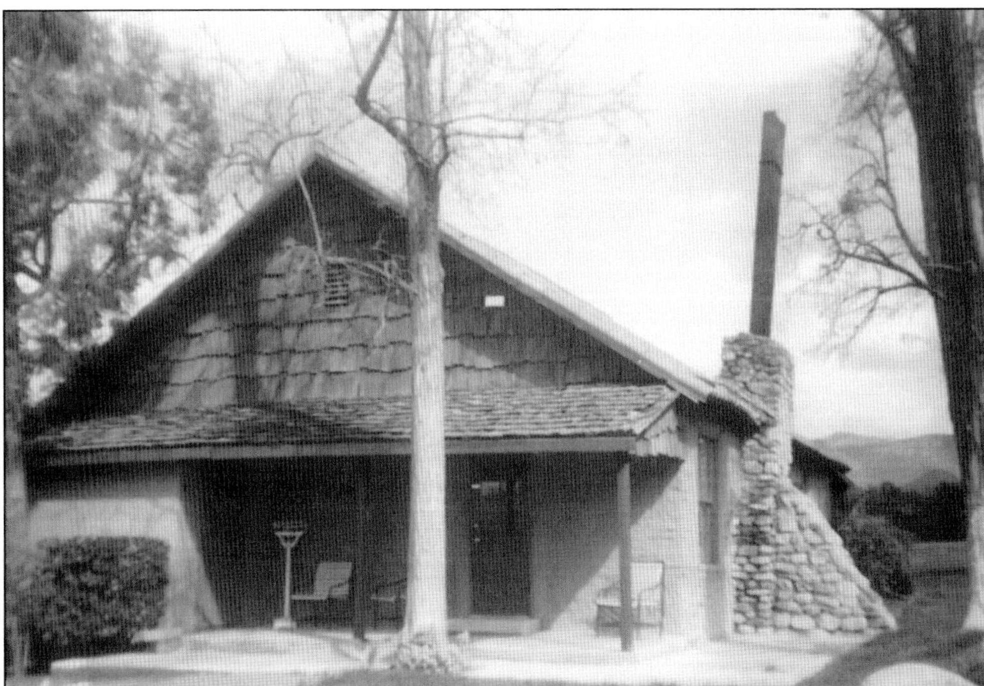

The Wrangler House was the home of Hank and Ma Smith for many years and is still there today. During World War II, this building was the headquarters of the Army recuperation hospital unit stationed there.

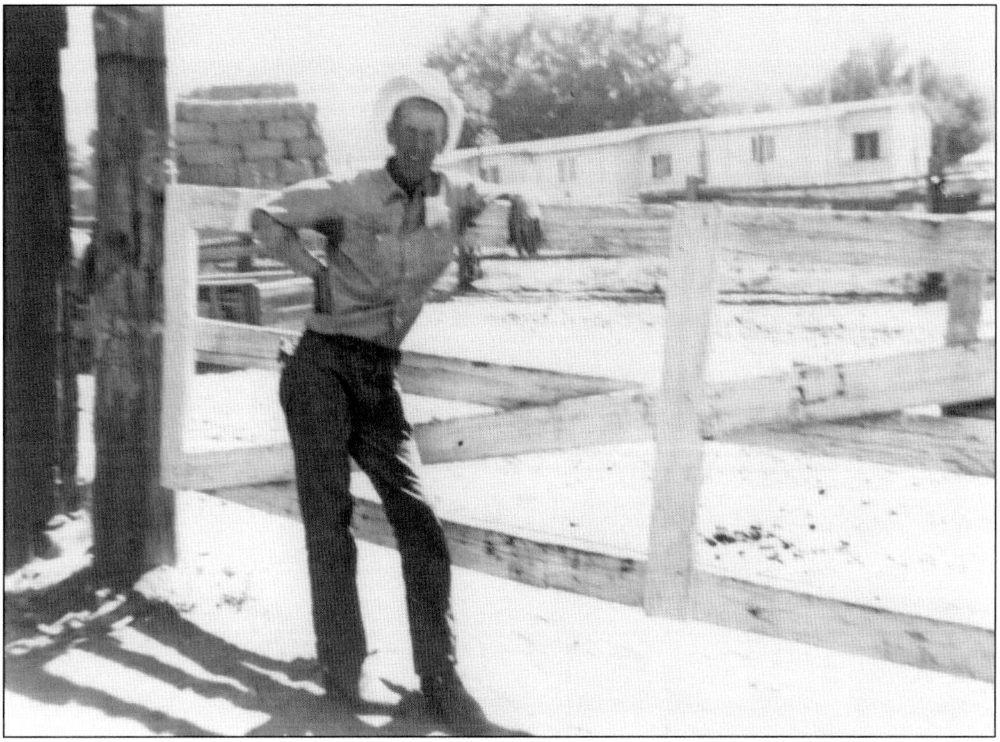

Longtime head wrangler Hank Smith not only ran the stables, he and Ma Smith also supervised the seasonal wranglers, most of them "bad girls" who were foster children of the Smiths and attended Warner Union School. Short on words but long on discipline, Hank was definitely in charge of both horses and teenagers.

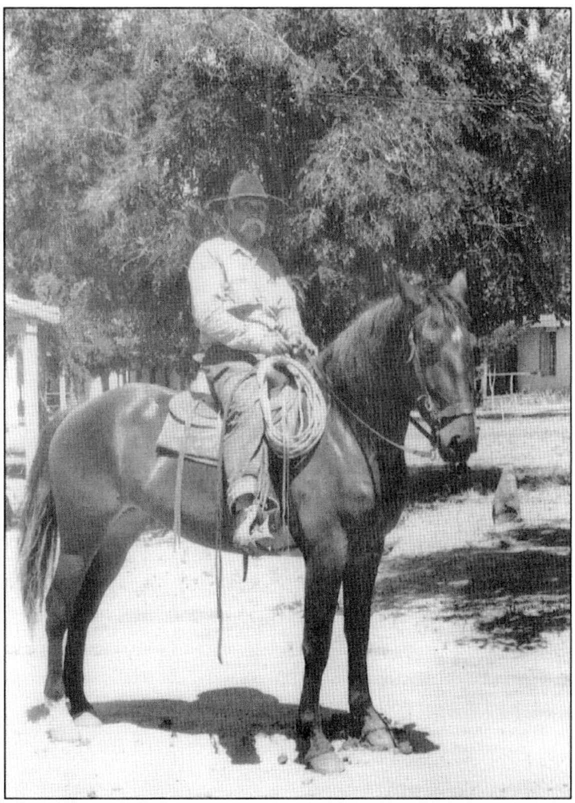

Longtime tourist guide and storyteller Julio Ortega is seen here on his horse, but he was frequently found on the porch of the Trading Post spinning tales for visitors. Julio's ancestors lived in the valley when Juan Jose Warner arrived. Ortega kept his old saddle, bridle, and spurs in the little cabin he lived in until he died because, as he put it, "If you were not a cowboy, you were not anything."

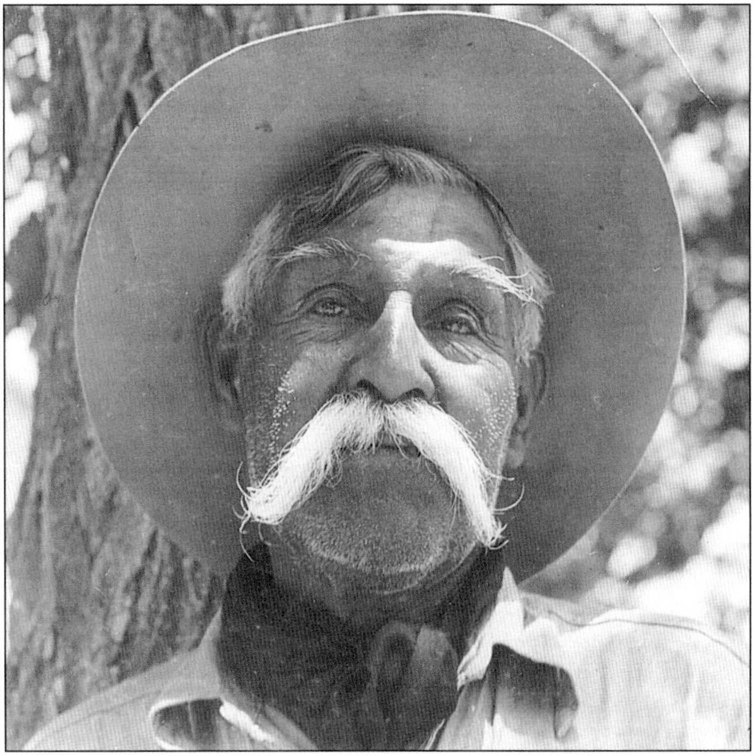

Julio said he was descended from the conquistadores of the Anza expedition and baptized by Fr. Junípero Serra, but Julio was known to embellish his stories to make them more colorful. White-haired in later years, he had bright blue eyes and the dark skin of an Indian but features more like a Spanish grandee, for he was of mixed blood. Many Ortega descendants still live in the Warner Valley.

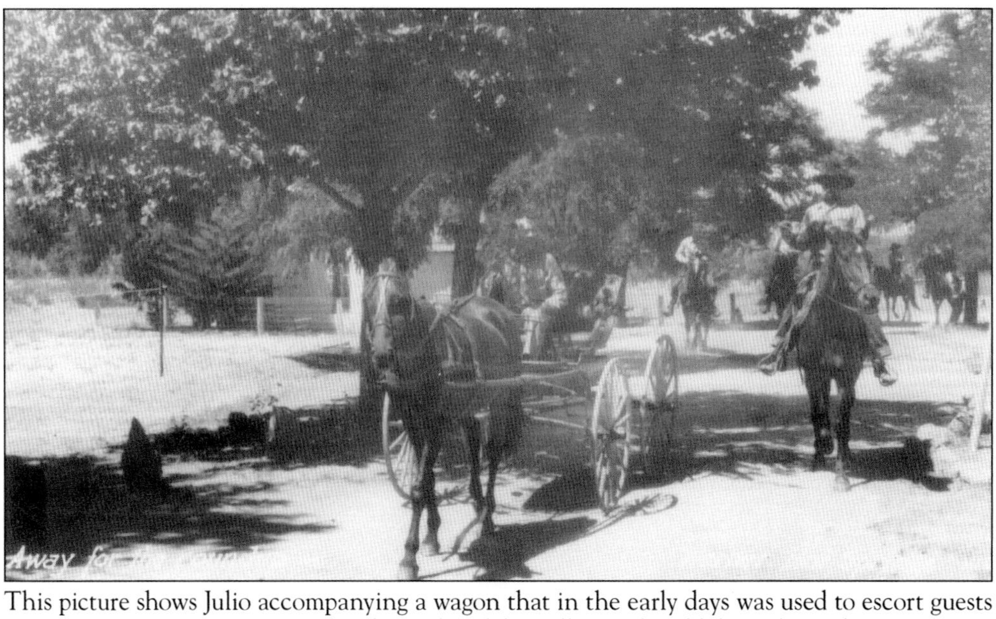

This picture shows Julio accompanying a wagon that in the early days was used to escort guests to their rooms. In a 1983 interview, he spoke of the valley in the old days when "there was water everywhere and the grass used to be so high. Now the irrigation district is milking the land dry, and even the grass does not seem to grow any more. Soon, it will be dry as the desert."

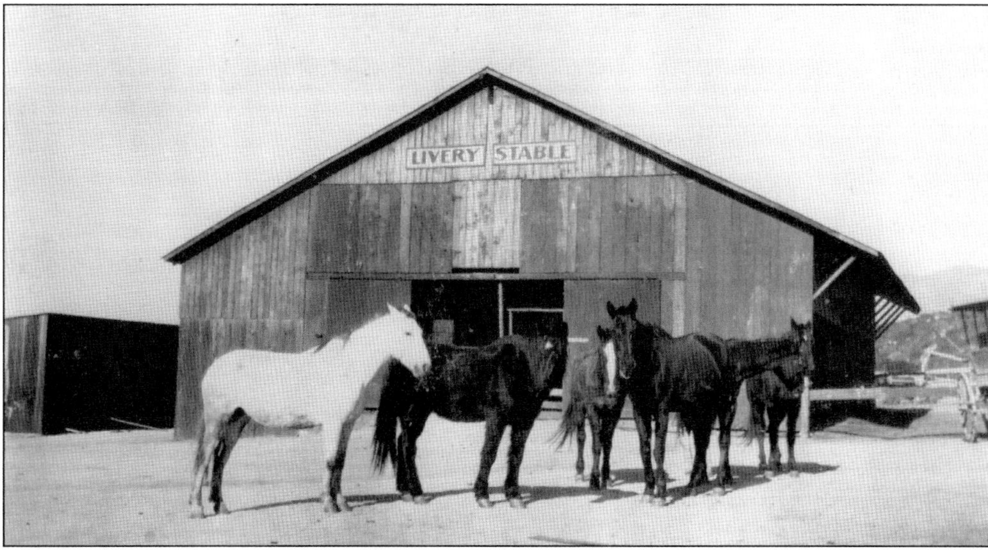

This is an early photograph of the Warner Hot Springs barn before signage and decorative trim were added. Tennis courts and a basketball court now occupy the area of the old barn.

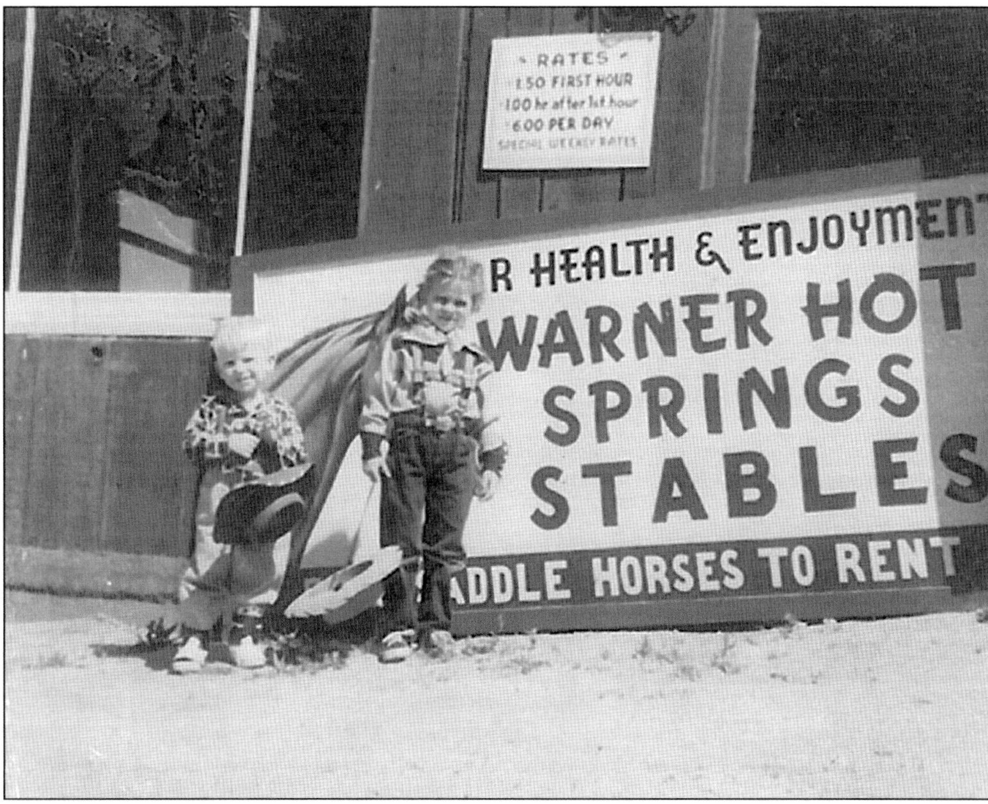

A picture from the 1950s shows Janie and Howard "Bud" Fletcher; one was never too young to ride. Above the big stable sign, a smaller sign shows the rates: "a dollar fifty for the first hour, a dollar for the second hour, six dollars for all day, weekly rates available." (Courtesy Howard Fletcher family.)

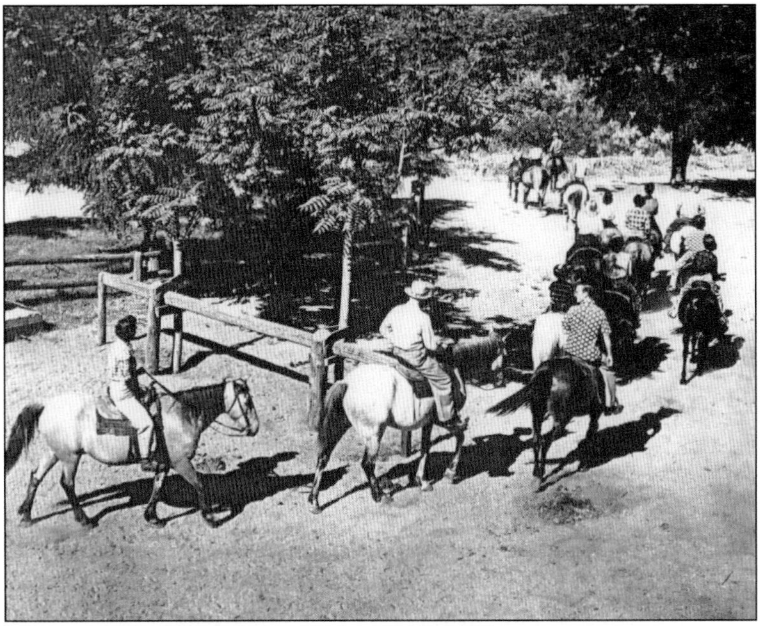

In this photograph, guests head out for a trail ride. There were no insurance forms, and a sign warned guests "Ride at Your Own Risk." Frequent visitors had their favorite mounts named Rowdy, King, Peanuts, Trouble, and the ever-unpredictable Joker.

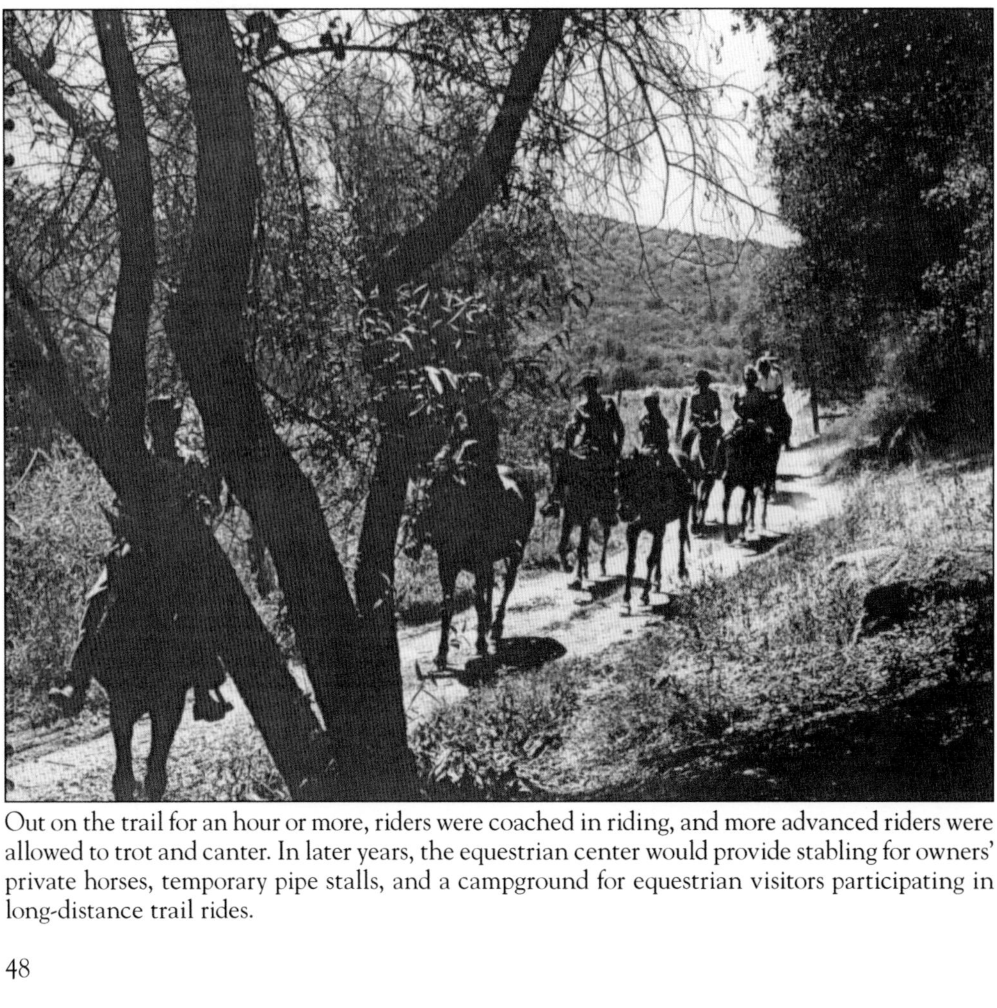

Out on the trail for an hour or more, riders were coached in riding, and more advanced riders were allowed to trot and canter. In later years, the equestrian center would provide stabling for owners' private horses, temporary pipe stalls, and a campground for equestrian visitors participating in long-distance trail rides.

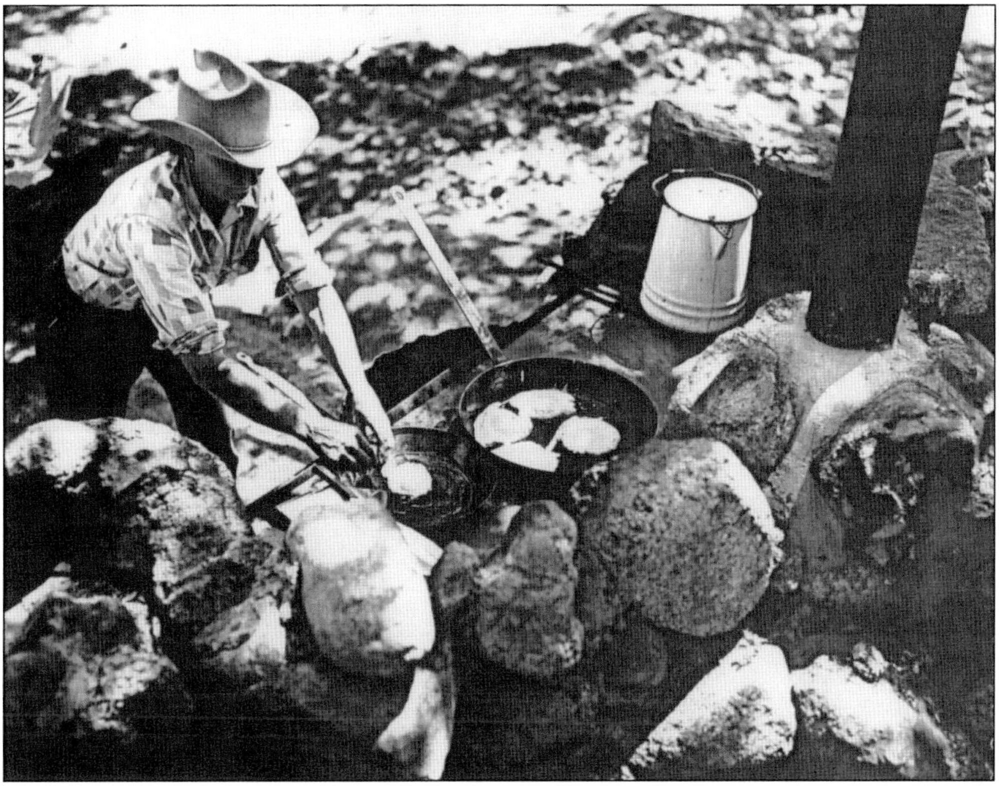

In this photograph, a cowgirl rustles up breakfast for guests on the breakfast ride, which started at 8:00 a.m. A trail guide was sent riding through the cabins early in the morning yelling "Get up for the breakfast ride" so that guests would be on time. After riding the trails, the guests would stop near the boulders and oak trees at Cold Spring for breakfast cooked over the campfire.

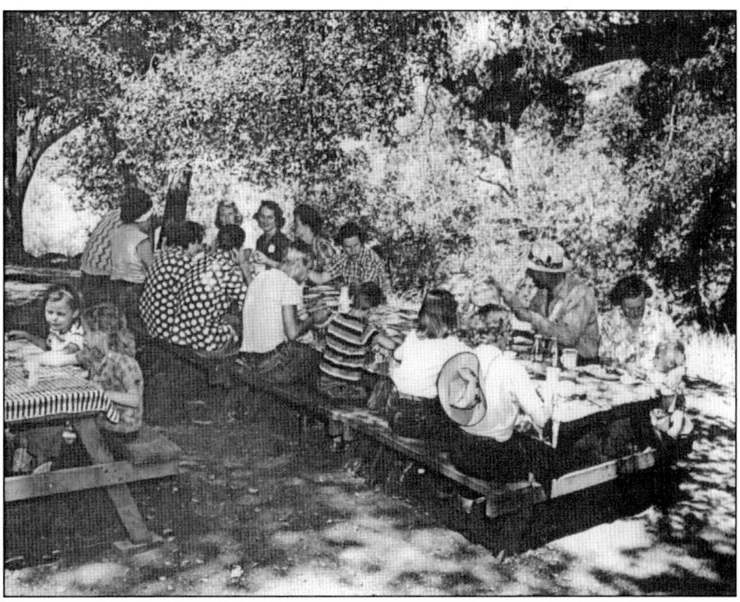

Children and adults alike enjoyed a great "all you can eat" breakfast of pancakes, eggs, bacon, sausage, coffee, juice, toast, and other breakfast items cooked over a campfire. In later years, the campsite would be moved to ranch property along the Agua Caliente Creek section of the Pacific Crest Trail, and a wagon was provided so that non-riders could enjoy the breakfast, too.

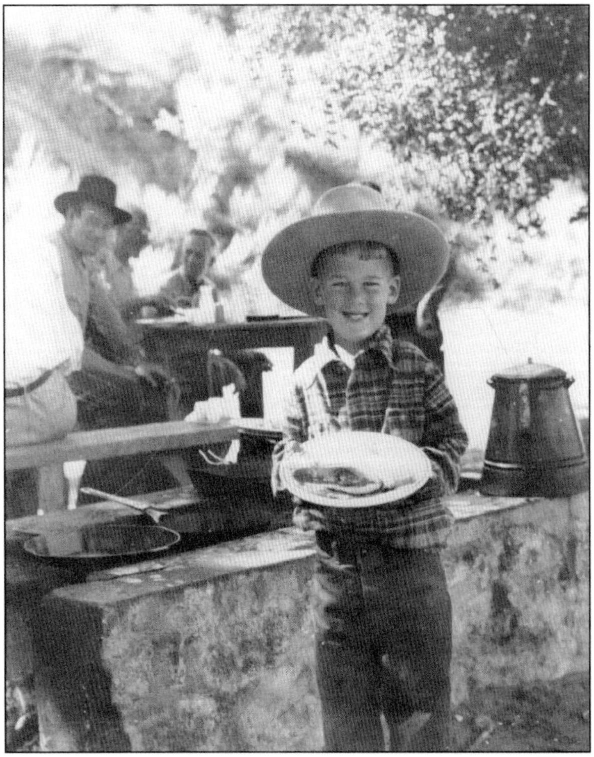

An early marketing brochure states that "kids take to this place like ducks to water." The boy shown is Johnny Coop, son of bartender and manager John Coop. Sitting in the background on the left is frequent visitor and movie star John Wayne.

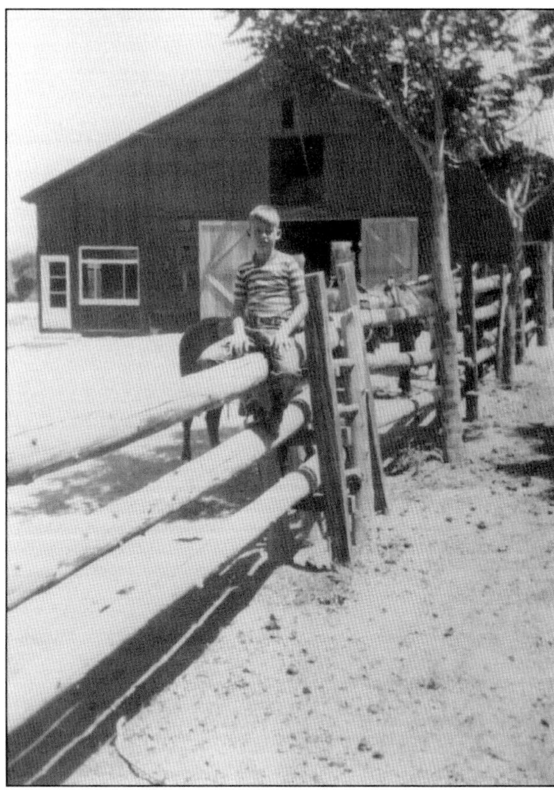

Kids loved to play cowboy, climbing the fence at the barn corral while waiting for the trail ride to begin. Hank Smith would size up children and adults alike and ask them about their riding ability, then assign them a horse. His word was final and he was not a man to be argued with.

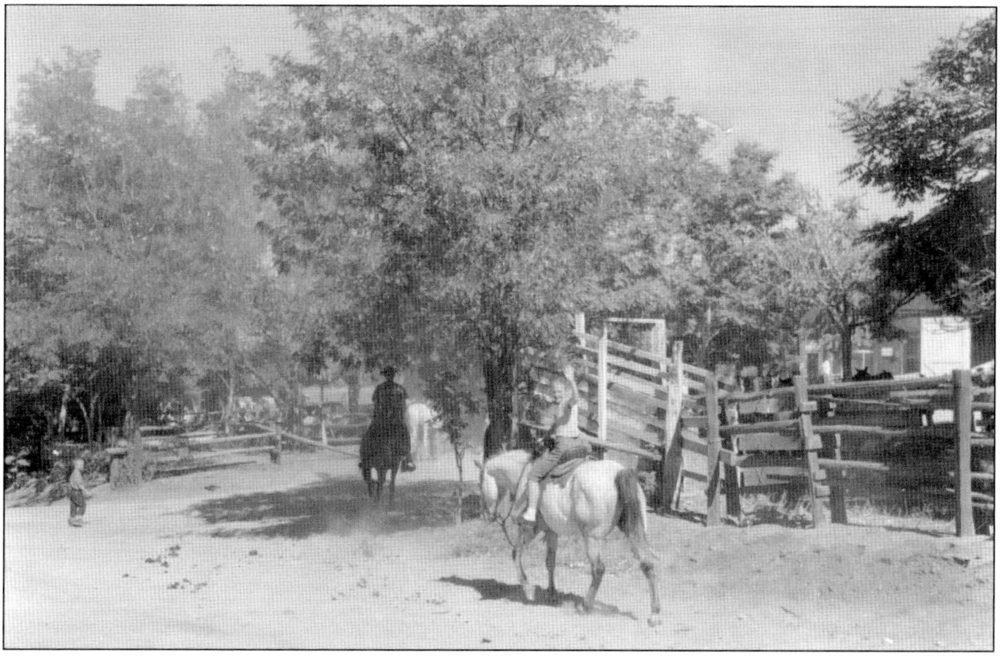

A happy cowgirl returns to the barn after a trail ride. Moonlight rides and wildflower rides in season were also offered. Head wrangler Smith's famous last words to riders were always "hold on tight on the way back to the barn," when the horses, anxious to return to the stables and be fed, would start to pick up the pace and throw many a rider.

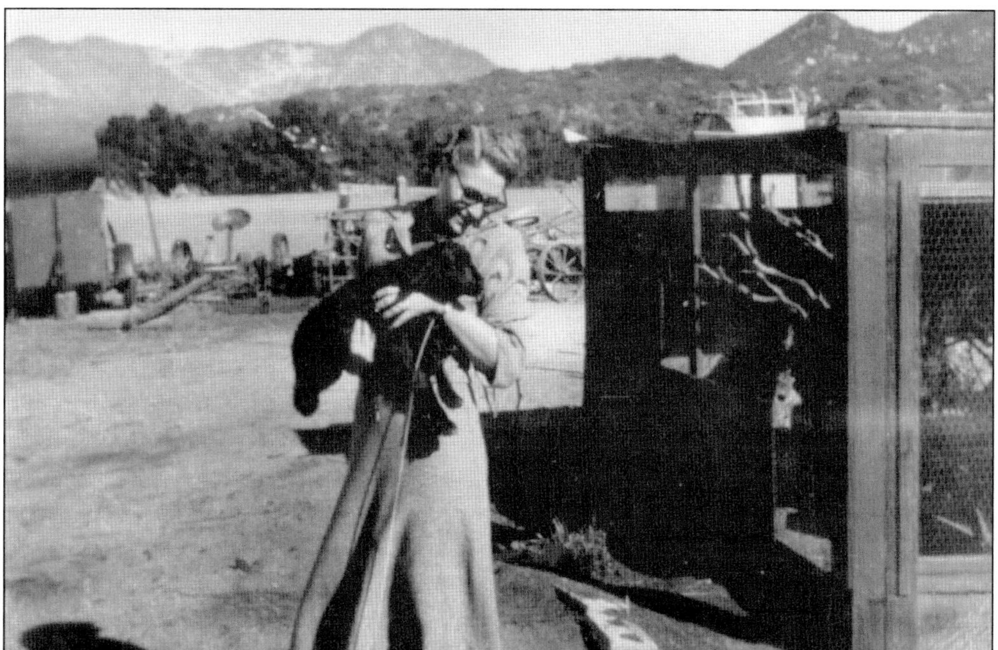

This woman is seen at the petting zoo next to the stables, where an odd assortment of animals like goats, sheep, foxes, coyotes, and a bobcat were kept. Some of these animals had been found injured and were rescued.

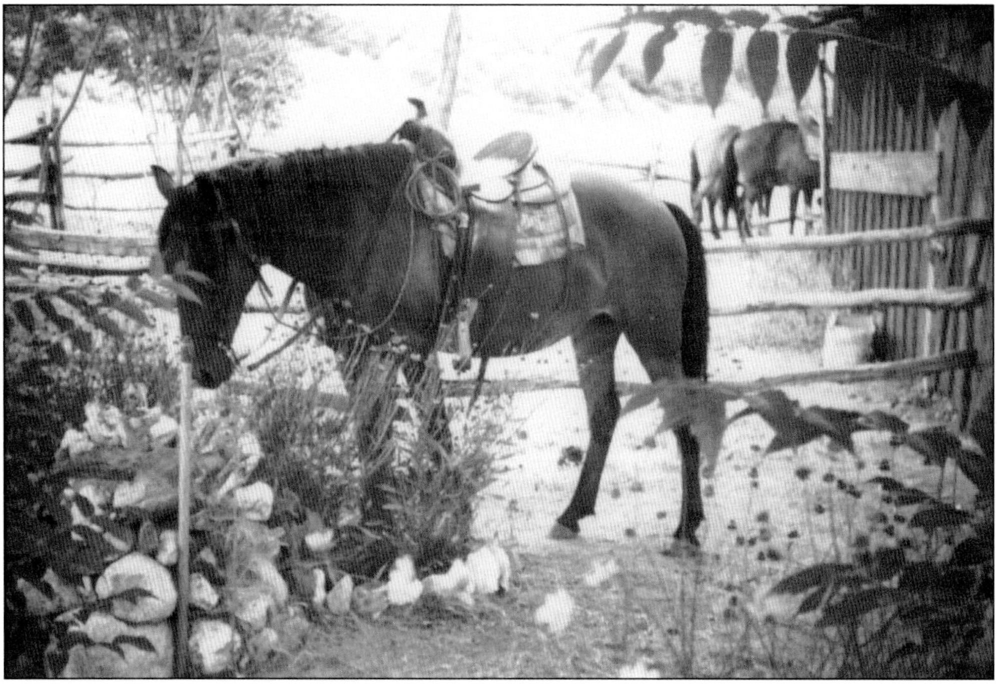

Julio Ortega's horse is shown eating Ma Smith's flowers after a trail ride.

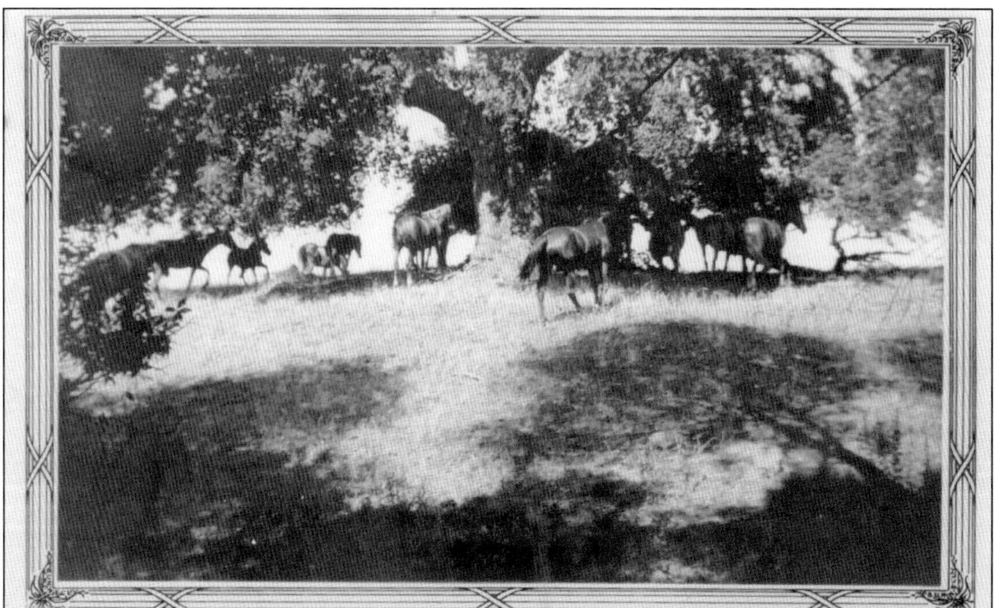

Stables horses are shown at pasture under the big oak tree in the meadow past Cold Spring in what now is a cultural preserve. They were also pastured in the commons field in Los Tules. William Henshaw started the development of the residential area of Los Tules and the Los Tules Mutual Water Company in 1939. Residents were able to use the facilities of the resort in the 1970s for $20 a month.

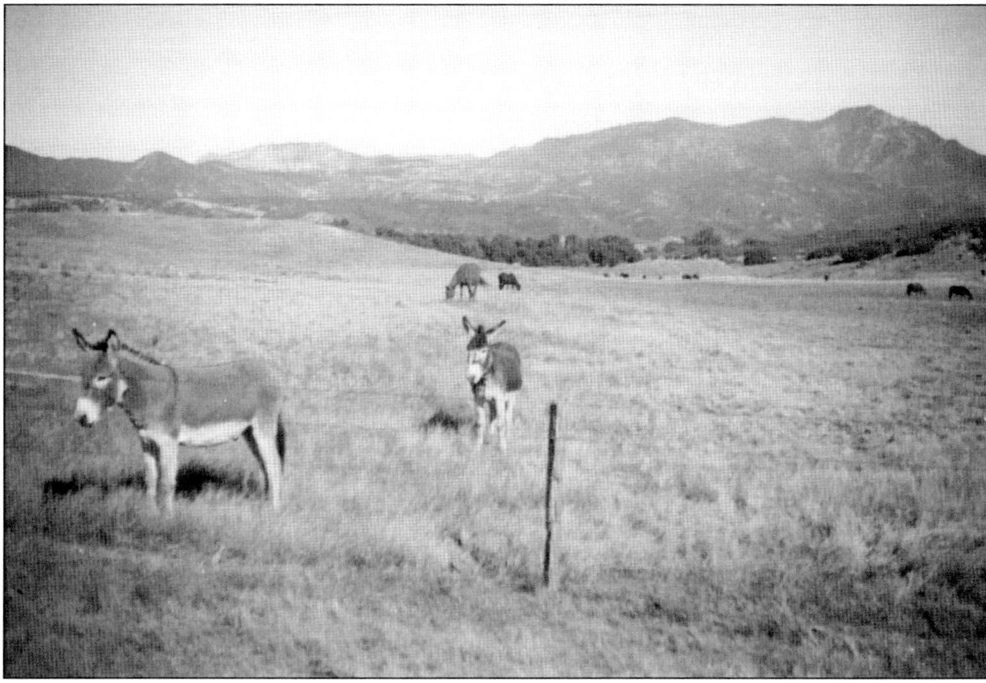

For longer time periods, horses were pastured out in the valley, where there was plenty of grass to eat, as were the burros shown here, who were used as pack animals for longer rides.

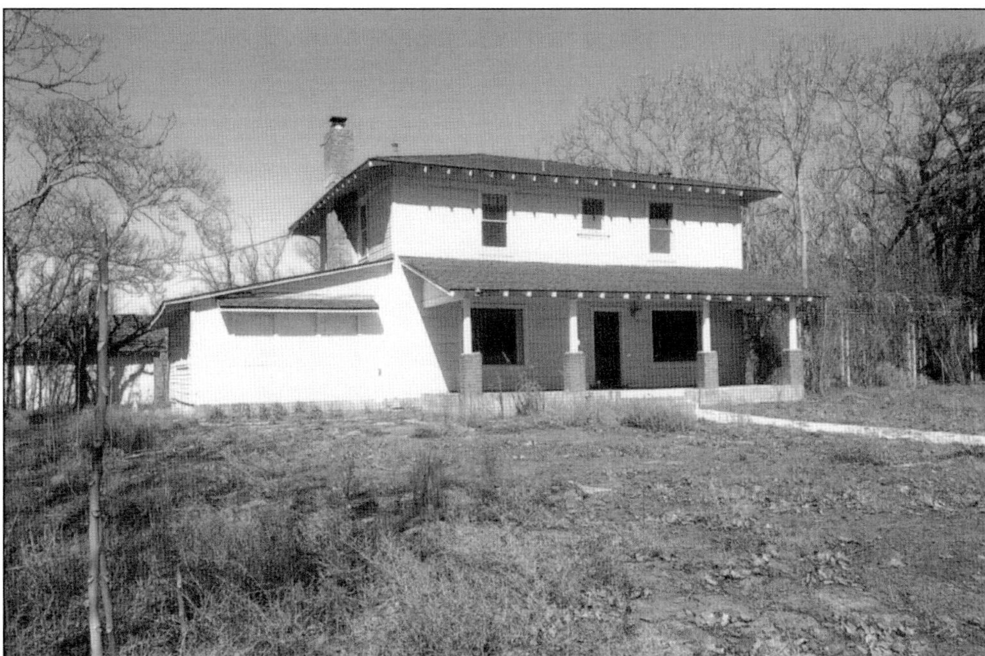

This farmhouse on the west side of the highway was built by Vail and Gates for their ranch foremen about 1915. One of several houses for long-term employees, it was home to many over the years, including the families of managers Jay Ream, Syd Furze, and John Coop. A hotel dairy nearby operated until the early 1950s, and the milk was sold locally and used at the hotel.

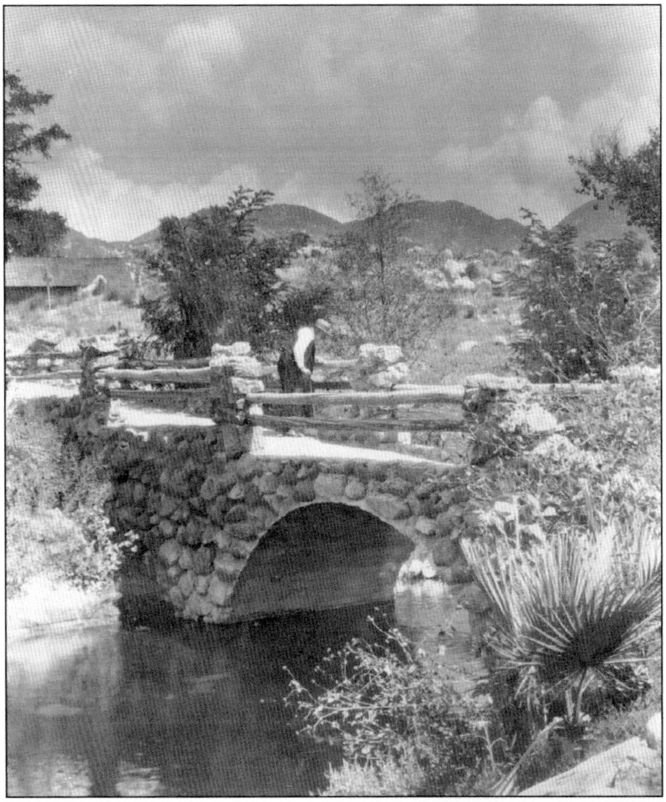

The stone bridge over the springs, which replaced the old wood bridge, and the stone walls were constructed in 1924. During World War I, there were lots of wooded paths around the springs, and the ranch was used as a recuperation center for soldiers. Sailors from the nearby survival school were allowed to use the pools during World War II as long as they were not too rowdy.

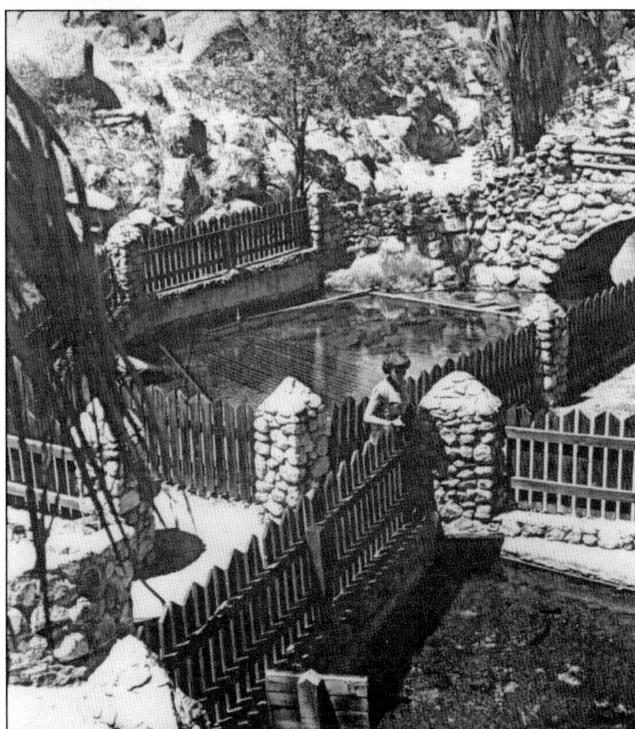

A picture from the 1930s shows the taller palm trees and picket fences installed to keep people and animals from entering the hot springwater and getting burned. One can actually see the springwater bubbling up from the earth.

Five

IT'S THE WATER

The most unique and fascinating feature of Warner Hot Springs is the world-famous hot springs themselves. Even prior to 1851, the springs were a flourishing source of income to the Indians, who charged for hot baths and laundry and came to recognize the tourist value of the warm waters, renting their adobes to early visitors. One can only imagine how wonderful soaking in the hot water must have been for riders of the Butterfield Stage or immigrants on the Southern Overland Trail. Continuously bubbling out of the ground century after century at a temperature of 110 to 140 degrees Fahrenheit, the mineral waters are famous for their healing qualities. The output rate is 150,000–200,000 gallons a day. It was said that many of the local Indians lived past 100 because of the springs. They drank it, bathed in it, and even slept in it on cold winter nights.

The first hot water at the resort was from the springs, and the water system was made on-site from concrete pipes for $2,000. At one time, besides being gravity-fed into the sulfur swimming pools, the water was piped into the early casitas. The hotel laundry was also washed in sulfur water. The US Geological Survey indicates that the springwater contains 16 different minerals, but it is the sulfur smell most people remember. It was often called "taking the cure," and early brochures promised it cured arthritis, rheumatism, emphysema, and even alcoholism.

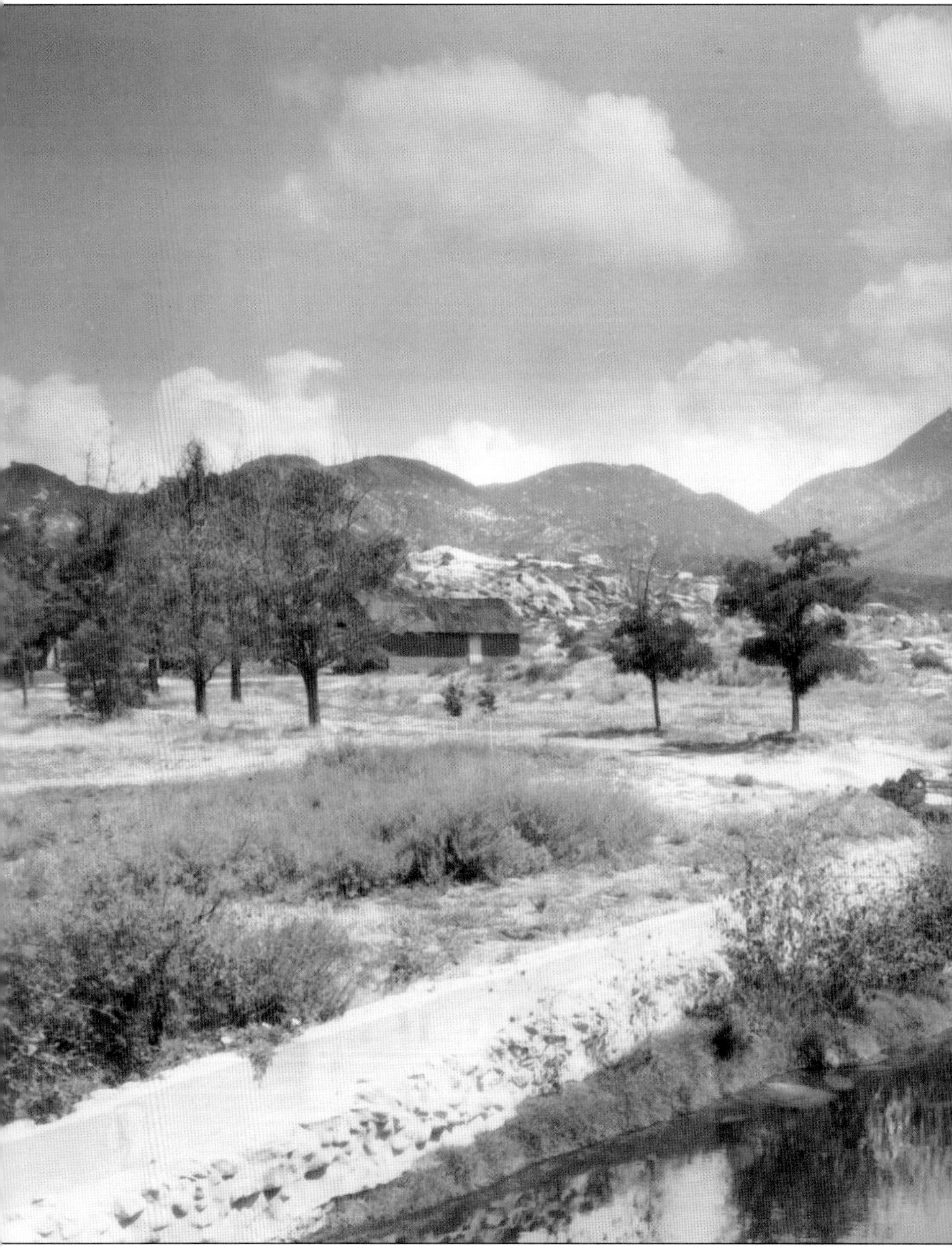

This photograph shows the hot springs on a beautiful clear day with Hot Springs Mountain rising in the background. A deteriorating, boulder-strewn granite path on the right leads up

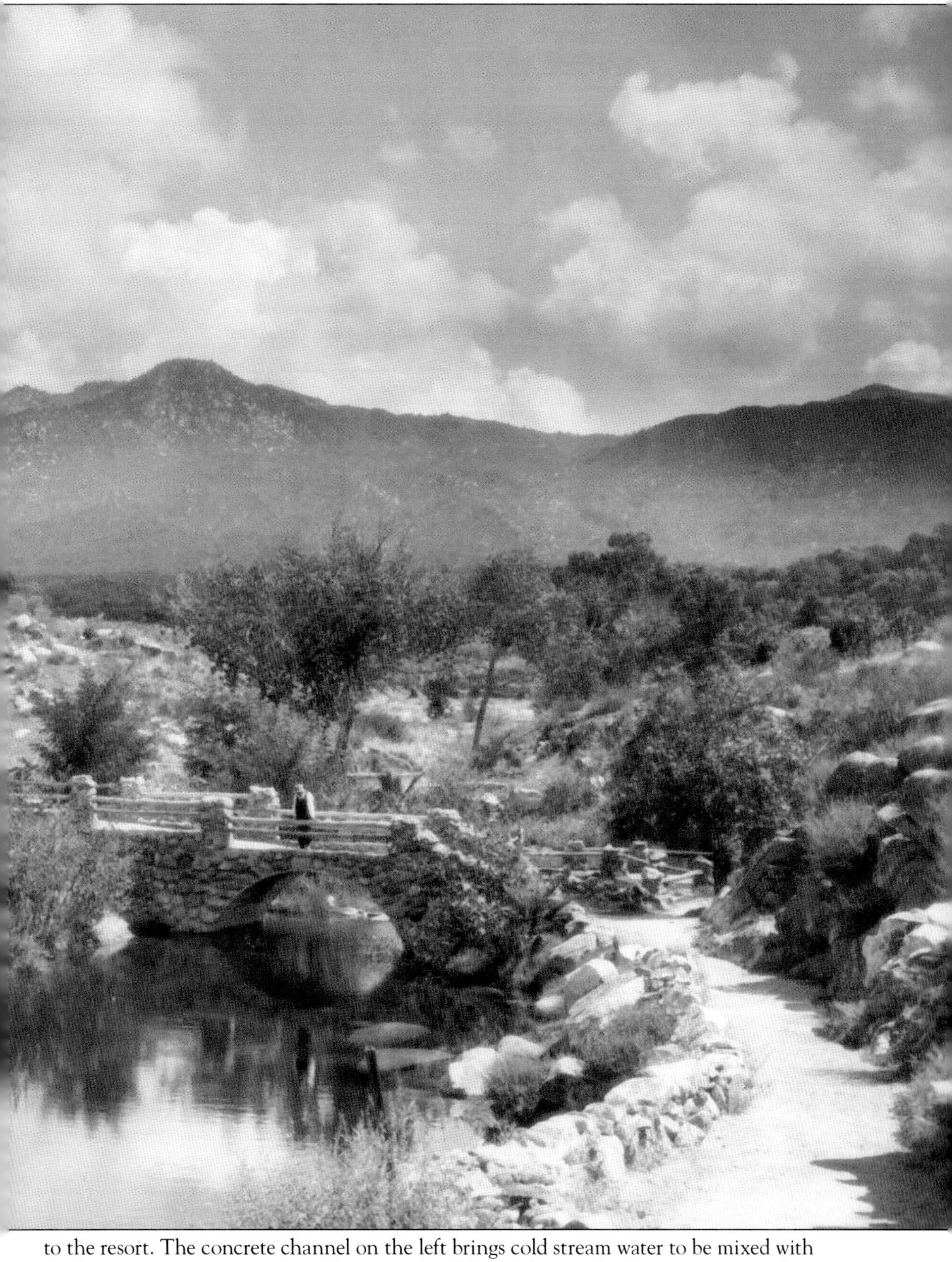

to the resort. The concrete channel on the left brings cold stream water to be mixed with the hot springs water to cool it off to a comfortable 104 degrees for the swimming pool.

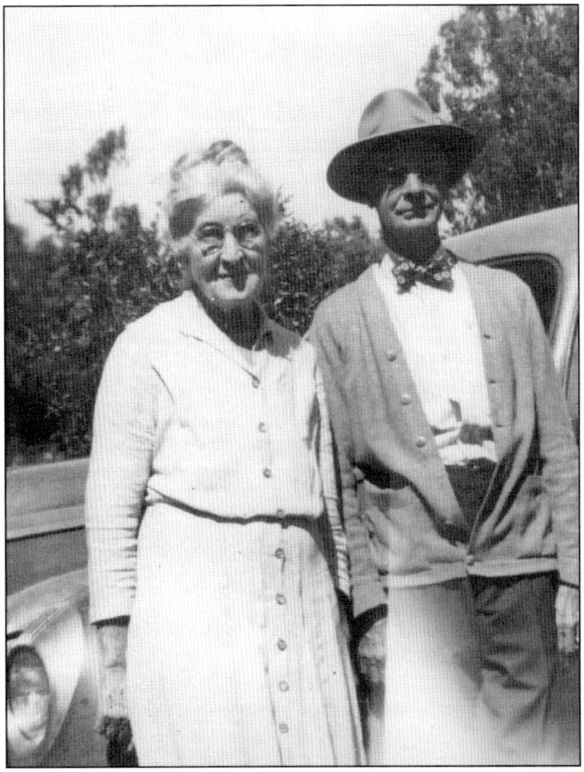

Mr. and Mrs. Fred Hewlett are shown in the 1930s. Fred was the general manager during that time and had the picket fences constructed around the springs. They resided in Los Tules in the old Riverside Cement manager's hunting lodge. Fred sent many "who's who at Warner Hot Springs" press releases to the *San Diego Union* society pages.

Visitors in the 1940s and 1950s will remember a slot in the rock wall of the hottest spring pool and a long metal dipper and paper cups so that those who were so inclined could "take the cure" by drinking the hot sulfur water.

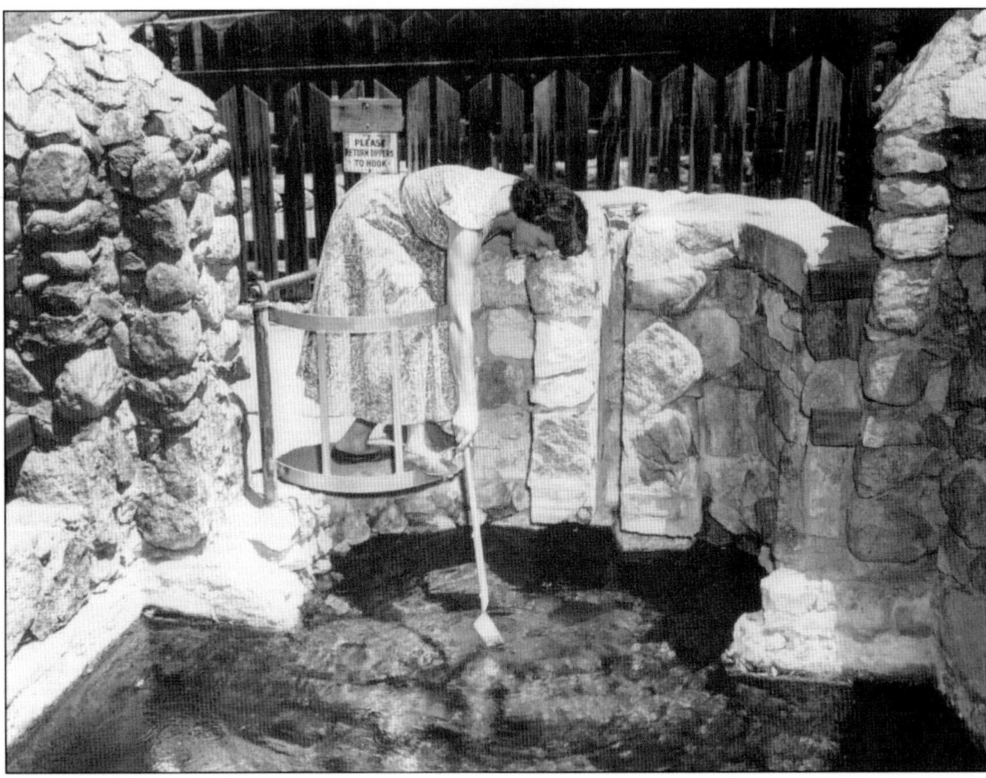

In this photograph, the picket fences have been replaced by split rails, and the California fan palms are taking their adult form. Palms at this elevation are not compatible with the winter cold, but because of the heat from the hot springs, the palms thrive.

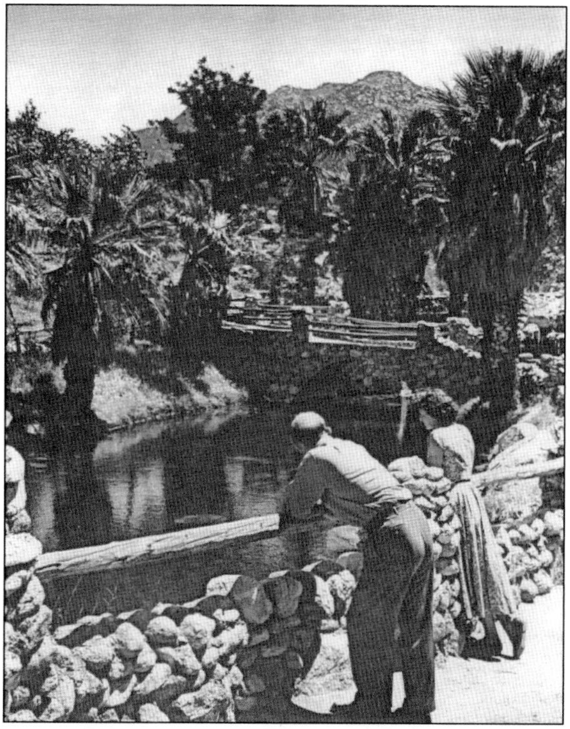

The palm trees in this picture are reaching their mature height and have been trimmed. Guests are shown photographing the springs and perhaps tossing coins into a concrete pot in the largest pool for good luck. A nearby sign indicated these coins were collected and given to the church.

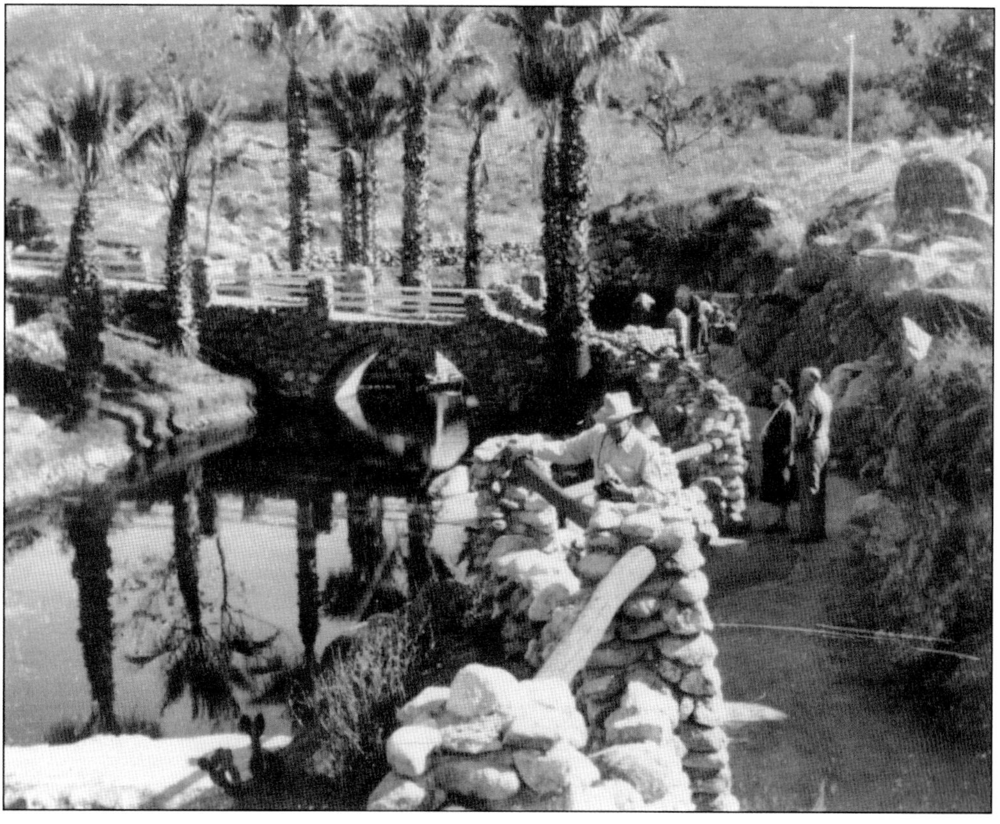

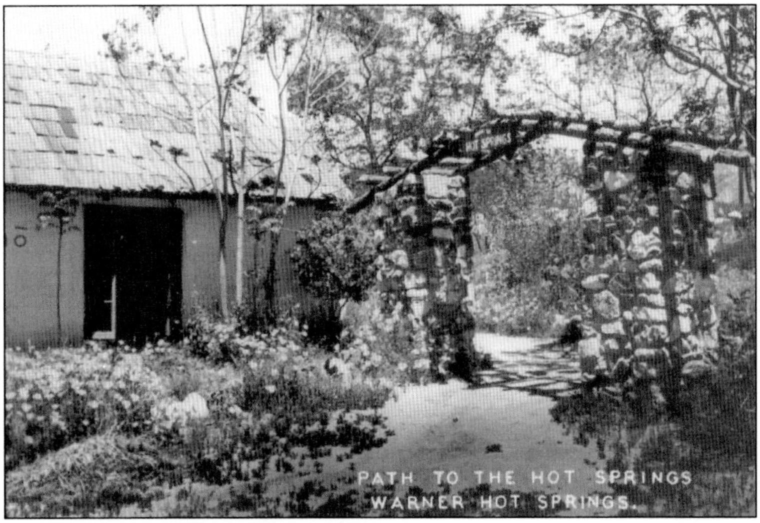

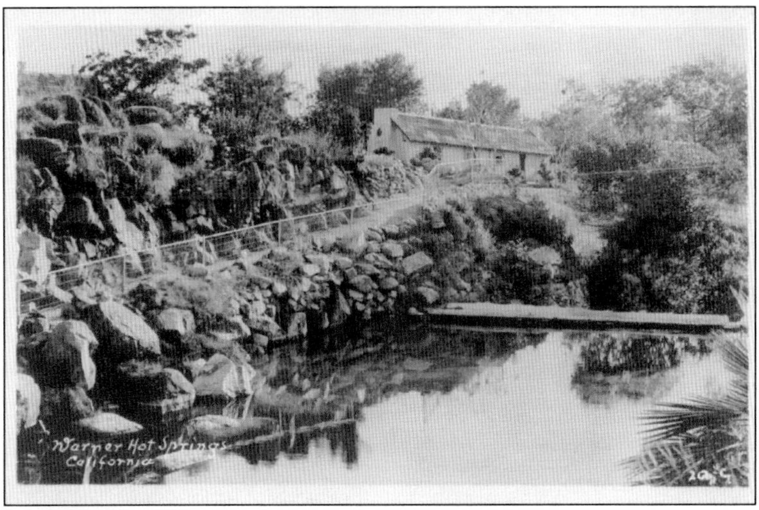

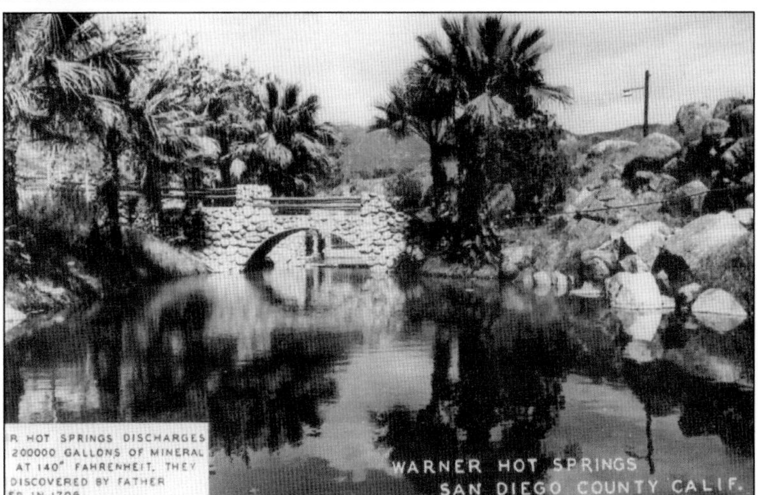

The vine-covered stone-and-wood arbor next to the Carson adobe still graces the pathway that leads to the hot springs from the resort area. In the middle photograph, the pathway is seen from the springs with the adobe at the top of the hill. A spillway releases the overflow, and pipes carry the water by gravity down to the swimming pools. The bottom photograph is a popular postcard that was sent by many visitors.

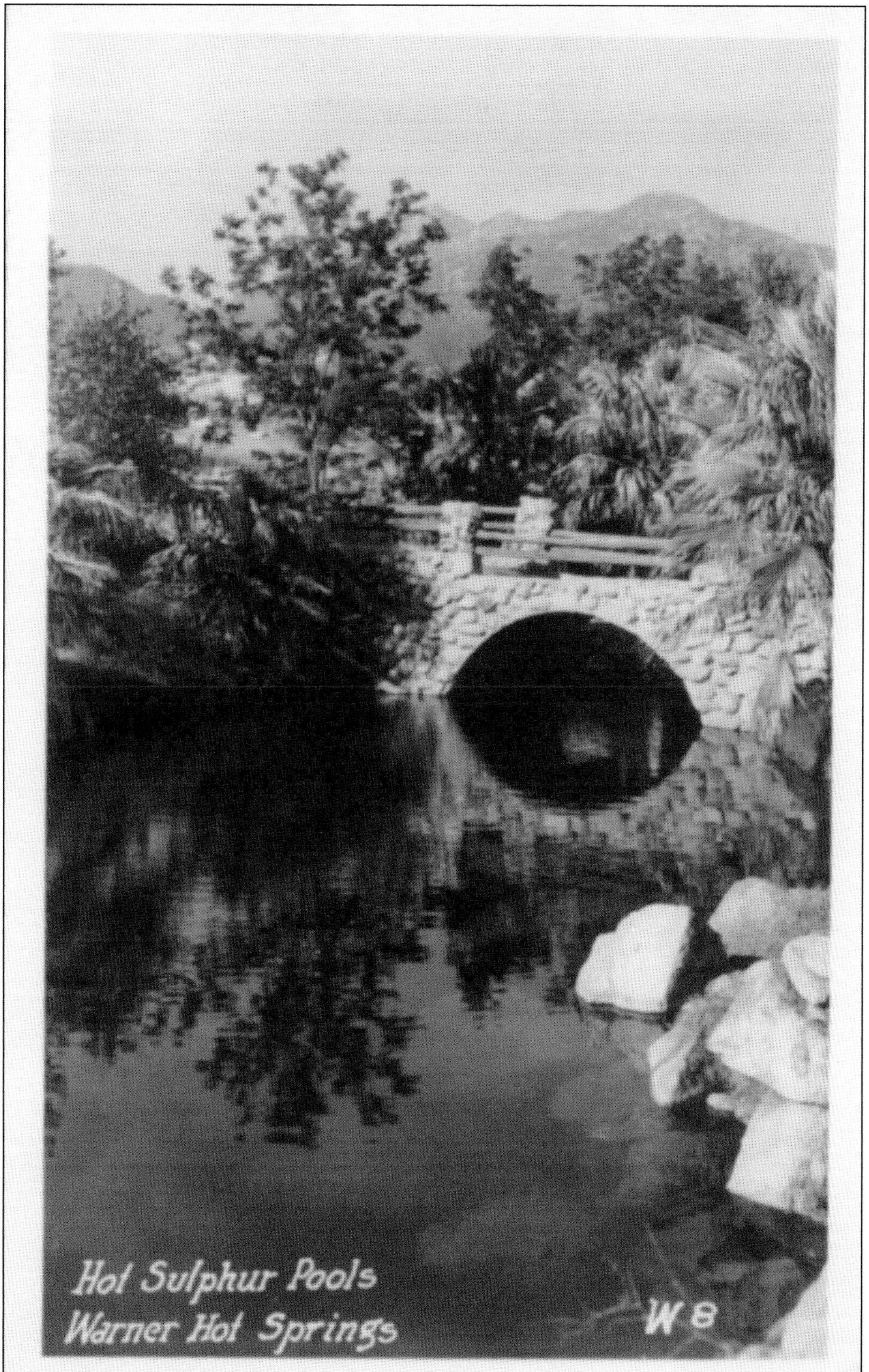

Another popular postcard image shows the stone bridge beautifully reflected in a full pond with Hot Springs Mountain and the growing palm trees as a backdrop.

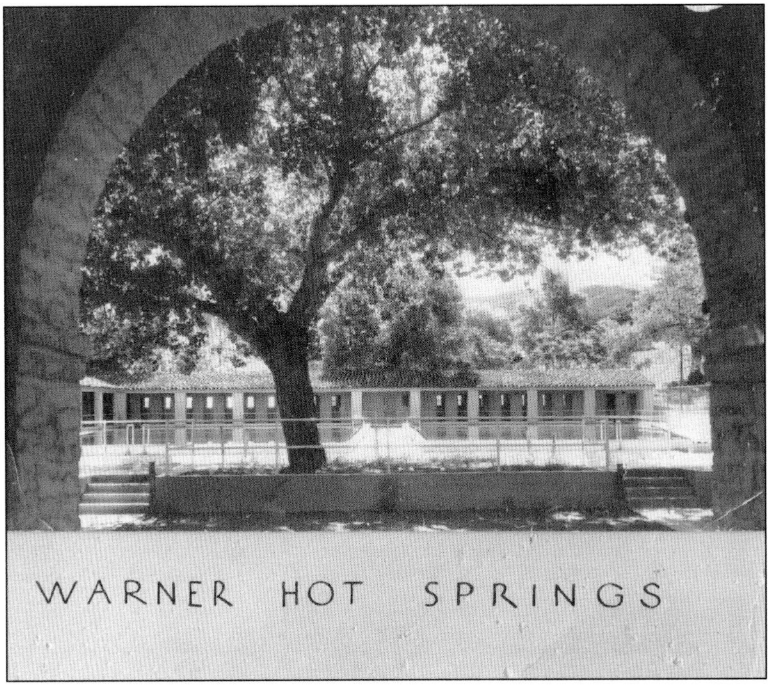

A 1940s marketing brochure picture was taken from the entry arches and shows the pool complex. A parking lot was where the present-day tennis courts are, and admission to the pool was 25¢ including parking. Guests could book an appointment for a hot soak or a mud bath in big concrete tubs or a massage from the masseuse or masseur.

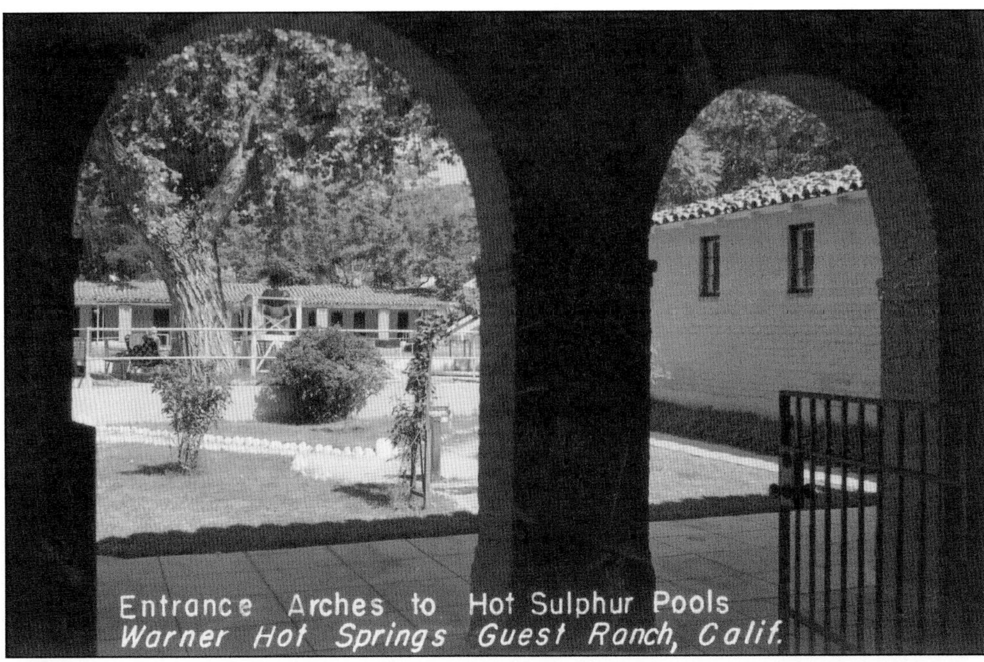

After the arches, guests entered a small garden between the bathhouses. A lifeguard is shown on a raised wooden stand under the giant cottonwood tree. This was a benefit that the parents of small children enjoyed so they could relax and soak in the hot pool. The guard also kept order, tended to bee stings, and administered first aid as needed.

Six

Taking the Plunge

The Plunge, a complex with Olympic-sized pools surrounded by dressing rooms on three sides, was constructed of "plastitite" cement. The first pool was built in 1922, and a second was built in 1928 so they could be alternately cleaned. The "hot pool" was cooled and the "cold pool" was drained and refilled with hot water from the springs, usually on Tuesdays. A Plunge booklet contained tickets that were collected at a window under the arches. The deep end was 12 feet to accommodate springboard diving, while the shallow end accommodated soaking. A 1940s *Warner Hot Springs Guest Ranch* handout given to arriving guests states, "You will have the most restful swim you've ever had and you'll come out feeling relaxed and with skin as soft as velvet" —even if one did smell a bit like a rotten egg. When sunbathing became popular and Mehitable "Hetty" Henshaw recommended tearing out most of the dressing rooms and flagstone decks, a snack bar and a raised sand area were added. Truck tire inner tubes were used for floating and fun in the 1950s.

The cement tubs in the bathhouse were removed about that time, the locker rooms remodeled, and saunas added. A playground just outside of the gate was a good diversion for children tired of swimming. The adjacent Palatingua Room was originally the resort laundry until the couple who ran it and the snack bar became too old and retired in the 1960s.

Later, a grassy, tree-shaded park along the cold stream was added and the spa for massage and other treatments moved to a former employee housing building. A freshwater youth pool was constructed along with a youth camp converted from another employee housing building. One sulfur pool was remodeled into a chlorinated water pool, and the practice of alternating pools stopped. Tennis courts were built on the old parking lot, and a building on the snack bar patio was constructed as a lunchroom first, then became tennis pro shop. The original purposes of ranch buildings changed with the times and ownership, but the Plunge was always a must-do for anyone visiting Warner Hot Springs.

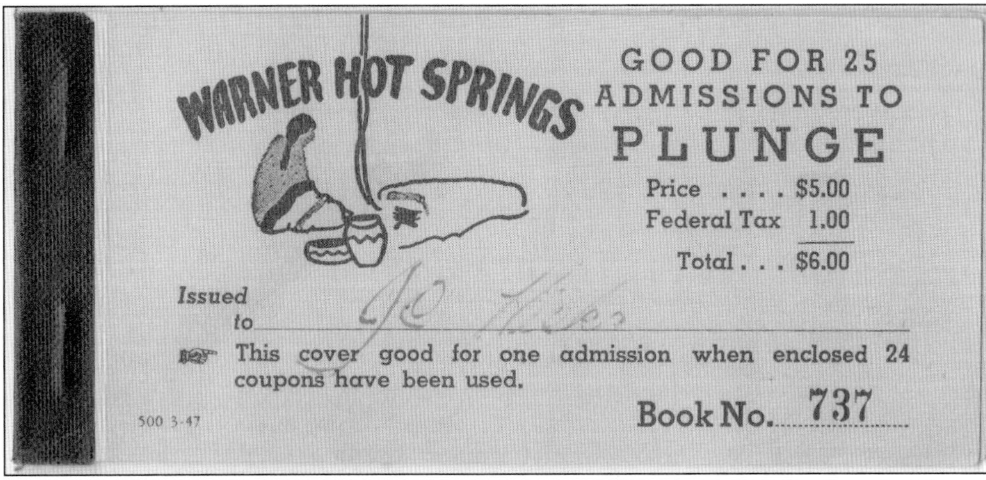

A booklet of Plunge passes like the one shown here was sold for $5 plus $1 federal tax for 25 visits to the pool. Inside were tickets for 24 visits (the cover was also a ticket).

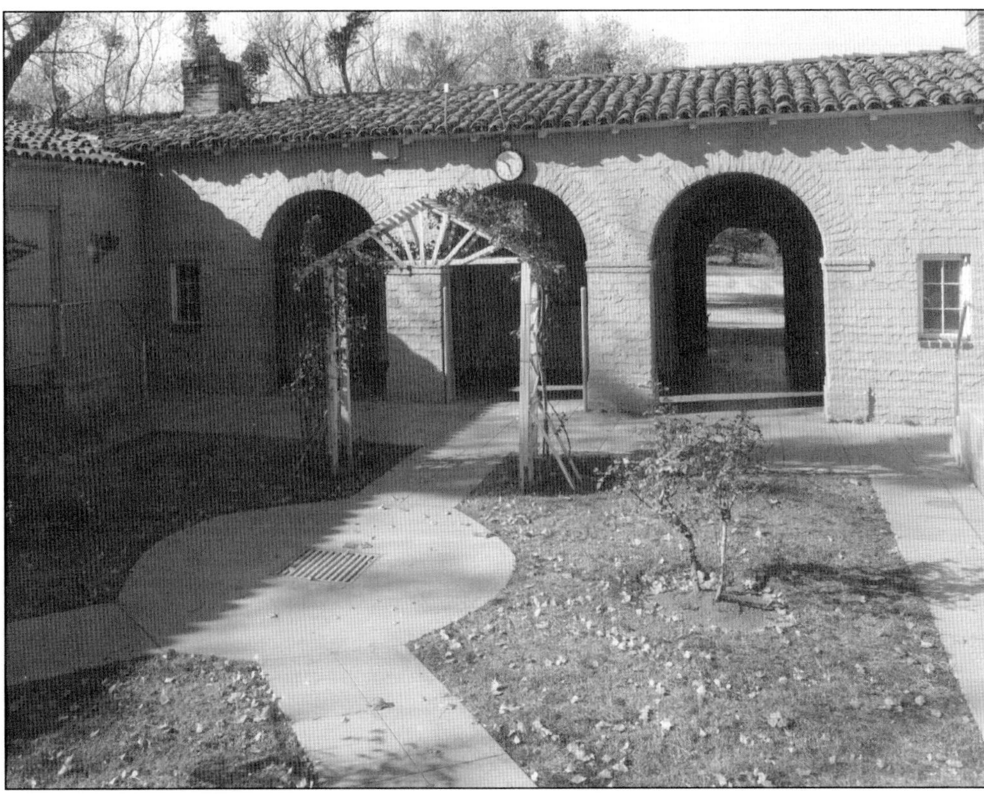

This picture shows the entry garden and pool office under the arched entryway.

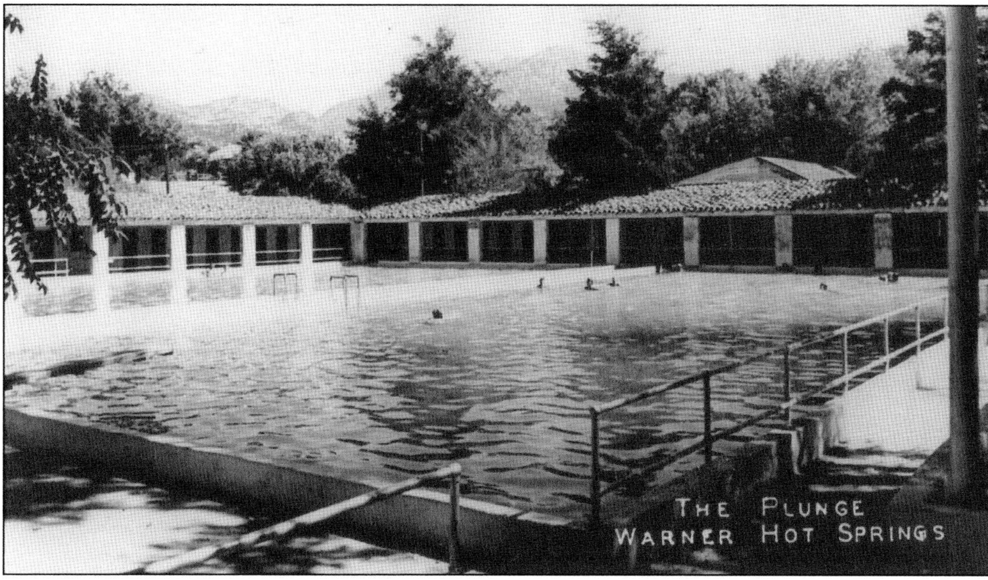

An early picture of the pool shows dressing rooms on two sides and the room of the laundry facility behind. Bed linens, tablecloths, and napkins were all washed in sulfur water from the hot springs, so the smell of sulfur was everywhere.

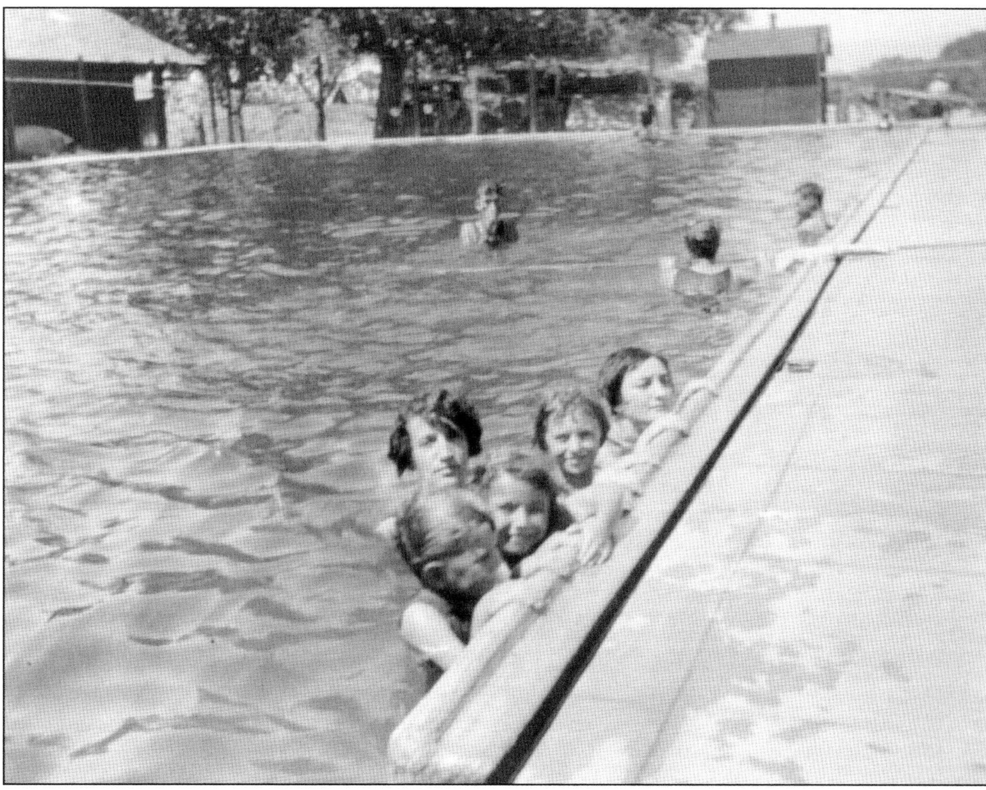

This 1922 photograph shows guests enjoying the first pool before the dressing rooms and new bathhouse complex were built. On the left is the wooden bathhouse that replaced the Indian bathhouse and that was torn down for the new buildings.

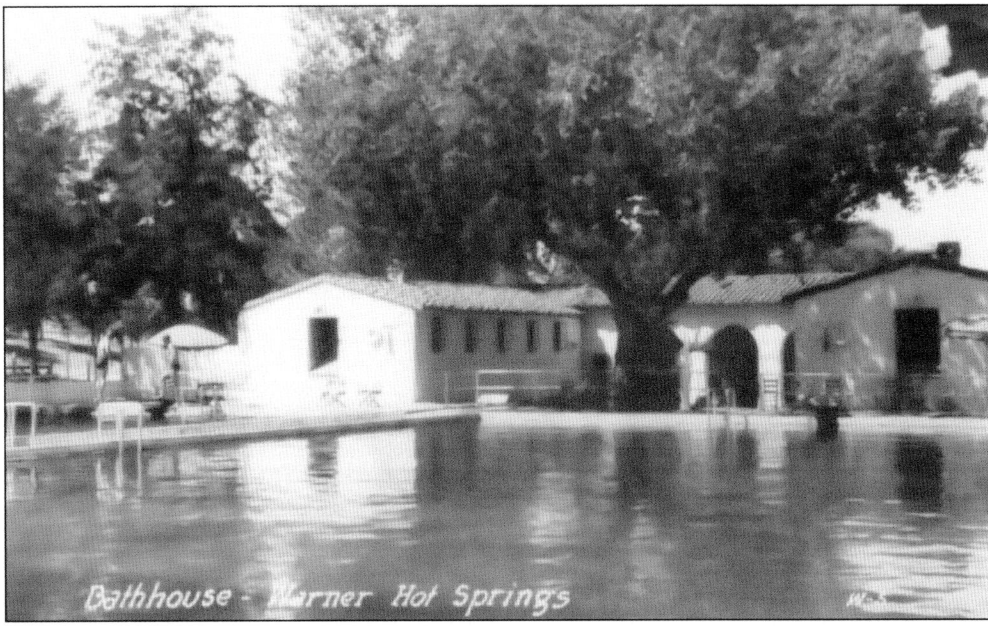

The new bathhouse complex is shown here at the deep end of the pools. The large cottonwood tree, which provided much-needed shade, is no longer there.

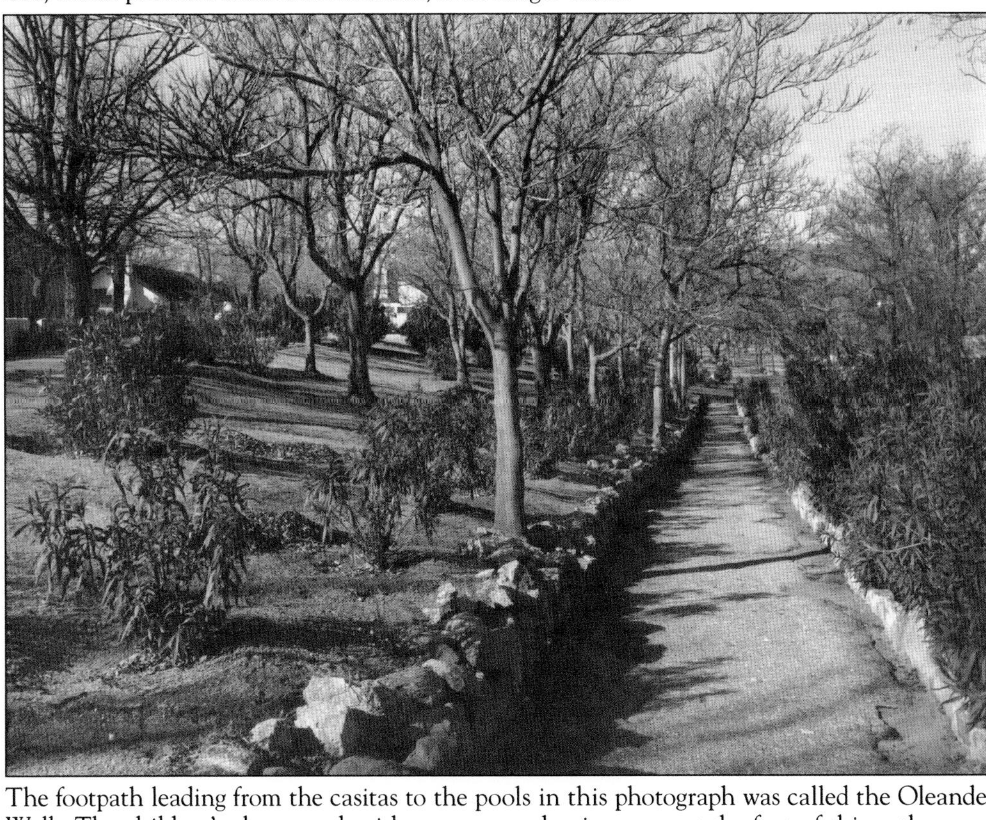
The footpath leading from the casitas to the pools in this photograph was called the Oleander Walk. The children's playground, with a seesaw and swings, was at the foot of this path near a side gate.

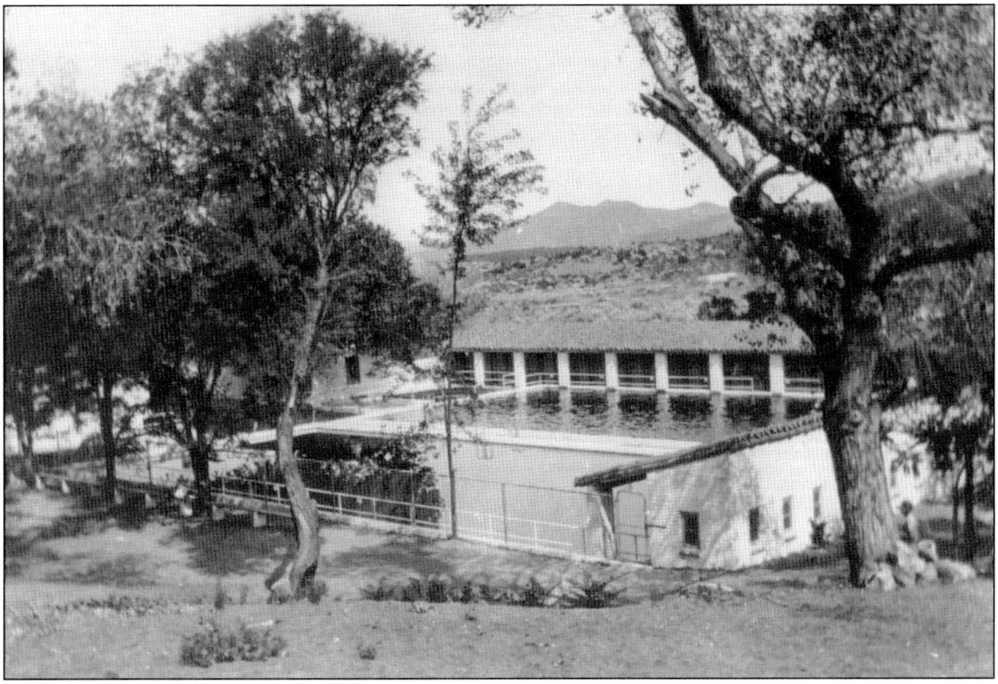

It must be Tuesday in this picture, which shows one pool drained and the other full and cooling. The "cold pool" was never really cold but pleasant at about 80 degrees.

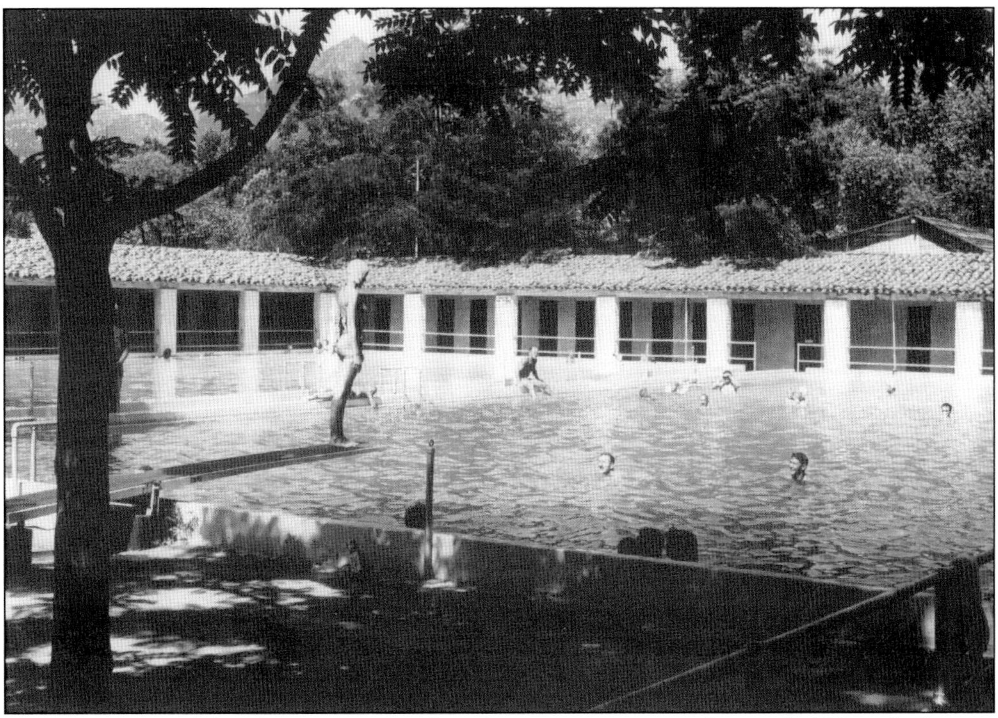

A diver on one of the aluminum springboards prepares to enter the pool. Although slippery from the sulfur water, these provided hours of fun before they were removed in the 1980s due to insurance concerns. The pool depth was raised from 12 to eight feet at that time.

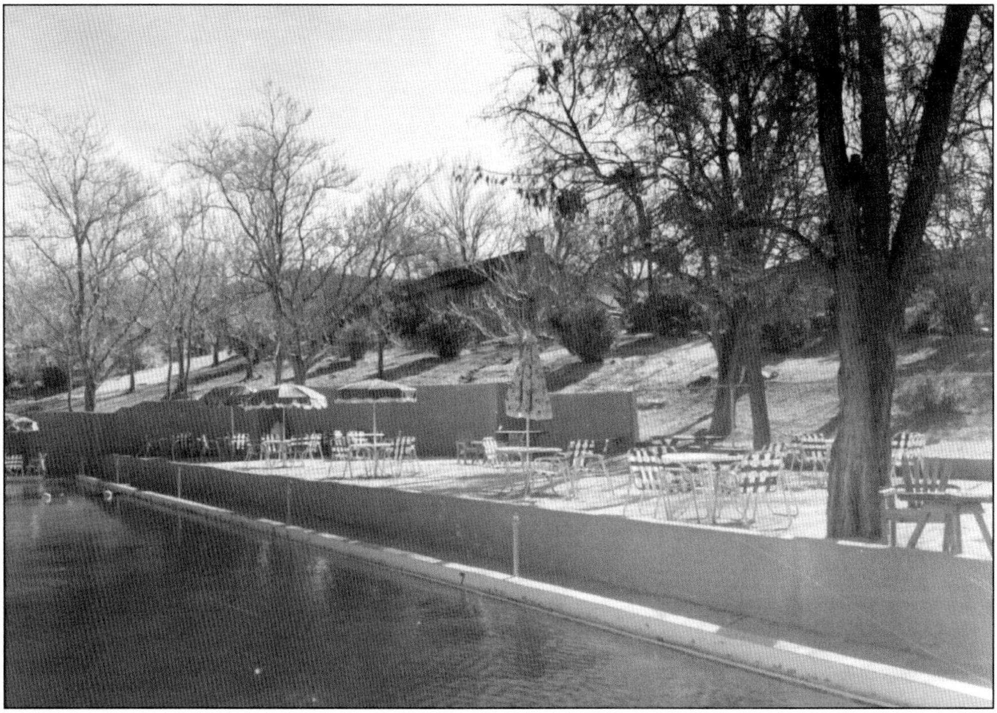

In this photograph, one can see the raised sand area that was added for more sunbathing. Although partially shaded, the sand would get burning hot in the summer, causing guests to make a hop, skip, and jump to their towels. The sand was later replaced with grass.

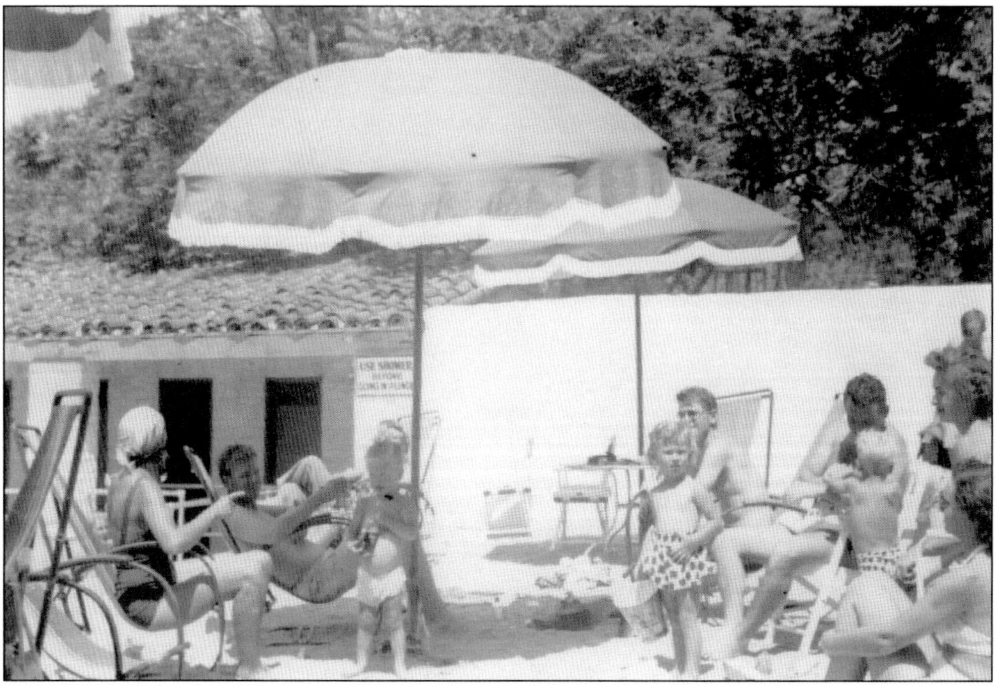

Adults and children alike are shown relaxing and having fun on the sand deck. For many, the pools were an all-day affair. (Courtesy Casey family.)

Longtime ranch lover Alberta Casey (now in her 90s), her husband, David, and children Julia and David are shown in this picture from the late 1940s. (Courtesy Casey family.)

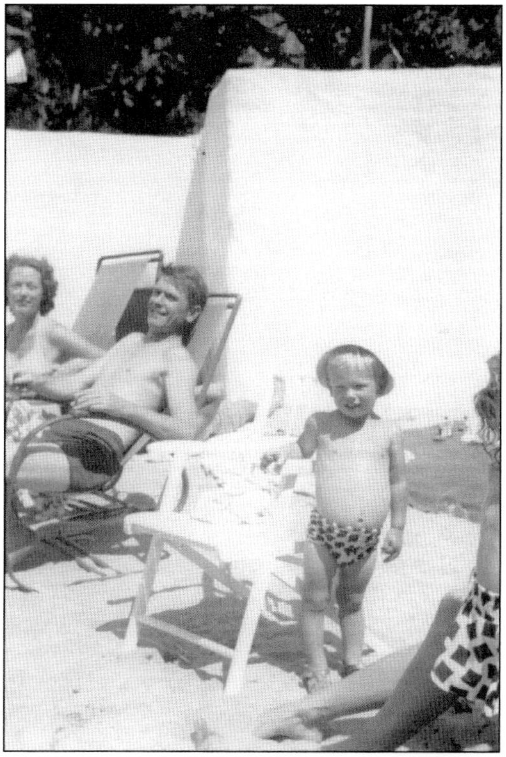

The Drip Bar, so named because one stood in line in a dripping-wet suit, was the snack bar at the pool and is shown with the patio beyond in this photograph. Hot dogs, hamburgers, milk shakes, and ice-cream cones were among the most popular items served from the small kitchen. It was a great way to feed families enjoying a long leisurely day at the pools.

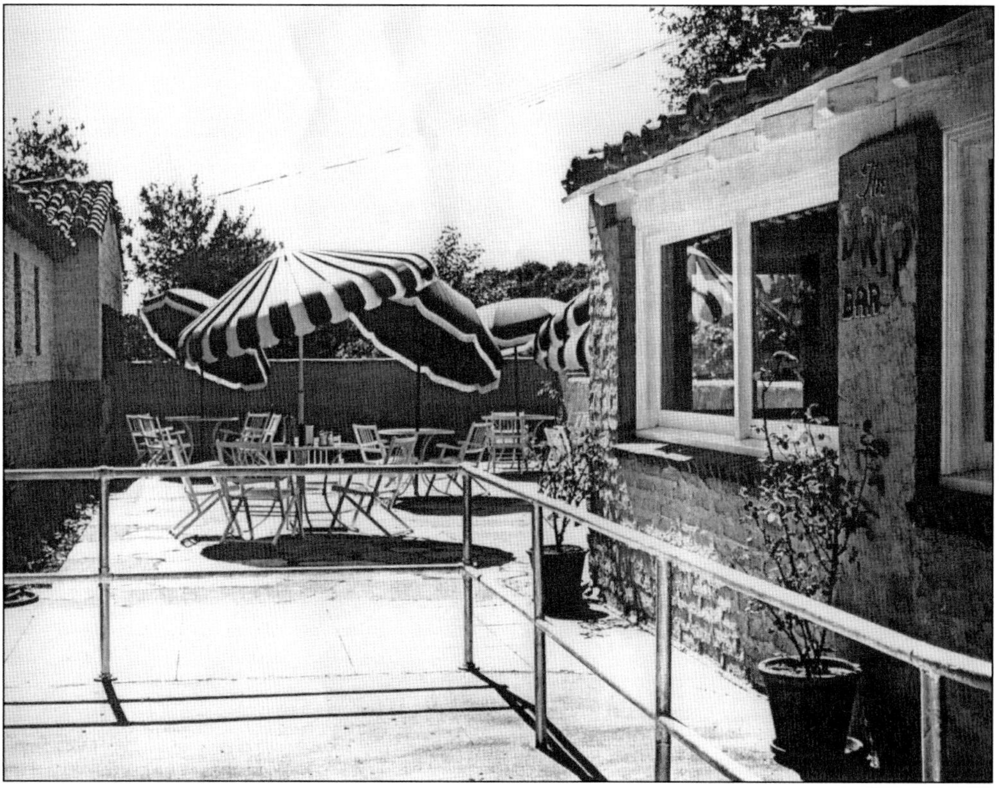

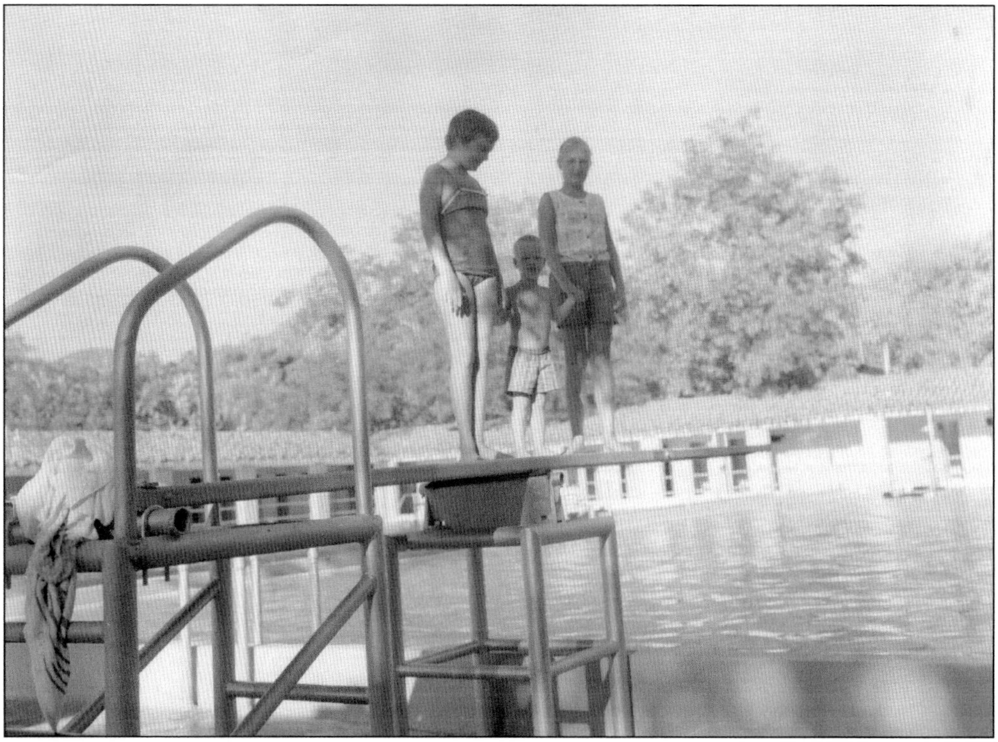

Siblings stand on the diving board for a family portrait. One benefit for parents was that after a day of swimming, kids were more than ready to hit the hay. (Courtesy Sharon Parker Mason.)

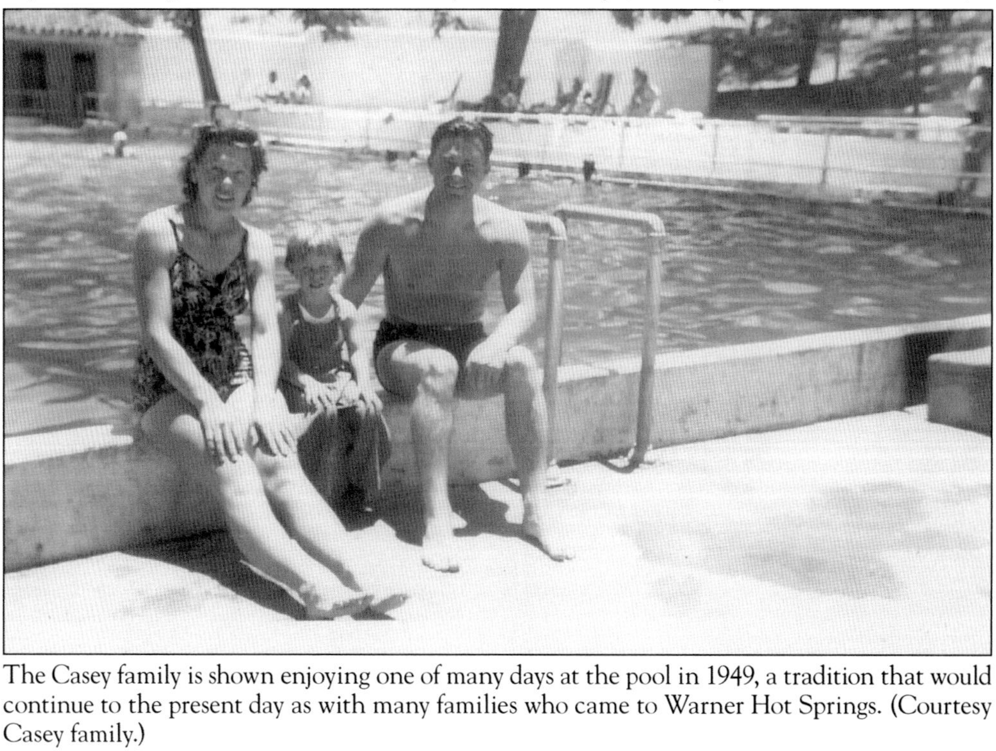

The Casey family is shown enjoying one of many days at the pool in 1949, a tradition that would continue to the present day as with many families who came to Warner Hot Springs. (Courtesy Casey family.)

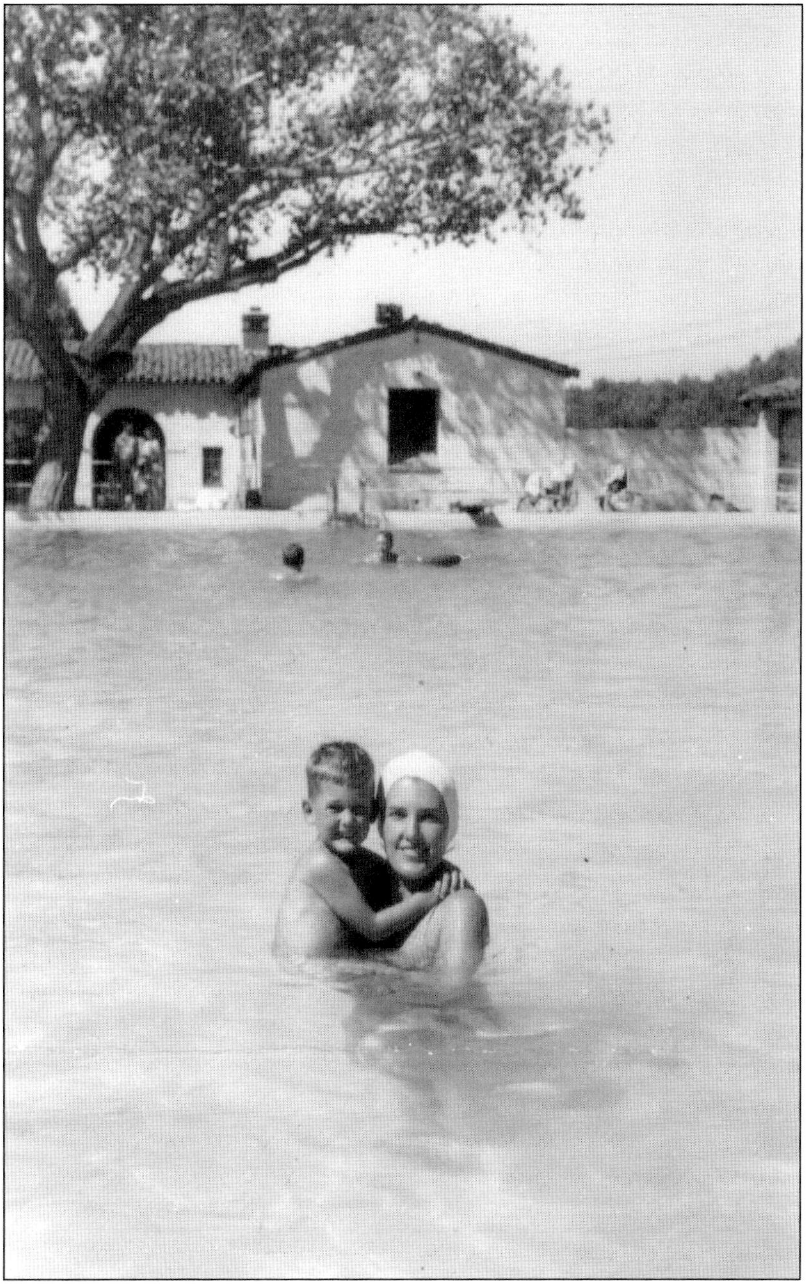

A mother and son are shown here enjoying family time in the pool in the 1940s. Quality time with family and friends, without today's modern devices and distractions, is what generations of guests at Warner Hot Springs remember the most. With no televisions or phones, no texting, and no computers, families spent time doing things together, enjoying the great outdoors and beautiful surroundings in this "resort for all seasons." Kids were free to roam and enjoy the experiences of a simpler time with each other, their parents, grandparents, and friends. This is what brought families back again and again, generation after generation. Just mention Warner Hot Springs to many people in Southern California, and they will recount with a smile the happy times they spent there. This is what makes great memories.

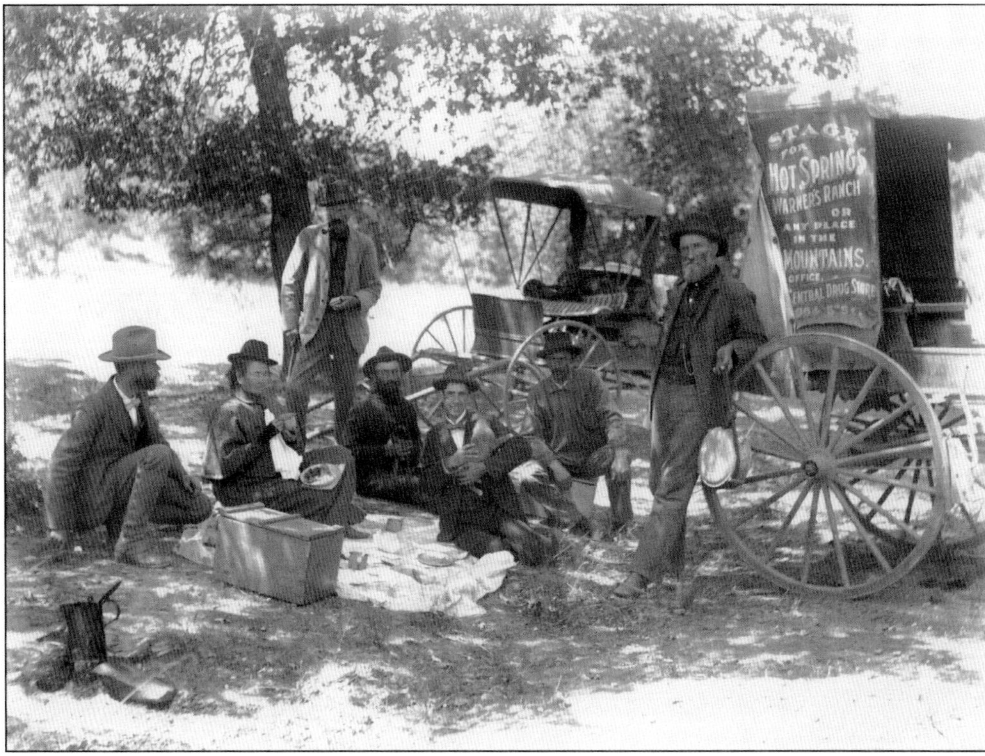

The Comstock Stage, pictured here, ran from San Diego to Warner's Ranch or "anyplace in the mountains," including Julian. Note the cultural diversity of the travelers in this photograph and one man holding a small dog.

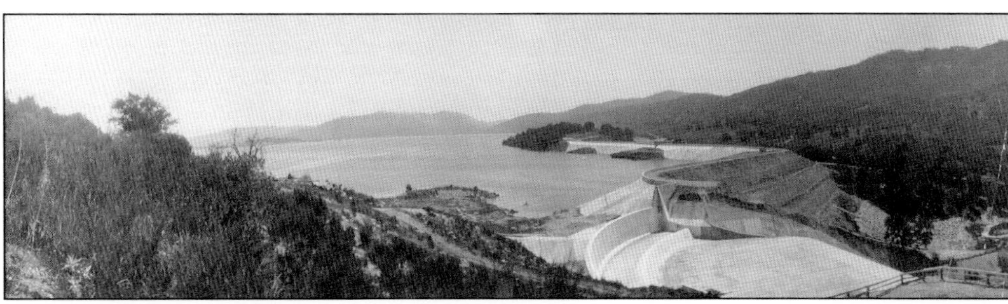

This photograph from 1928 shows the dam at Lake Henshaw, which was completed on Christmas Day 1922. Designed to hold 203,580 acre-feet of water, it extended around Monkey Island in the distance and up to the junction of Highways 76 and 79. Earthquake faults running through this area and the failure of the Van Norman Dam in 1972 caused the water level of the lake to drop. (Courtesy Vista Irrigation District.)

Seven

Getting Here Was Half the Fun

Getting to Warner Hot Springs was not an easy task in the late 19th and early 20th centuries. Roads were rough, with steep grades, streams that had to be crossed, and bridges that were frequently washed out. The earliest transportation was a horse-drawn stage that left the Central Drug Store on Fifth Street in downtown San Diego early in the morning and with luck arrived at the springs by nightfall. A long step forward in transportation was the establishment by Thomas O. Fewell of an automobile stage line. Offering triweekly service, it left San Diego on Tuesdays, Thursdays, and Saturdays at 9:00 a.m. and reached the springs about 3:30 p.m. with "automobiles driven by skilled chauffeurs providing a quick and comfortable service." A daily service on the San Diego, Cuyamaca & Eastern Railroad to Foster's, then by stage, left the city about 9:00 a.m. and reached Warner Hot Springs at 8:30 p.m.

The oiled dirt road was improved but still not paved until the 1930s. The year 1935 was an important one for the development of the resort, as with the completion of the Henshaw Dam, a paved highway now connected Warner Hot Springs with San Diego, and soon Los Angeles, and commercial electricity was brought in. A 30-mile, 12-kilovolt line was put in from Ramona (originally called Nuevo), and Warner Springs Ranch was the only customer. Power was out for days during storms, accidents, and floods, and the voltage fluctuated greatly, burning out motors and lights. The service improved as more customers were added.

Later highway improvements made the Pauma Grade and other roads easier for visitors and eliminated many dangerous hairpin turns. Coming from San Diego, Los Angeles, Oceanside, and later Orange County got better over time. Warner Hot Springs enjoyed a great deal of popularity during World War II, when gas rationing limited the distance people could drive. A tank of gas could get visitors to the springs and back from San Diego or Los Angeles.

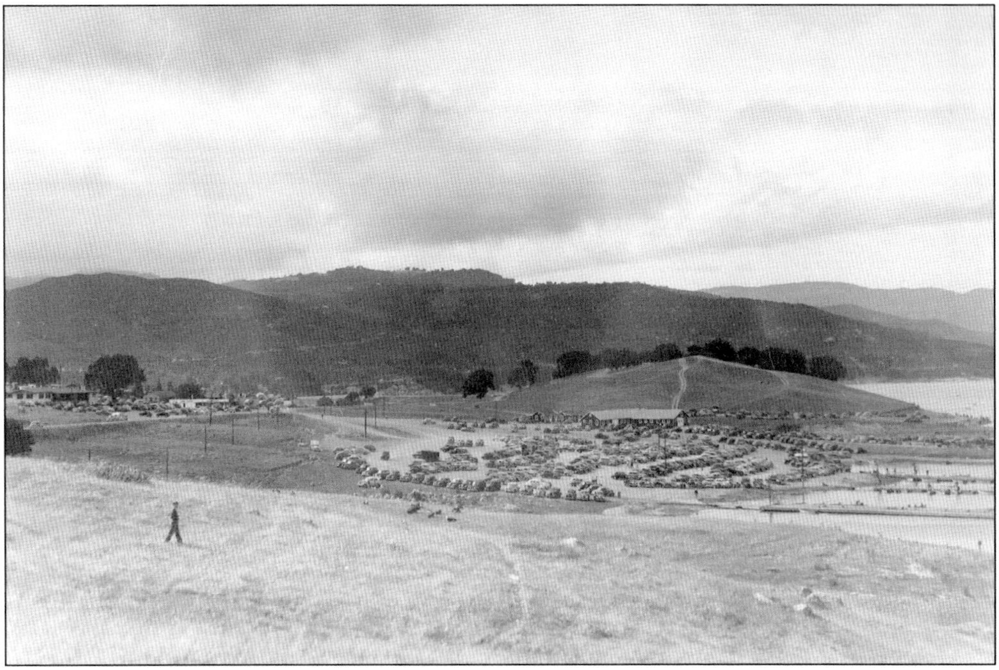

A photograph of the parking and boat launching areas of Lake Henshaw shows a full crowd of people. The West Fork and East Fork of the San Luis Rey River, along with a number of streams, empty into the lake. Popular with fishermen, the lake contained bass, bluegill, crappie, channel catfish, and red-ear sunfish. (Courtesy Vista Irrigation District.)

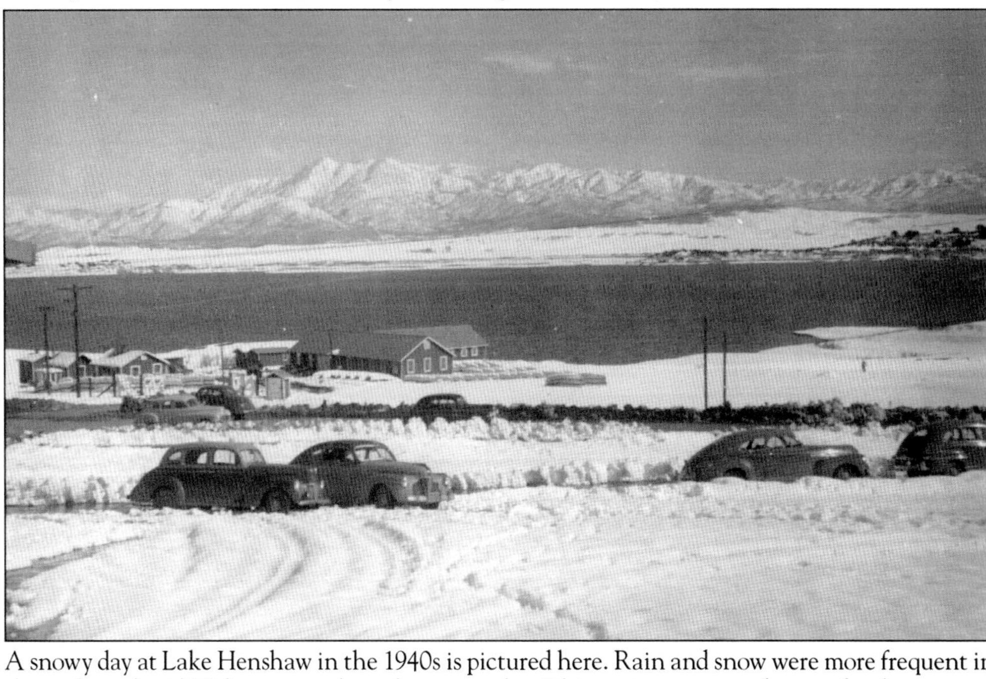

A snowy day at Lake Henshaw in the 1940s is pictured here. Rain and snow were more frequent in the early and mid-20th century than they are today. This entire area was famous for the amount of water just about everywhere and thousands of acres of green grass. There were lots of artesian wells, one or two of which ran into the 1960s.

Boats, motors, tackle, permits, and licenses for both fishing and hunting were available at the Lake Henshaw Resort store, which looks much the same today. The cabins at the resort were originally in Los Tules on the site of the old Henshaw Riverside Portland Cement Hunting Lodge and were relocated to the lake when Los Tules was developed in the late 1930s.

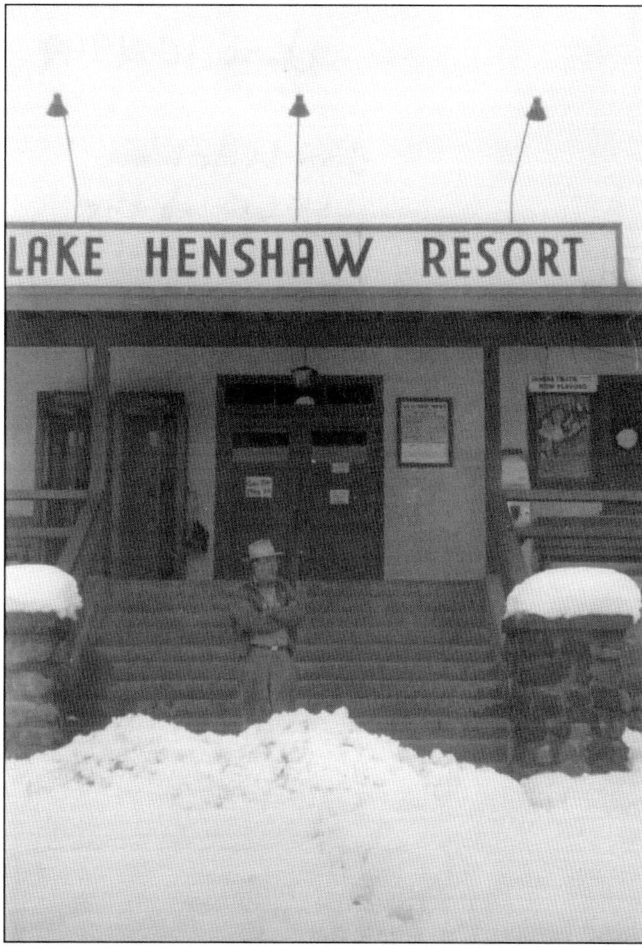

At the dirt crossroads of Highways 67 and 79, a sign let drivers know they were only 20 minutes from their destination of Warner Hot Springs. It was known as Morettis Junction, and there was a small store and gas pump here at one time.

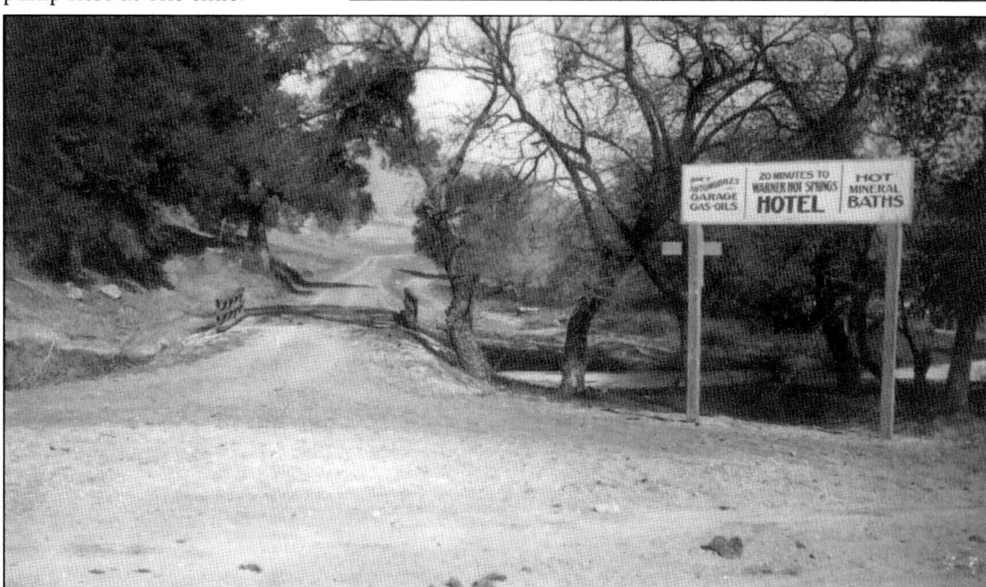

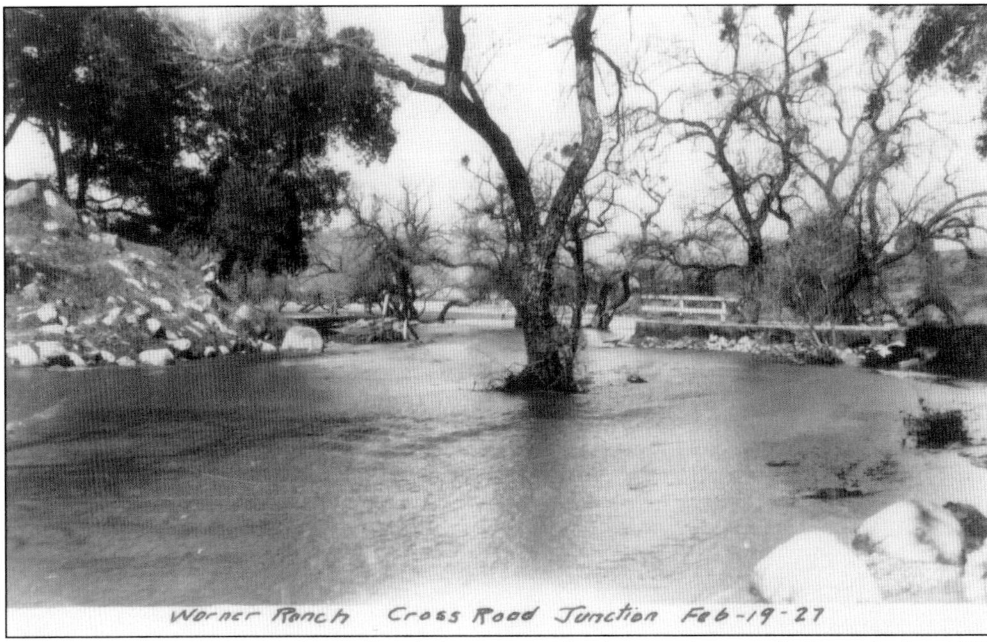

This photograph from 1927 show a flooded junction. Floods were always a challenge before 1935, when the road was paved, especially in 1916, the year of "the Great Flood." In 1968, floods washed out parts of the golf course. Much of the valley was swampy, and cattle and cars would frequently get stuck in the muck.

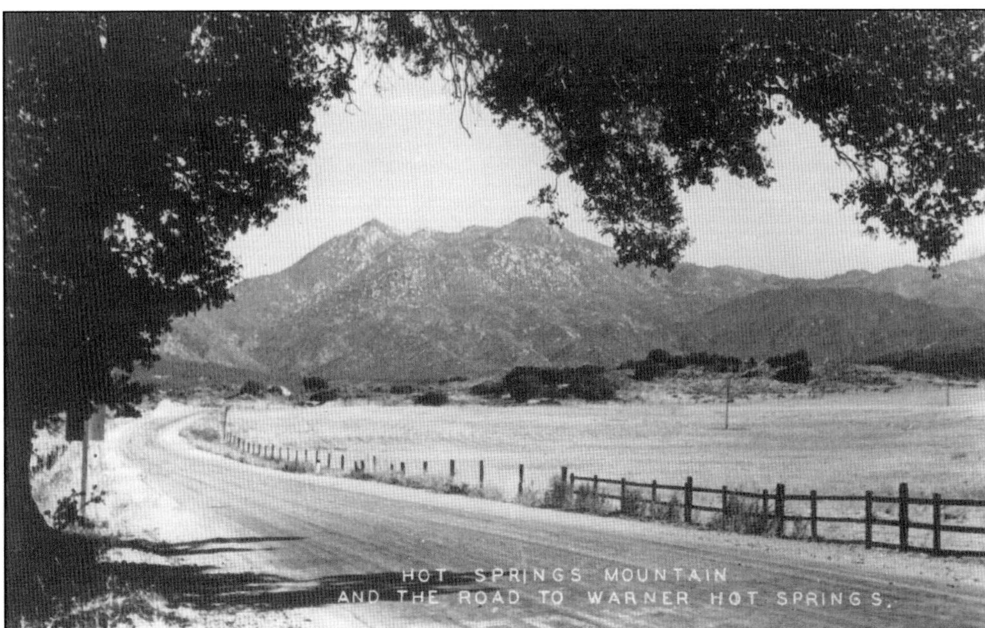

With Hot Springs Mountain rising in the background on a sunny day, travelers on the oiled highway knew they were almost to their destination of Warner Hot Springs.

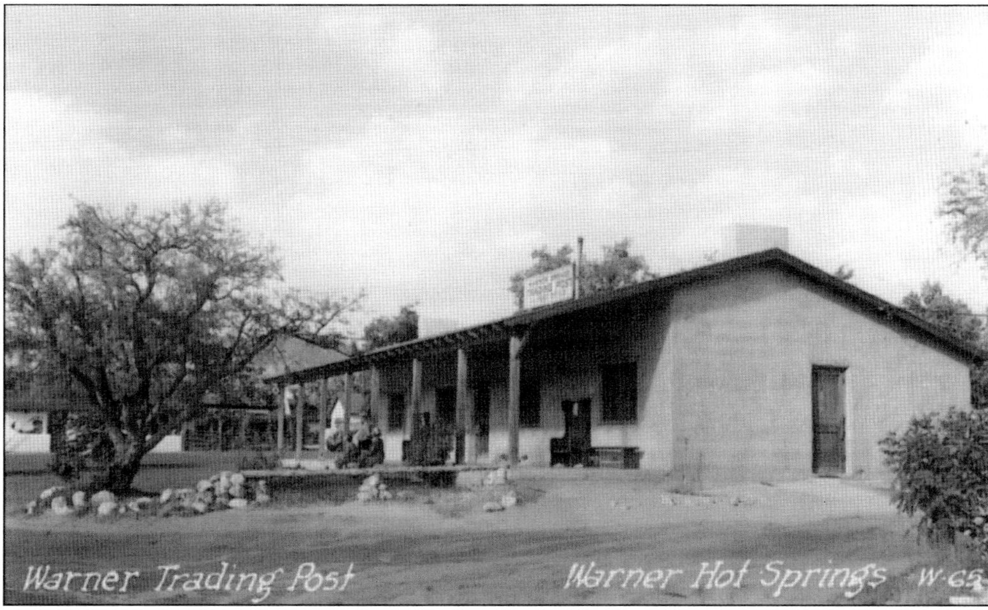

The Trading Post on Highway 79 and, in the background, the original cantina signaled one had arrived. This building was constructed about 1947 and was run by Alfred Iller and his wife, Alice, in the 1950s. It contained the post office and sold Western clothing, jewelry, trinkets, food, magazines and newspapers, and a fine array of wine and liquor. The Illers, originally from La Jolla, built a home in Los Tules.

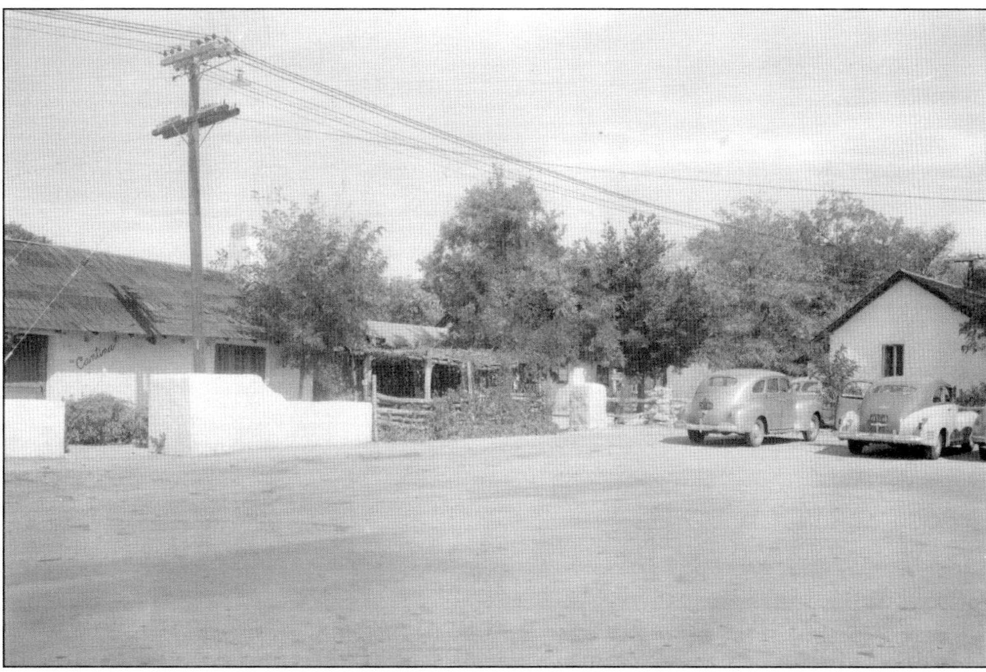

The original cantina, shown here across the parking lot, had an alcove and a "five cent one armed bandit" slot machine, according to Griff Henshaw's letter to Terry Chambers, founder of the historical committee. The cantina was later moved to an old adobe within the resort grounds and connected to the lodge. This building was converted into a hotel room.

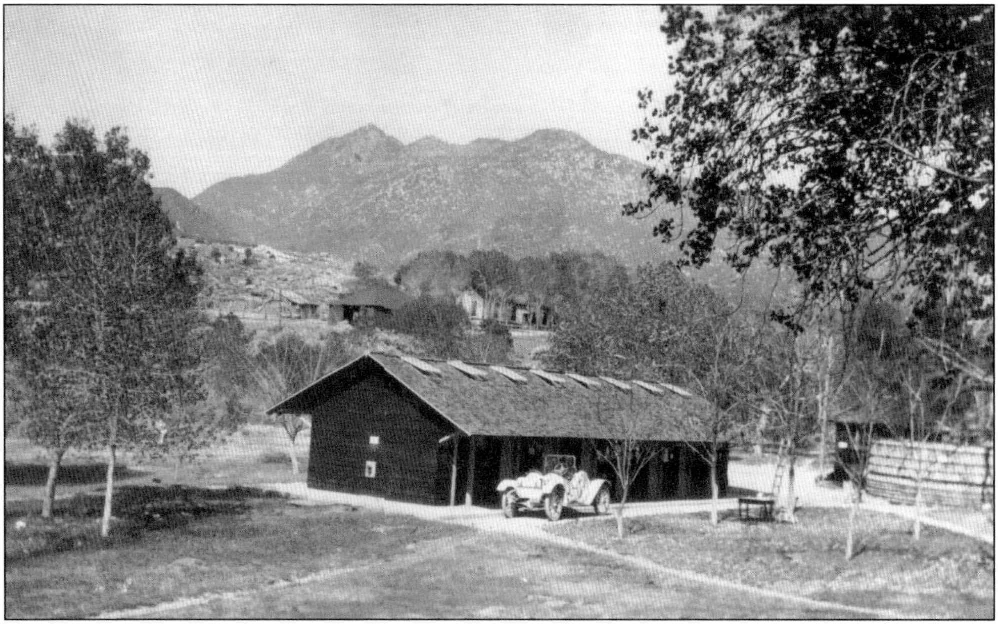

A photograph from before 1920 shows an open car in front of the second bathhouse. There was a small garage on-site for minor repairs.

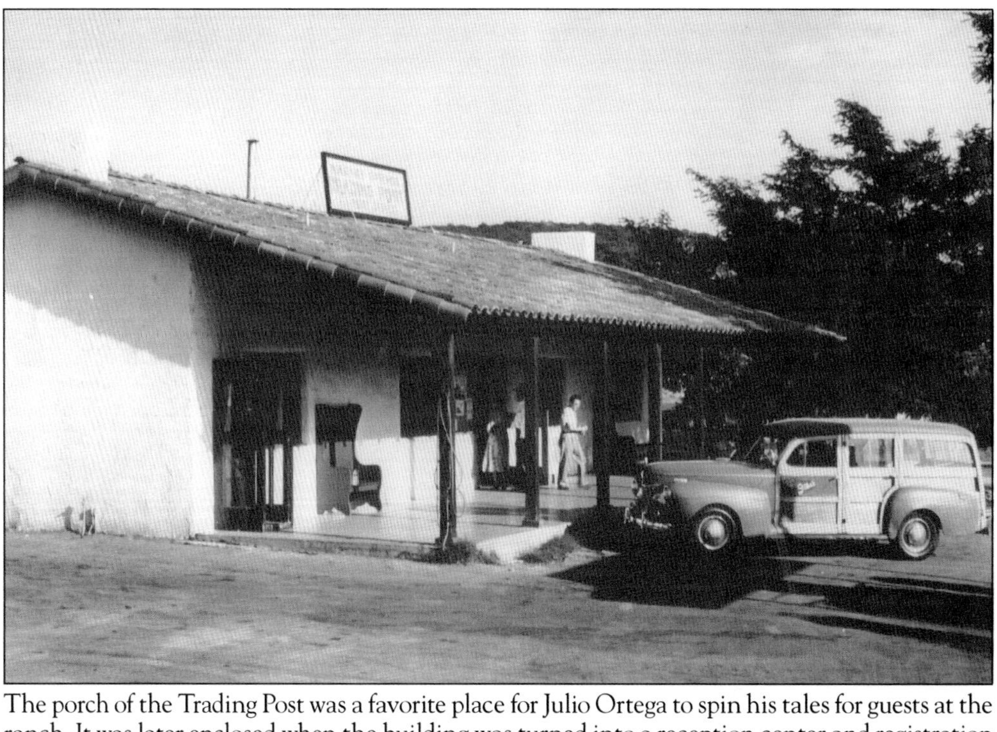

The porch of the Trading Post was a favorite place for Julio Ortega to spin his tales for guests at the ranch. It was later enclosed when the building was turned into a reception center and registration was taken out of the lodge building. The woody parked out front has "Iller's" painted on the side. An Englishman, Les Wesmakot, and his wife ran the post after the Illers.

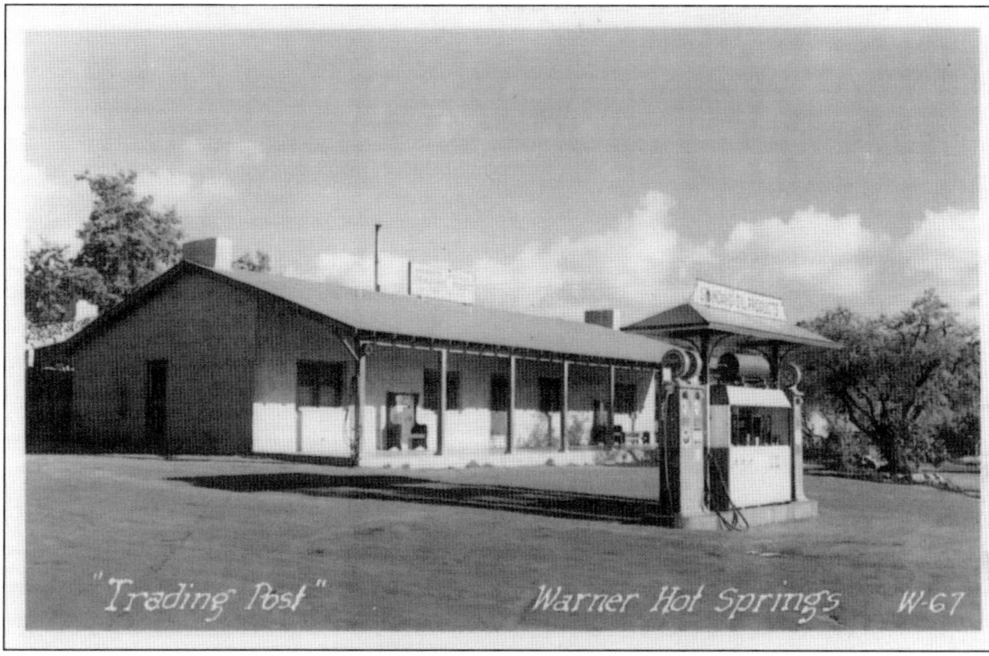

Pictured here are the gas pumps in later years that were installed in front of the Trading Post. Other opportunities to buy gas while going to and from the springs were limited. The highway now runs closer to the building where the tanks are shown here. Crossing to the other side of the highway has always been dangerous. Caltrans offered the new developers of the ranch in the 1980s an opportunity to realign the highway behind the golf course and connect it near the airport, but they declined because of the cost. This would have eliminated a safety concern that still exists. In later years, the Trading Post became the reception building, and the post office was moved to a double-wide next door.

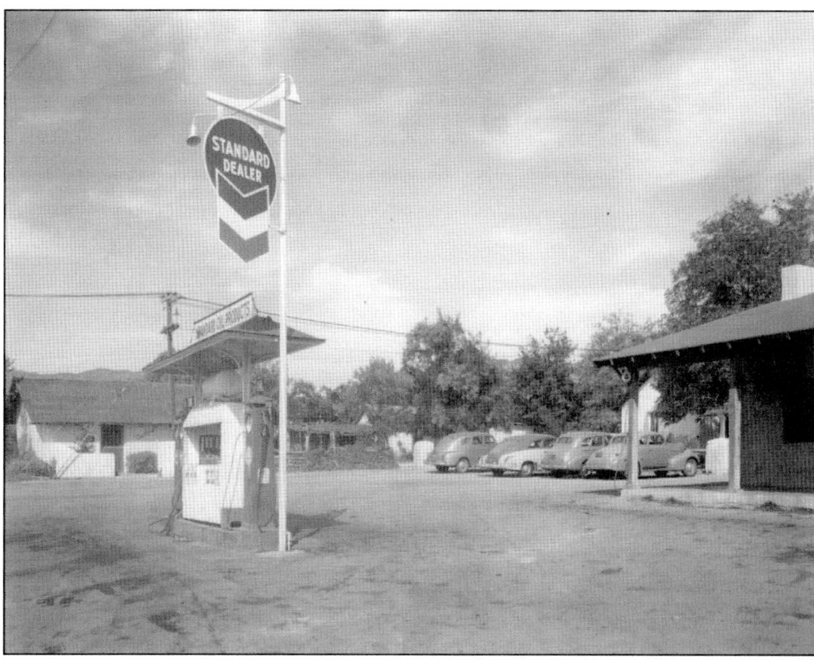

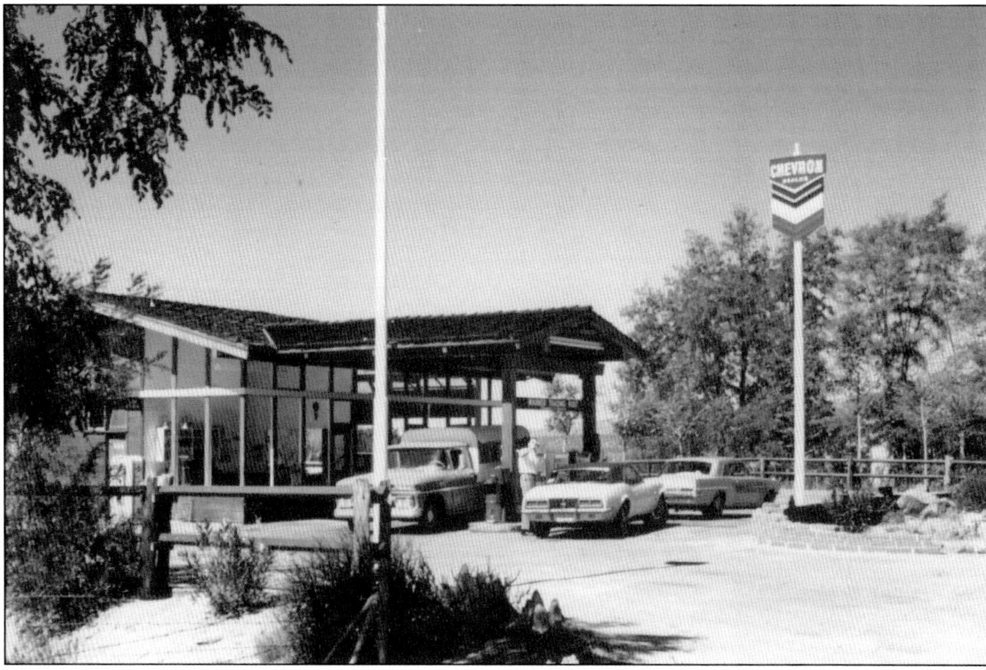

After Highway 79 was realigned, a modern gas station and garage were built for guests and local residents and a minimart was added. After the garage service closed, the ranch fire truck was stored here. Current plans call for this building to be renovated and gas service renewed.

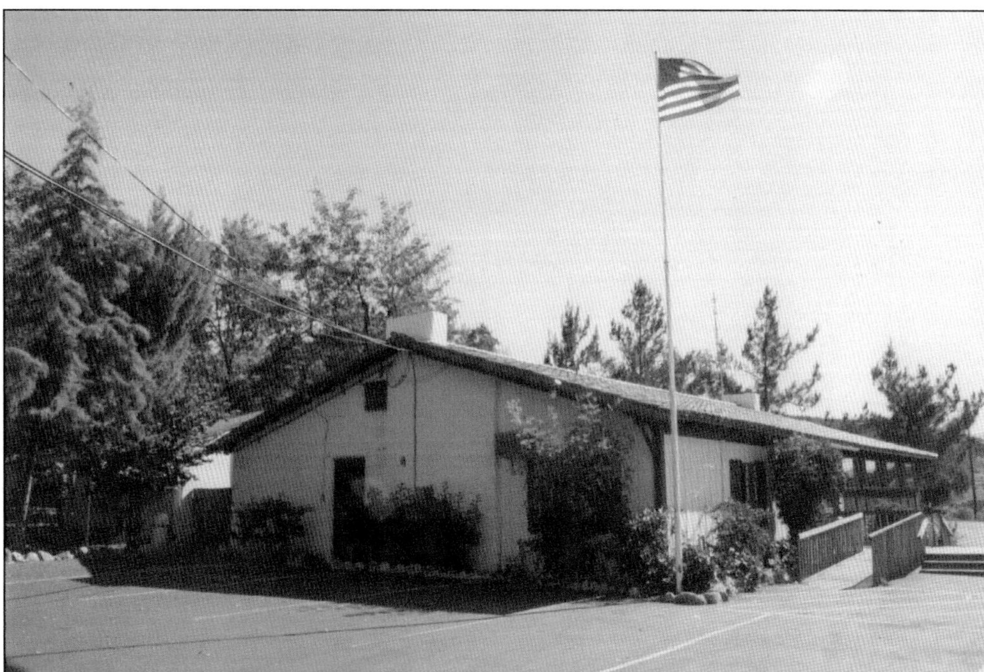

This photograph shows the former Trading Post with its porch enclosed during the mid-1980s and the guard gate entry installed. It was then used as the reception area and administrative offices.

Eight

A Resort for All Seasons

Summers at Warner Springs are usually temperate because of the altitude, while beautiful autumn leaves make a show of color. Winter brings rain and a bit of snow with wood fires in the lodge and cabins. Spring follows with green grass, flowering fruit trees, and wildflowers in the valley. An article in the June 14, 1908, *San Diego Union-Tribune* states:

> Life in camp is pleasant. Formalities are largely laid aside. Acquaintances are soon formed and there is little excuse for being lonesome. The mornings are an inspiration. Many of the sojourners are up soon after daylight for walking and driving, while others are out hunting. The baths are taken either in the late forenoon or early afternoon; either event occupying about two hours. Meals are served at seven, twelve and six. Frequent pilgrimages are made to the springs and picnic parties are common, not a few climbing the mountains to Eagle Peak, overlooking the desert.

Many people have fond memories of the Henshaw years, particularly after the Warner Resort Company was formed in 1945 as a separate entity from the San Diego Water Company, which was sold and became the Vista Irrigation District. A $500,000 renovation begun during the management of Syd Furze saw many improvements. A gracious lodge was built with a reception desk, offices, a soda fountain, a new dining room, a cantina, and a dance hall. The former lobby became the Palomar Room and with the Ortega Room was connected to the lodge and the freestanding adobe that became the new cantina. New recreational facilities built at this time set the stage for the glory days of Warner Hot Springs.

During the 1940s and into the 1950s, all sorts of things were grown and produced for use in the kitchen or sold in the Trading Post. The dairy supplied milk and cream; vegetables of all kinds, grapes, and other fruits were grown; ducks and chickens were raised; and, from time to time, George Sawday provided meat. Sensible and healthy farm-to-table management practices were supplemented by items brought in weekly from Young's Market in San Diego.

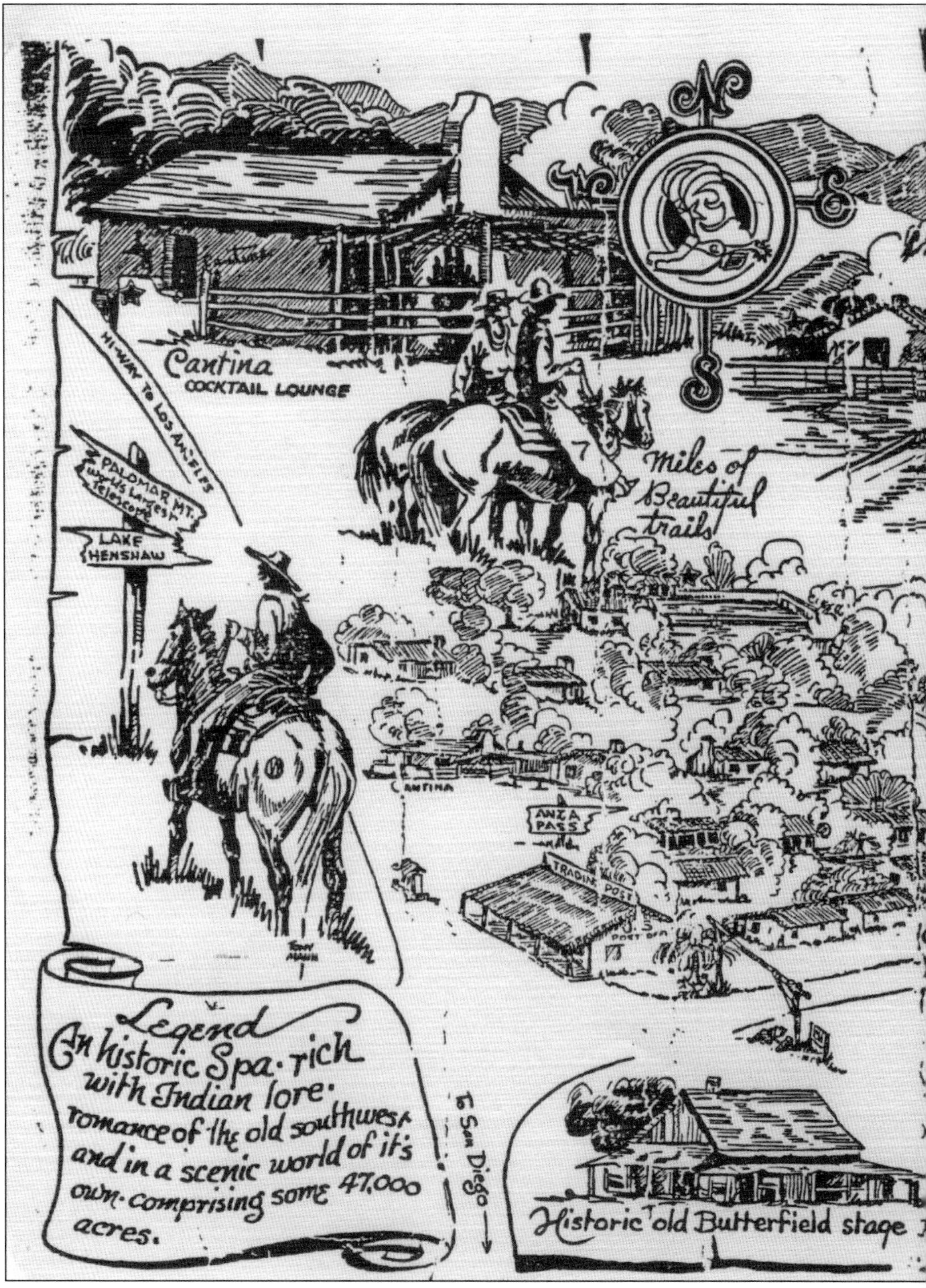
Cantina
COCKTAIL LOUNGE
HI-WAY TO LOS ANGELES
PALOMAR MT.
LAKE HENSHAW
Miles of Beautiful trails
CANTINA
ANZA PASS
TRADING POST
Legend
An historic Spa · rich with Indian lore · romance of the old southwest and in a scenic world of it's own · comprising some 47,000 acres.
To San Diego
Historic old Butterfield stage

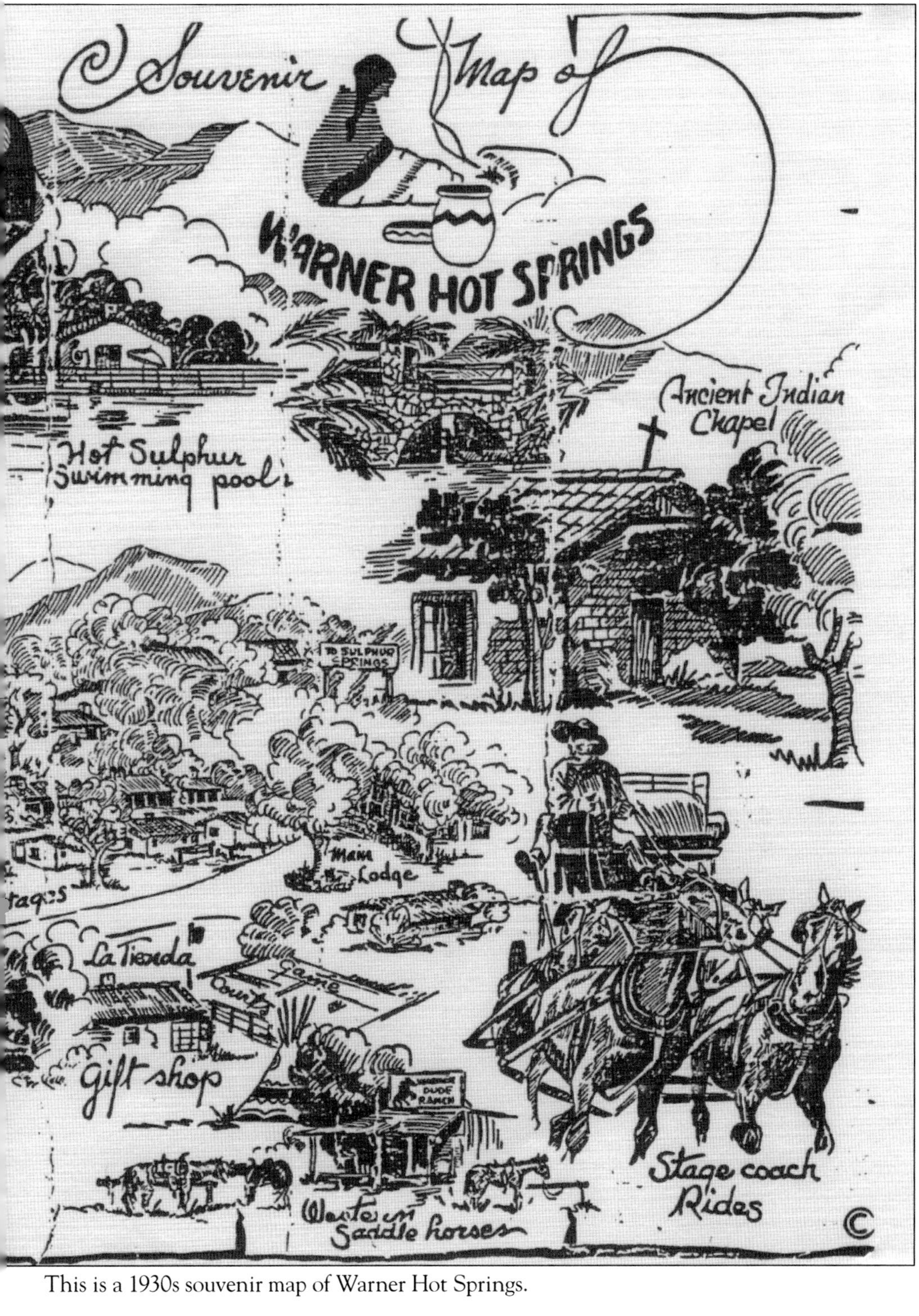

This is a 1930s souvenir map of Warner Hot Springs.

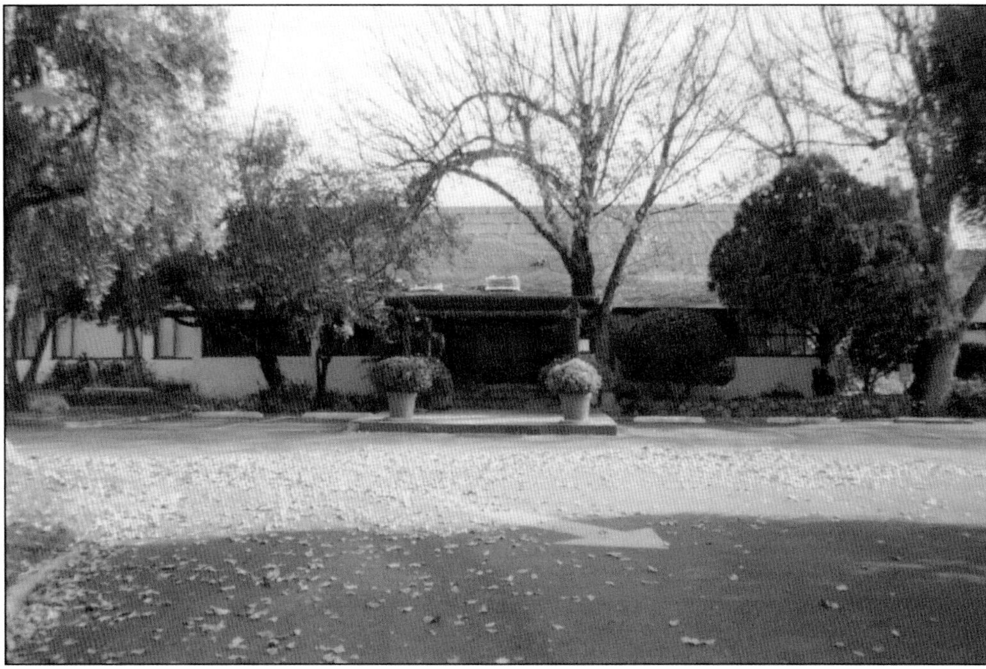

This building was the reception area and lobby until 1949, when it was incorporated into the new lodge. Known as the Palomar Room, it had a screened porch that later became an area for Ping-Pong. Then it was enclosed as a small library and historical museum. Old grinding stones are set into the entry steps.

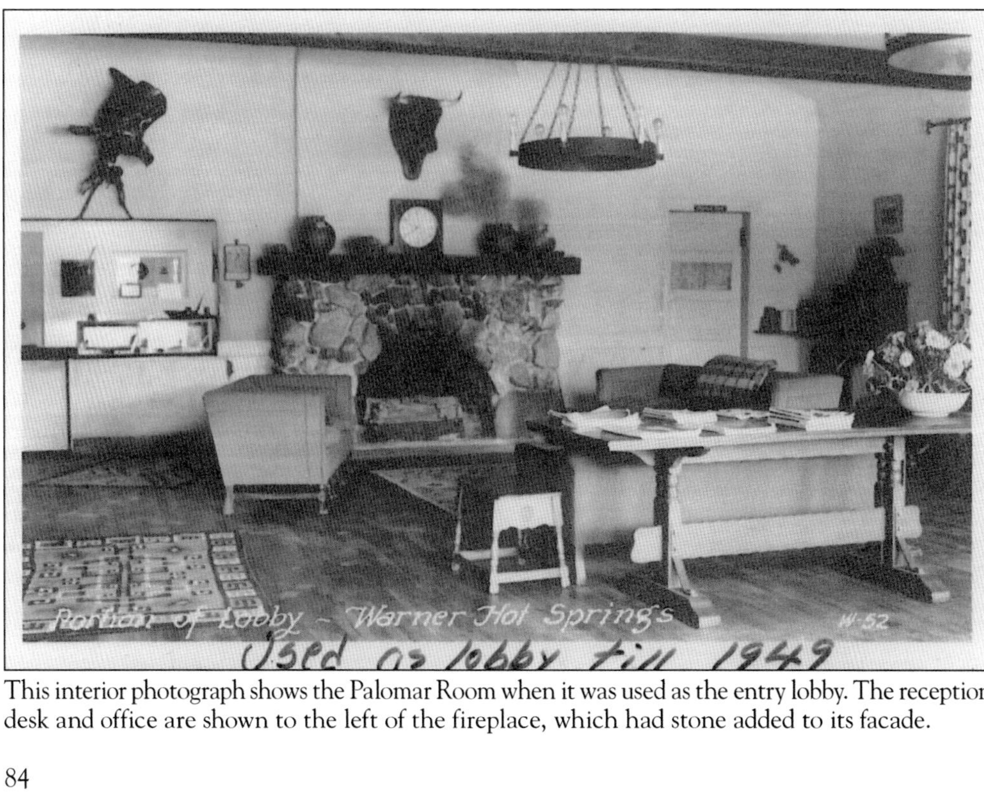

This interior photograph shows the Palomar Room when it was used as the entry lobby. The reception desk and office are shown to the left of the fireplace, which had stone added to its facade.

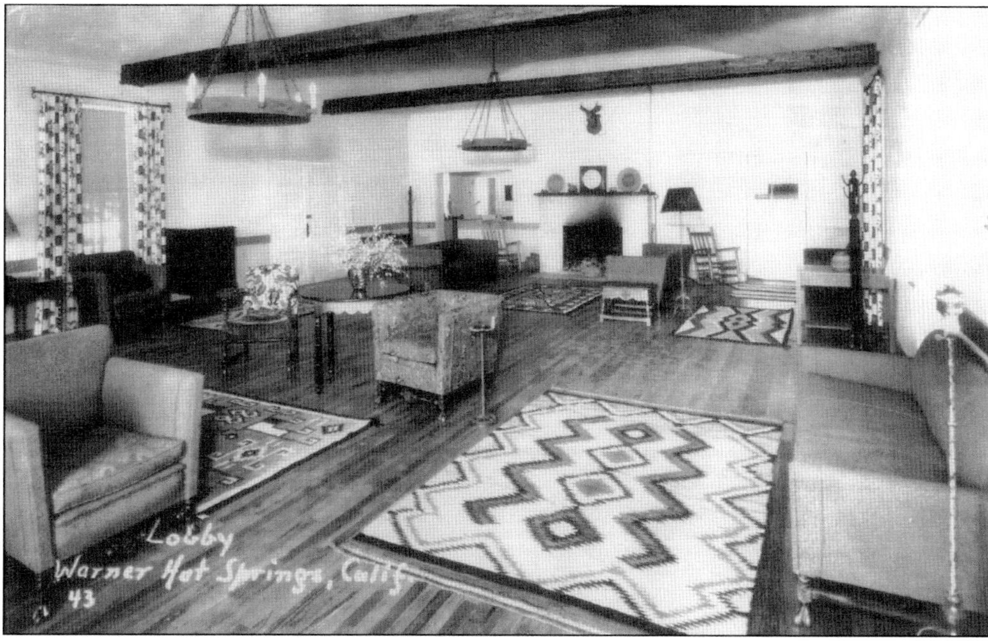

A 1943 photograph shows the gracious interior, fine furniture, and Indian rugs of the Palomar Room. Note the fireplace before the rocks were added and the open beam ceiling and light fixture. Later, it became a ballroom for dances popular in the 1940s and 1950s and a multipurpose room for reading, cards, and special programs.

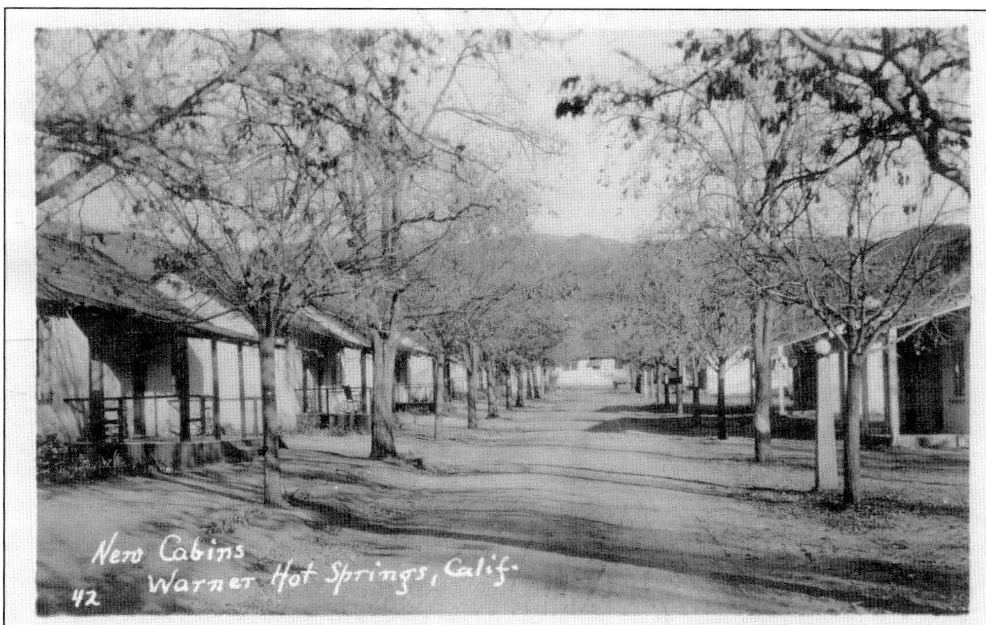

These new cabins were built prior to 1920, and the entry road, called Broadway, ran between them to the original reception building up on the hill. When the next era of cabins was built, the road was moved south and became the Anza Walk, and grass was planted beneath the shade trees.

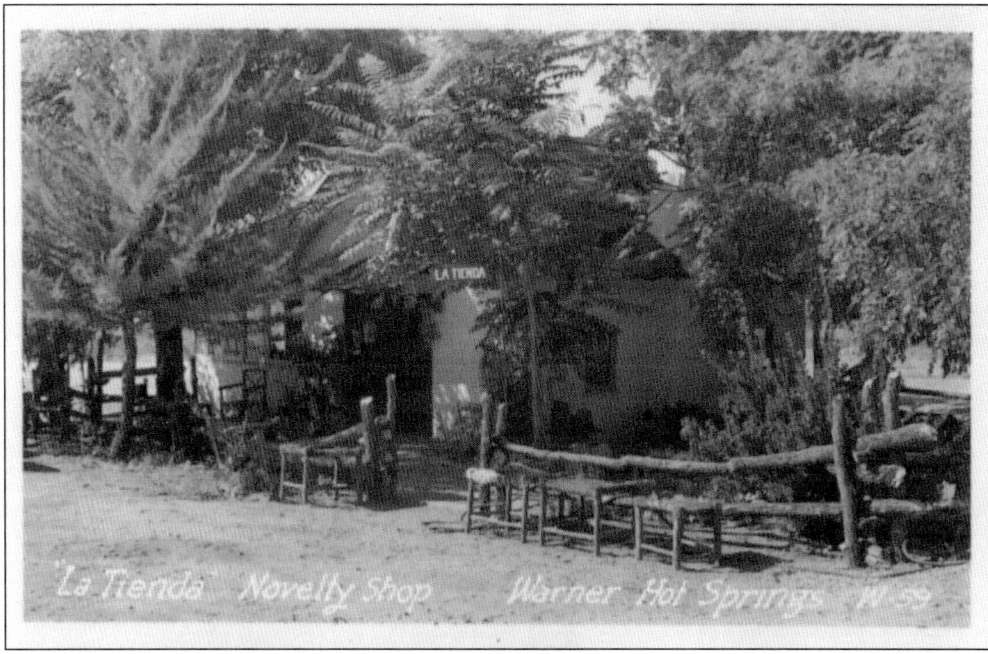

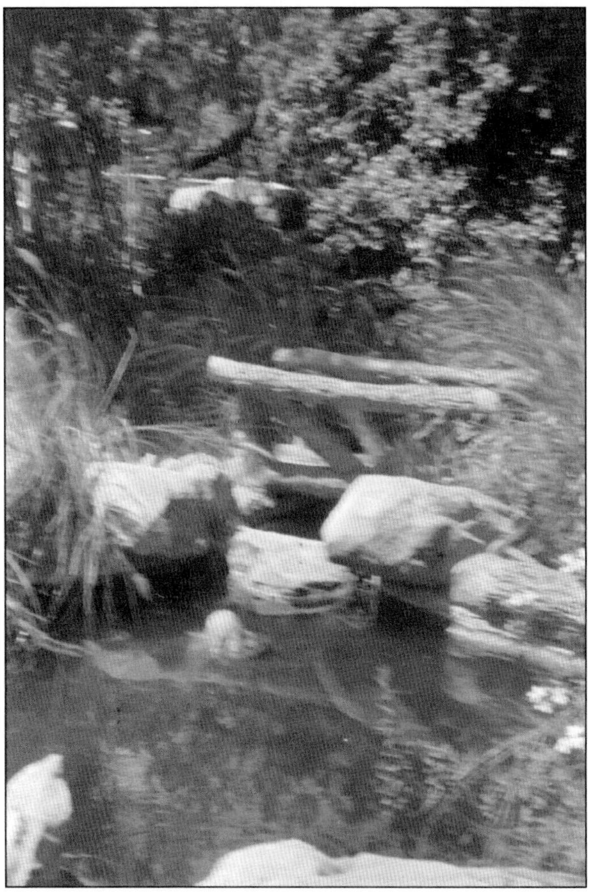

La Tienda, meaning "the store" in Spanish, was an adobe near the lodge and original tennis court. It sold mainly arts and crafts. It later became a deluxe cabin with a sitting room and fireplace.

This picture shows a small bridge over a pond at La Tienda. The pond is no longer there.

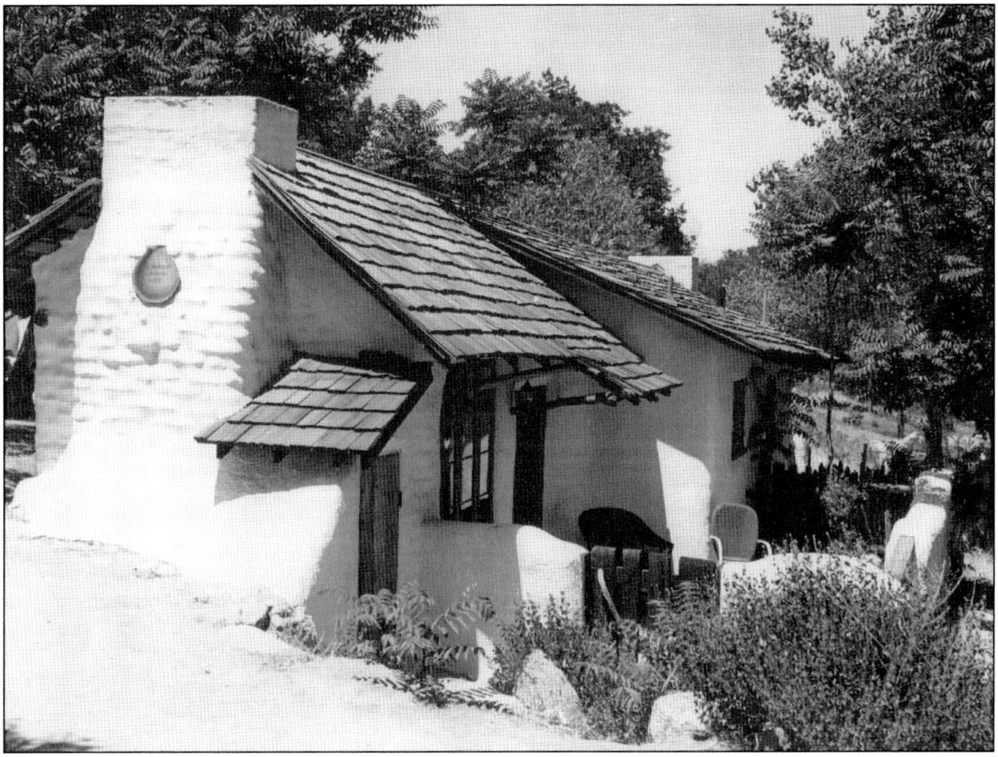

The most photographed adobe at the top of the pathway to the hot springs has often been called the Carson Adobe, as it was reported to be where Kit Carson stayed in the 1800s. But it was originally the home of Cupeño Indian Juan Cibimoat, who was captain in 1903.

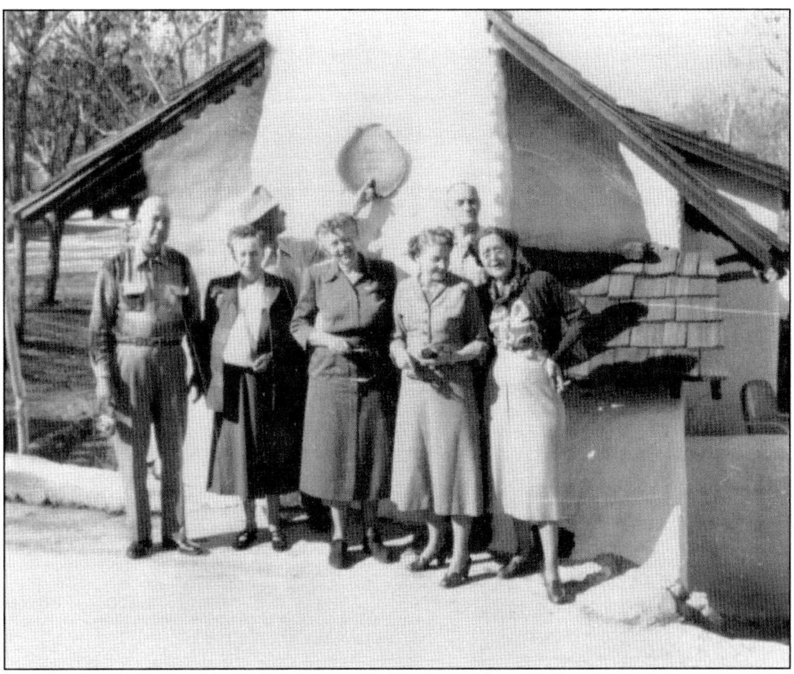

One member of a group of happy guests points to a historic sign on front of the Carson Adobe on the way to the hot springs.

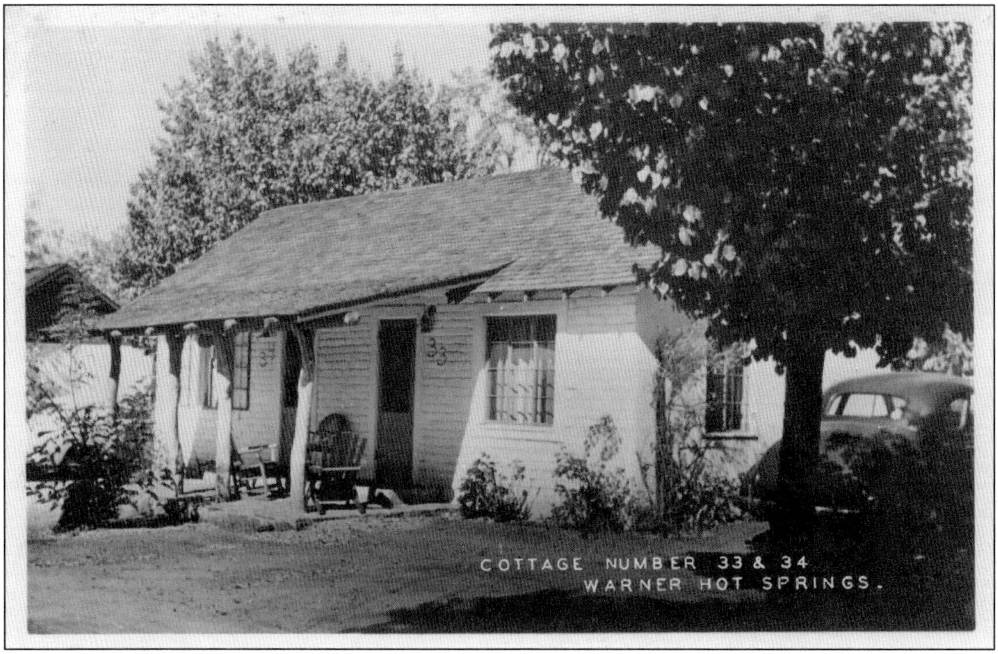

These new cabins on Broadway, shown in the 1940s, were duplex units, each with a single room and a porch. The original adobe walls were painted white in later years. Adobe bricks for these cabins and later additions were made on-site.

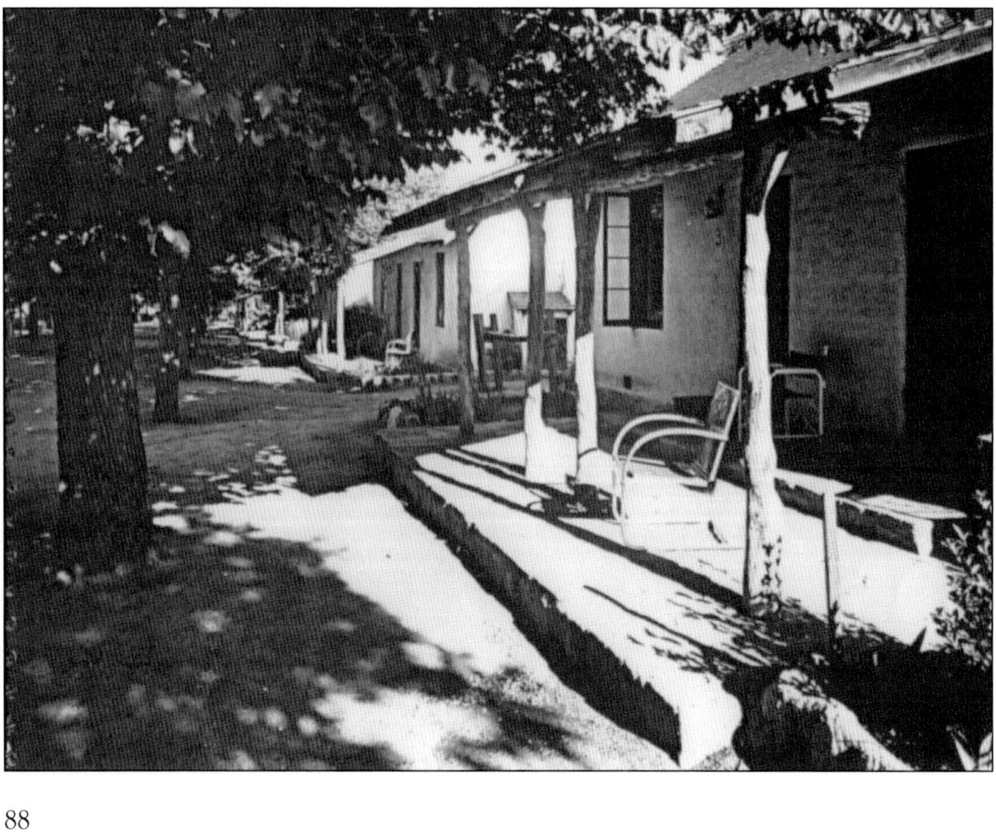

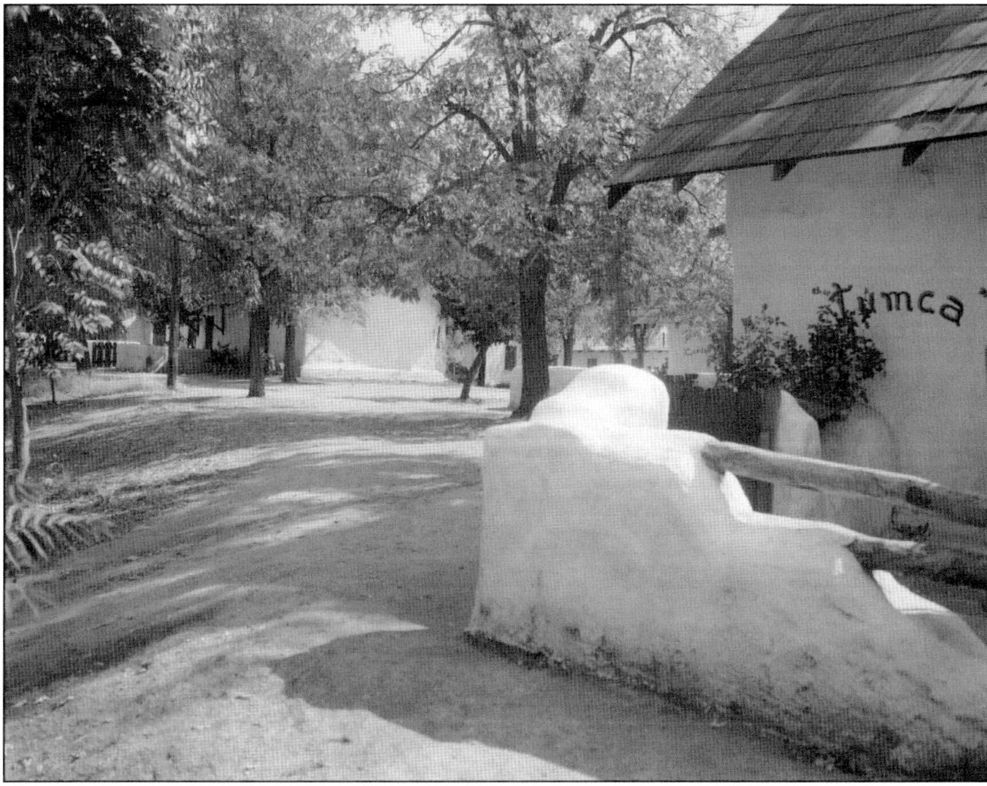

Most of the original Cupa village adobes sit at the top of a grassy and tree-shaded hill overlooking the pools. They were remodeled many times over the years, with bathrooms and water heaters added. Considered deluxe casitas, many had fireplaces, sitting rooms, and patios. They were often referred to by the Indian words painted on the front and were very popular with visitors. On the outside of many, one can see where the original beams were before the roofs were added. The original thatched roofs did not protect the foundations from rain, so many had to be rebuilt with concrete and the roofs extended. There are several existing original adobes on the west side of the highway, but others that were originally there do not remain.

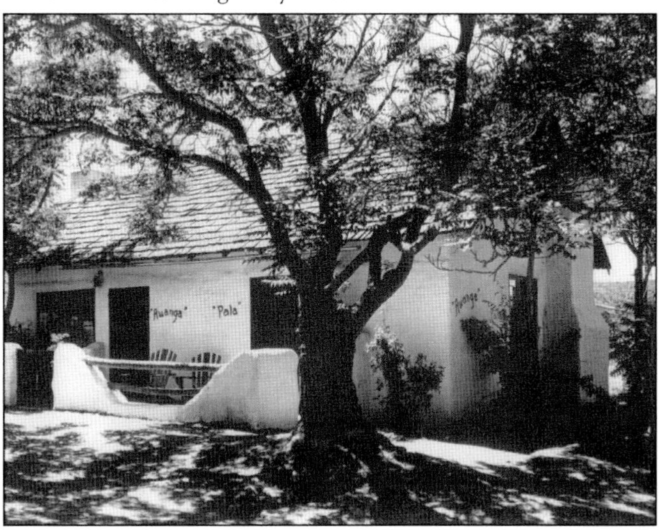

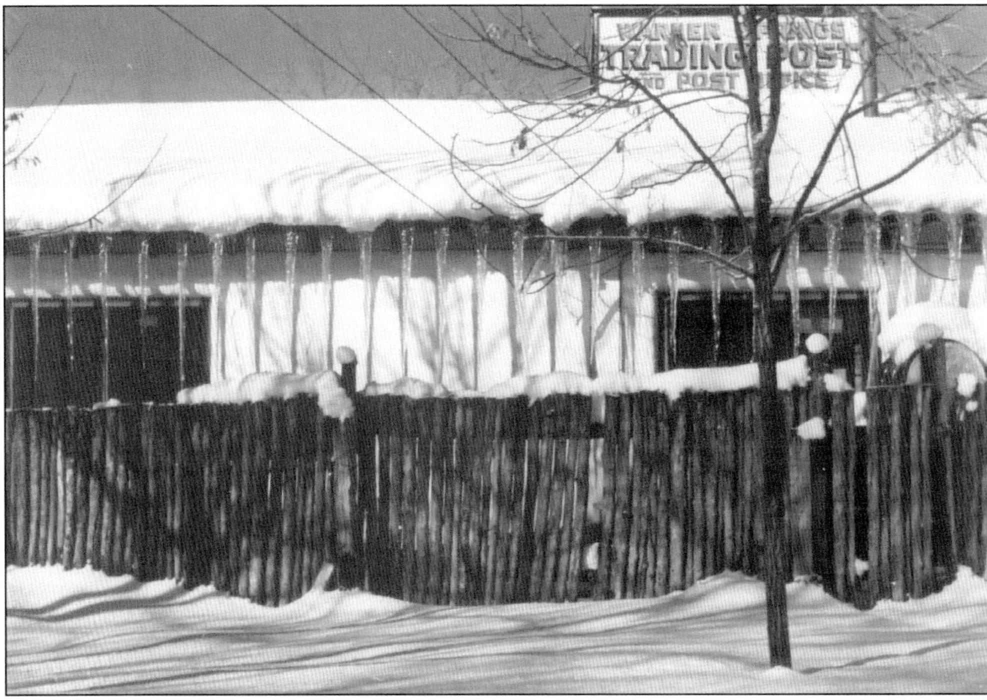

This photograph shows the original Trading Post with long icicles hanging from the roof. Snow was not uncommon at Warner Hot Springs and afforded guests a rare Southern California winter experience.

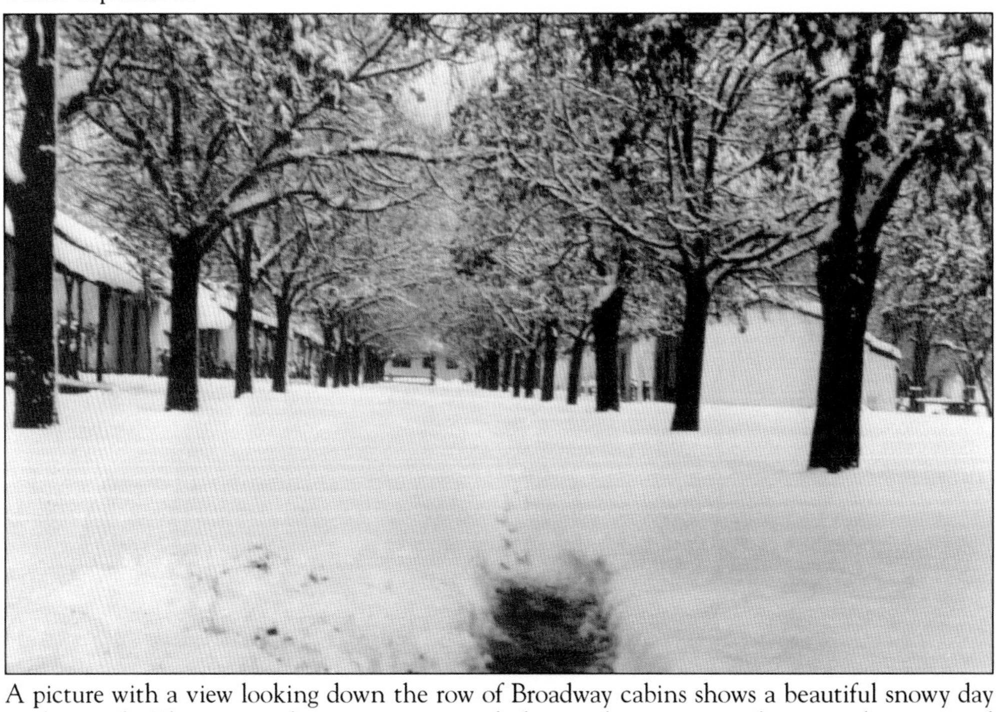

A picture with a view looking down the row of Broadway cabins shows a beautiful snowy day at the ranch. The surrounding mountains and plants take on a special magic when covered with snow.

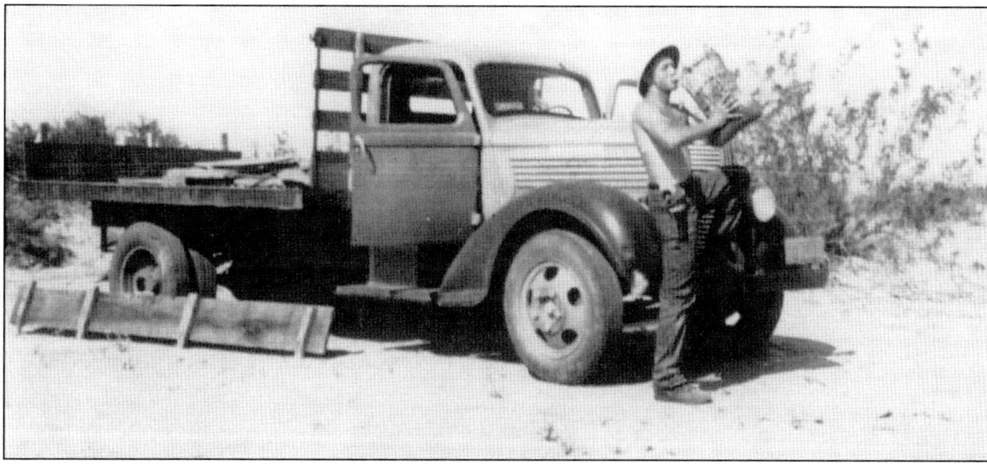

After World War II, returning soldiers, their wives, and the baby boom generation created a demand for more rooms and facilities at Warner Hot Springs and an important period of growth for the ranch. In this picture, a workman is taking a break from loading flagstones into a flatbed truck in the Borrego Desert to be used for patios and porches.

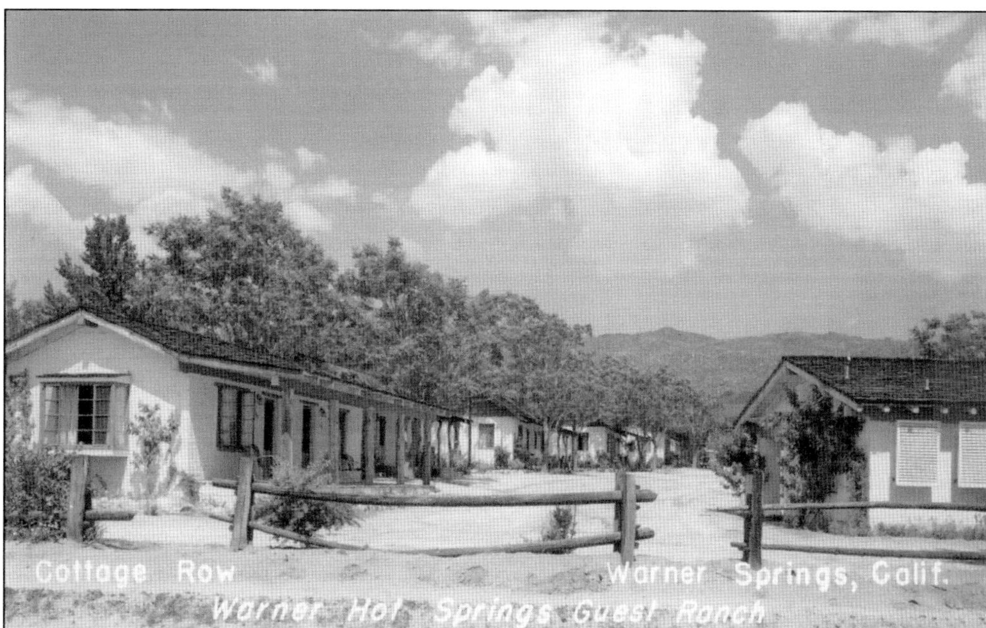

This photograph shows Cottage Row, new semi-deluxe casitas on the south side of the Broadway cabins, and the new entry drive. Local residents Joe Grammar and Chet Taylor were involved in building the casitas and worked for Eddie Cardinal, who hand forged the metal hinges, door hardware, and other metal fixtures at the ranch.

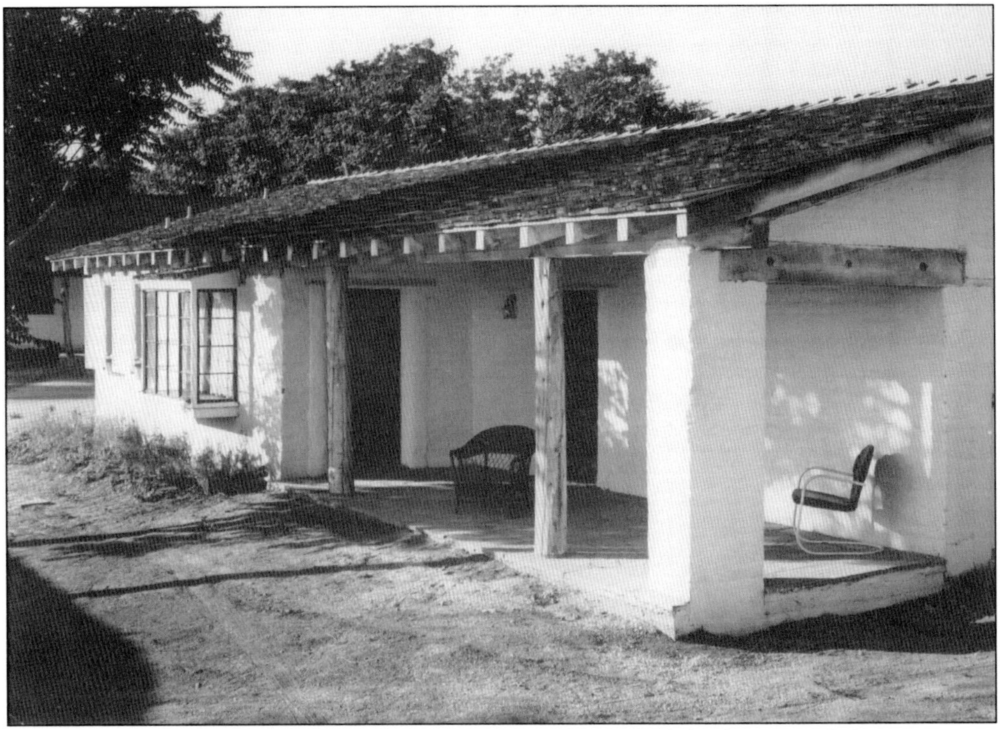

A marketing brochure states "these contain living-room with bedroom and dressing room combinations which have been pleasantly designed with beautiful, restful colors and are equipped with private baths and electric heat."

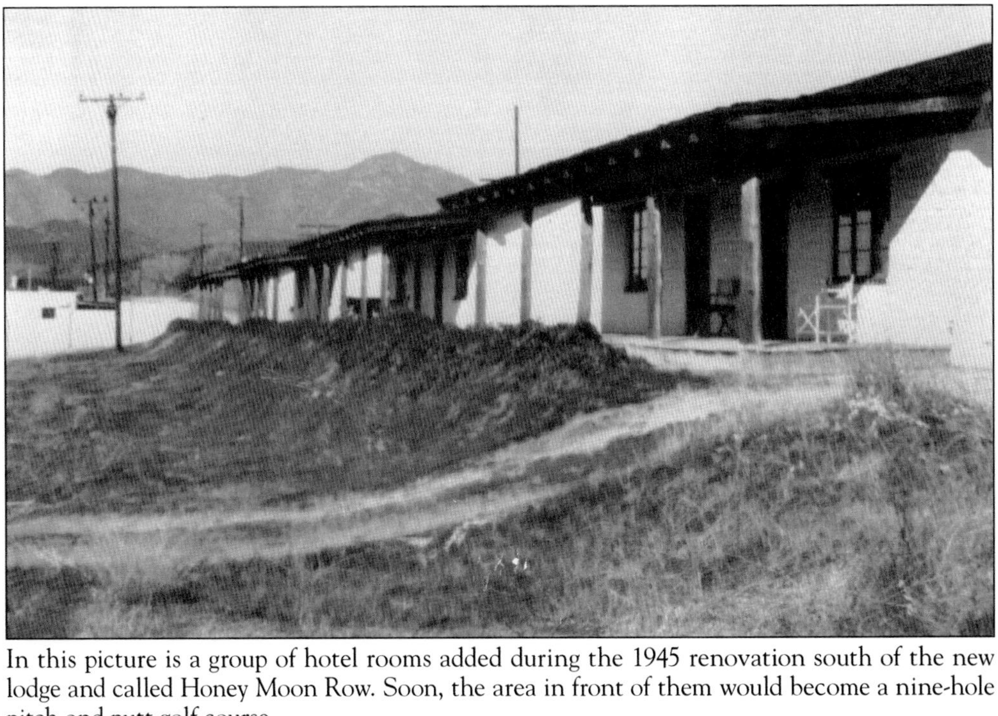

In this picture is a group of hotel rooms added during the 1945 renovation south of the new lodge and called Honey Moon Row. Soon, the area in front of them would become a nine-hole pitch-and-putt golf course.

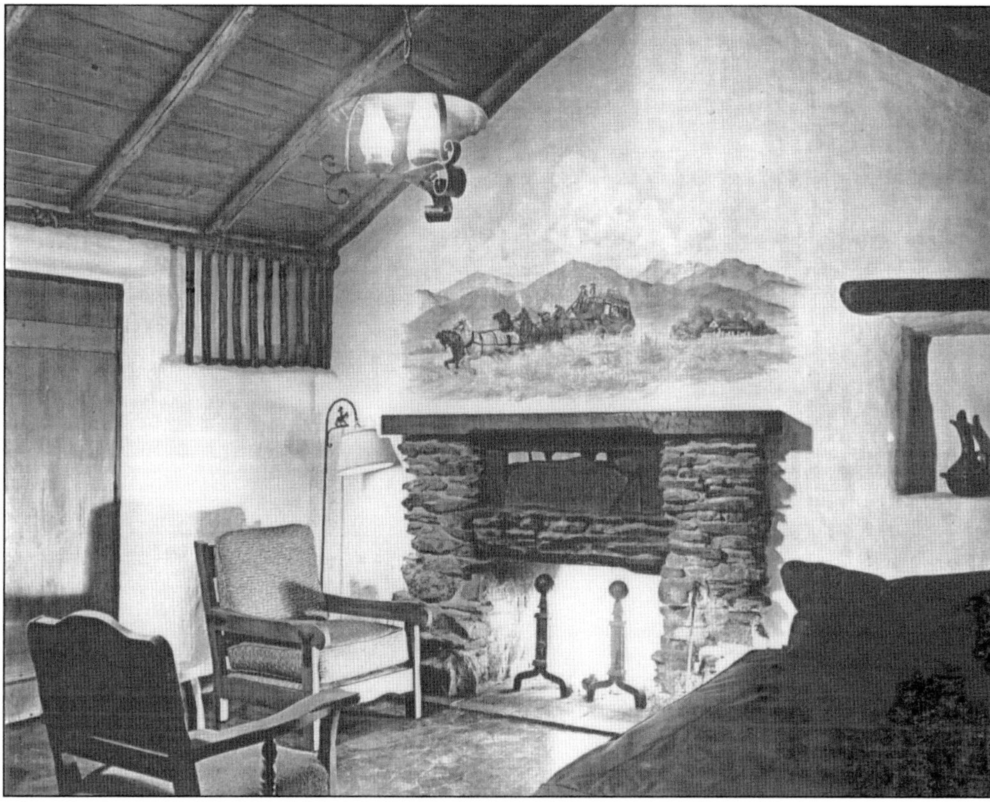

This photograph shows the deluxe cabin interior in one of the original Indian adobe cottages, advertised as having "all the charm of early American Indian Buildings." The mural above the fireplace is by artist and dishwasher Paul Matthews. Rock facades and wood mantels were added to the fireplaces at this time, which accounts for their unusual depth.

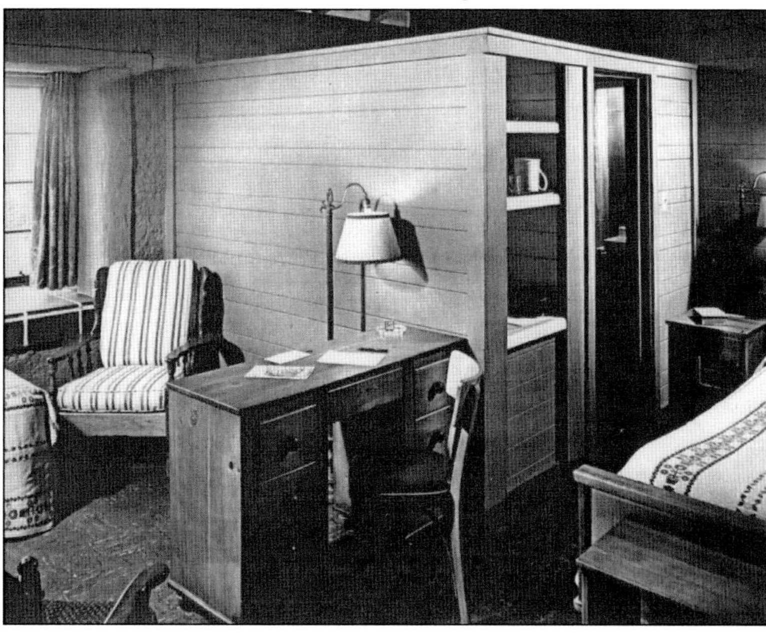

This picture shows a Cottage Row interior with a built-in wooden closet and dressing combination room divider, desk, and bay window.

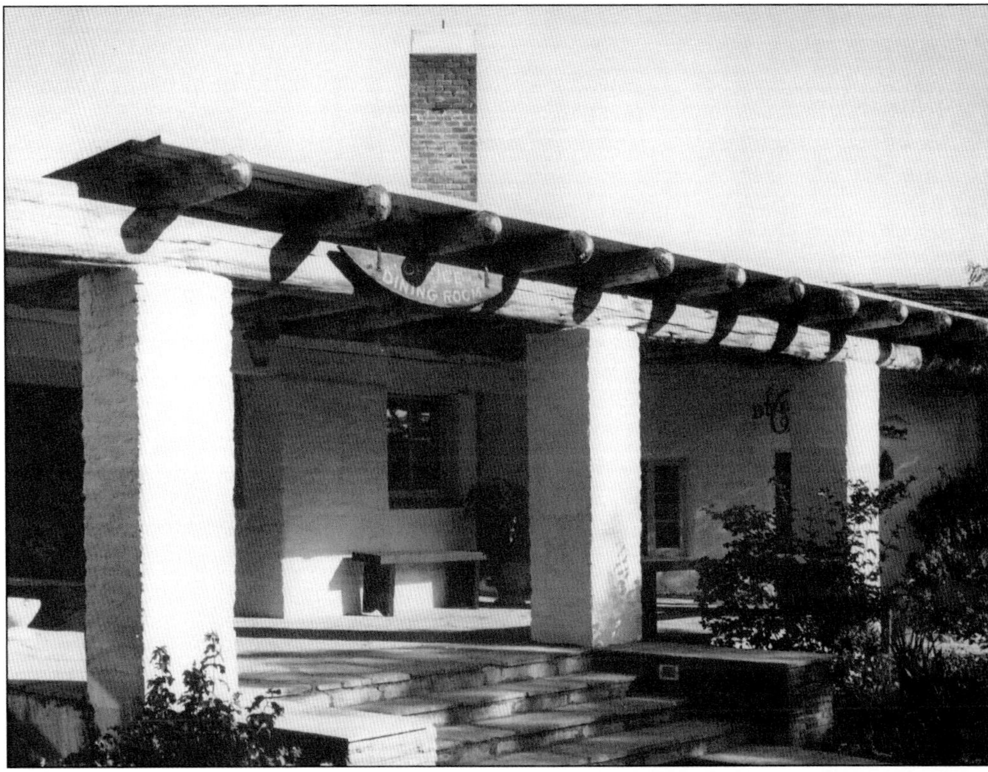

A big part of the 1940s additions was the connection of existing structures in a new lodge building. This photograph shows the entry to the lodge, where "your vacation begins, reminiscent of the old West. Here we have our offices, lounge, dining room, soda fountain, and recreation area," according to the advertising.

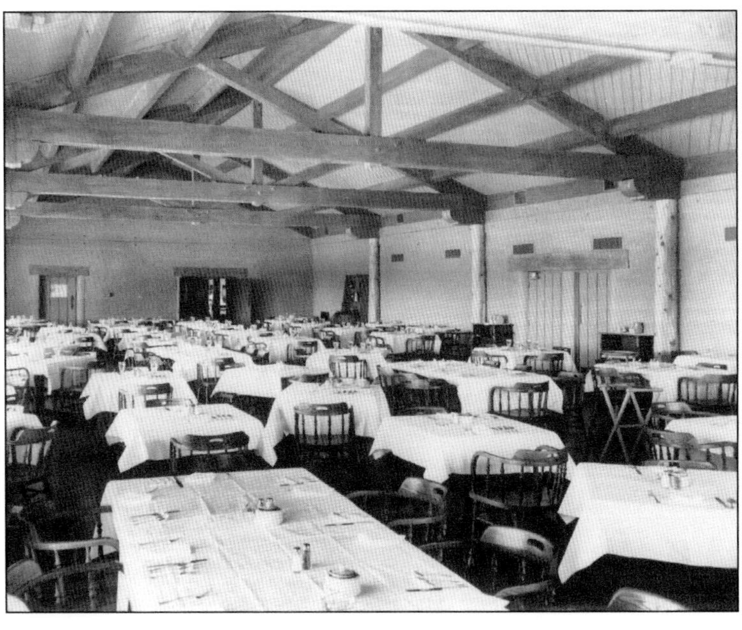

The Anza Dining Room and a new, larger kitchen were built to accommodate more diners. Linen tablecloths and napkins, turquoise glassware, and china with the Warner Hot Springs logo graced the tables. A strict dress code required diners to dress for dinner. During popular weekends, there were two or three sittings with a bell rung to announce them.

Steps from the Anza Dining Room led to this flagstone patio for outside dining and cocktails before dinner. A window from the back of the Butterfield Bar to the patio and to the dining room allowed waitstaff to service these areas easily. The waitresses were dressed in "Indian attire" complete with braided wigs at this time to resemble the logo of "Wa-ner Ran-Cha," an imaginary Indian woman. Fortunately, these uniforms were abandoned for more sensible and culturally sensitive garb.

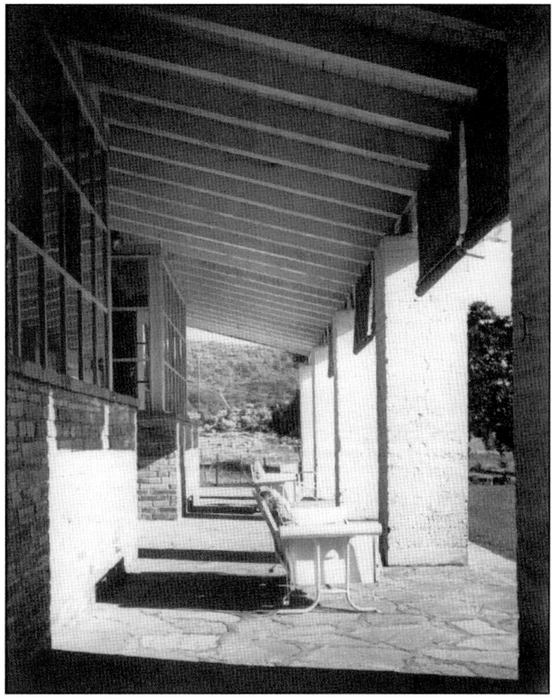

Delicious Food - Wide Selection
Reasonable Prices

IN THE LODGE:
- The Butterfield Cantina
  - Open weekdays at 2
  - noon Saturdays, Sundays & Holidays
- Anza Dining Room
  - Ranch Breakfast 8 to 10
  - Dinner 6 to 8
  - Dinner, Friday & Saturday, 6 to 9:30

AT TWIN POOLS:
- The Cedar Room
  - Luncheon noon to 2 p.m.
- Fountain Counter
  - Snacks, ice cream, beverages from 9 a.m. to 4:30 p.m.

ON THE TRAIL:
- Horseback Ride and Ranch Breakfast.
  - Leave stables at 8 A.M.

FAIRWAY HOUSE:
- At Championship 18-hole course.
  - Snacks and beverages

HIKER'S DELIGHT —
- Our delicious box lunches. Order at Front Desk.

Under the "Ranch Plan," breakfast and dinner were covered in the cost of the room. Lunch was available at the Chatter Box soda fountain and Drip Bar at the pool. Hikers and horseback riders could also order a box lunch to be consumed on their adventures.

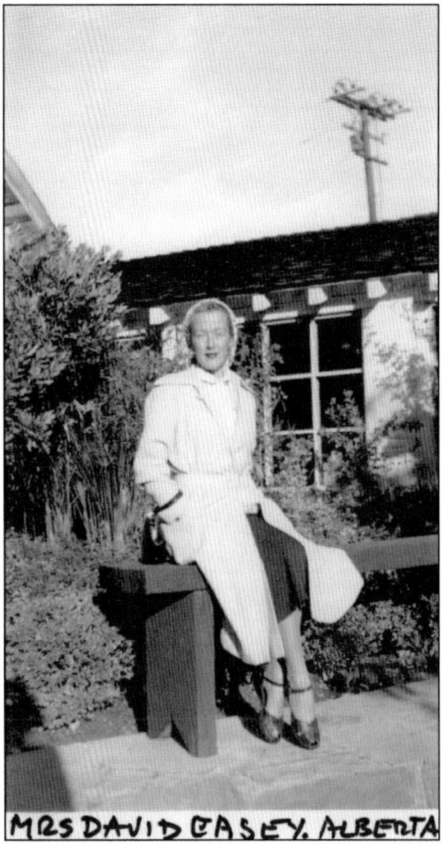

Alberta Casey, longtime visitor and a resident of La Jolla and Los Tules, is shown outside the lodge dressed for dinner. Many visitors from Point Loma, La Jolla, and other San Diego communities, as well as residents from Los Angeles and Orange County, would frequent Warner Hot Springs for years. (Courtesy Casey family.)

One of the buildings that became attached to the lodge was an original adobe where Juan Jose Warner was reported to have lived before his house on the Southern Immigrant Trail was built. This building was used as the manager's office in the early days, with a bell outside for late arrivers to ring. It became the new cantina and was called the Butterfield Bar.

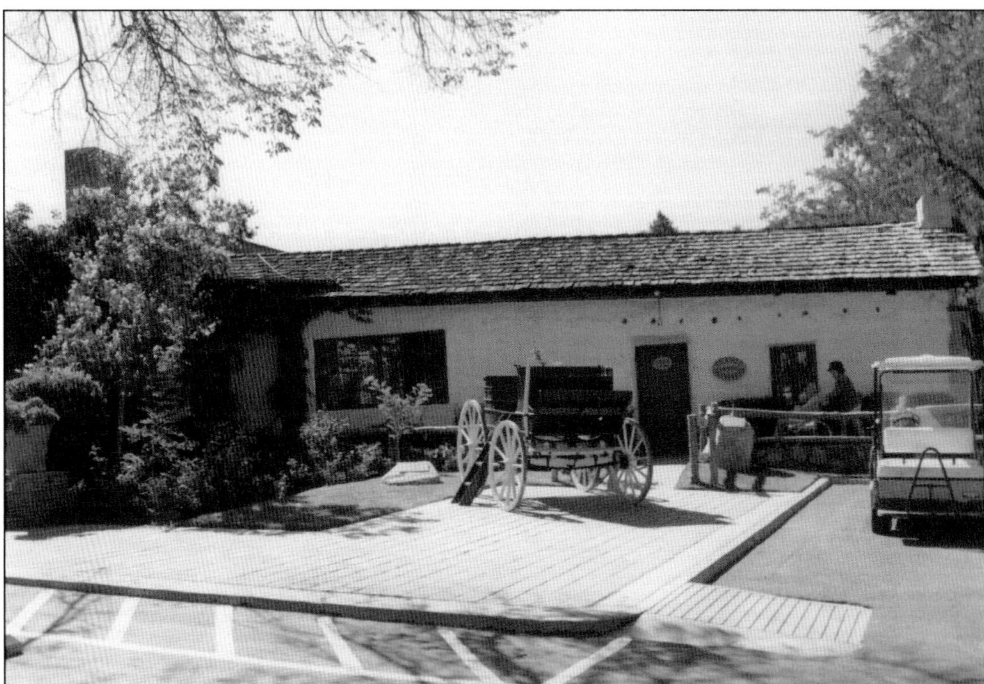

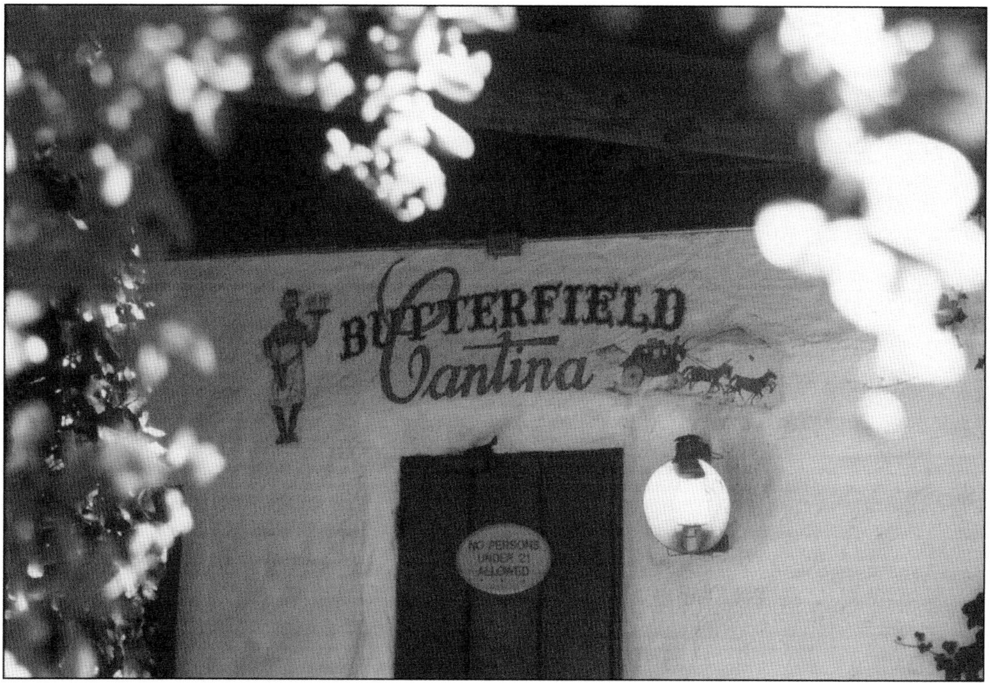

A sign above the entry door reads "Butterfield Cantina," and a light on means the bar is open. This charming building of two rooms became a favorite gathering place and is still today a place for cocktails and entertainment.

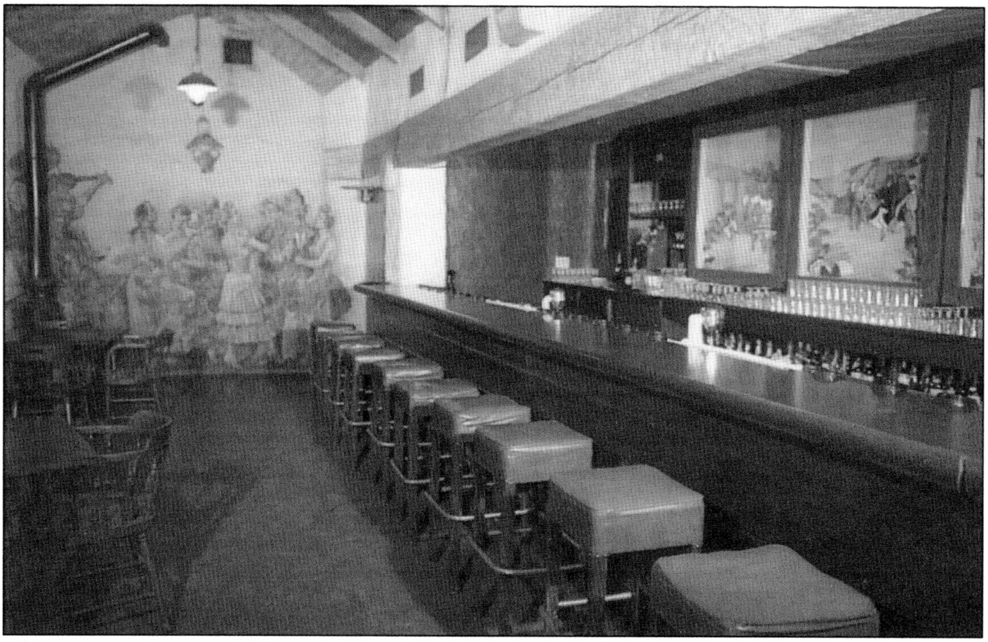
This interior photograph shows the long bar with the original dioramas behind it, the potbelly stove in the corner, and the mural done by artist Paul Matthews, all of which have been preserved.

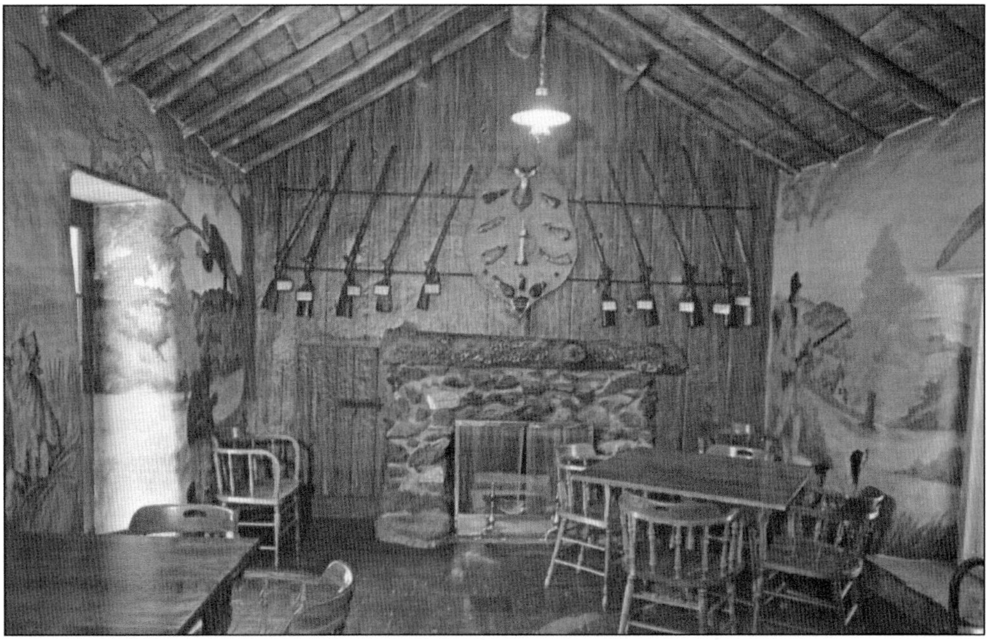

A step down from the bar, the lower room of the cantina featured more murals by Matthews, a stone fireplace surrounded by antique guns, and at one time a player piano. Note the thickness of the adobe walls.

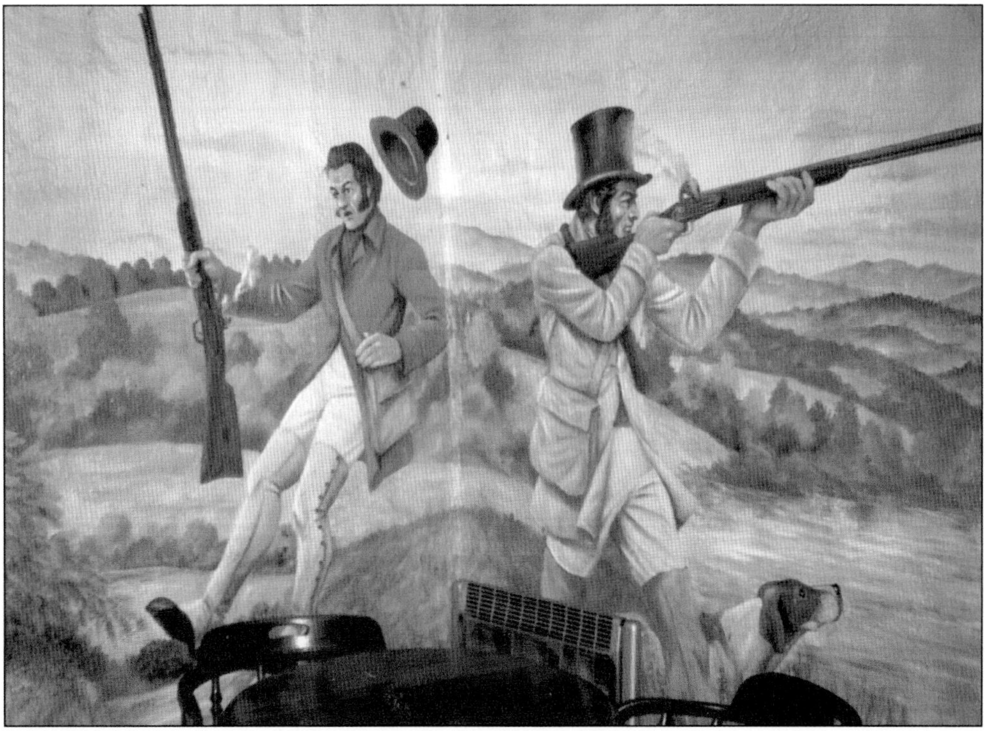

This photograph shows a close-up of part of a mural. Walt Disney, a visitor to Warner Hot Springs, was so impressed with Paul Matthews's talents as an artist he hired him to work for Walt Disney Studios.

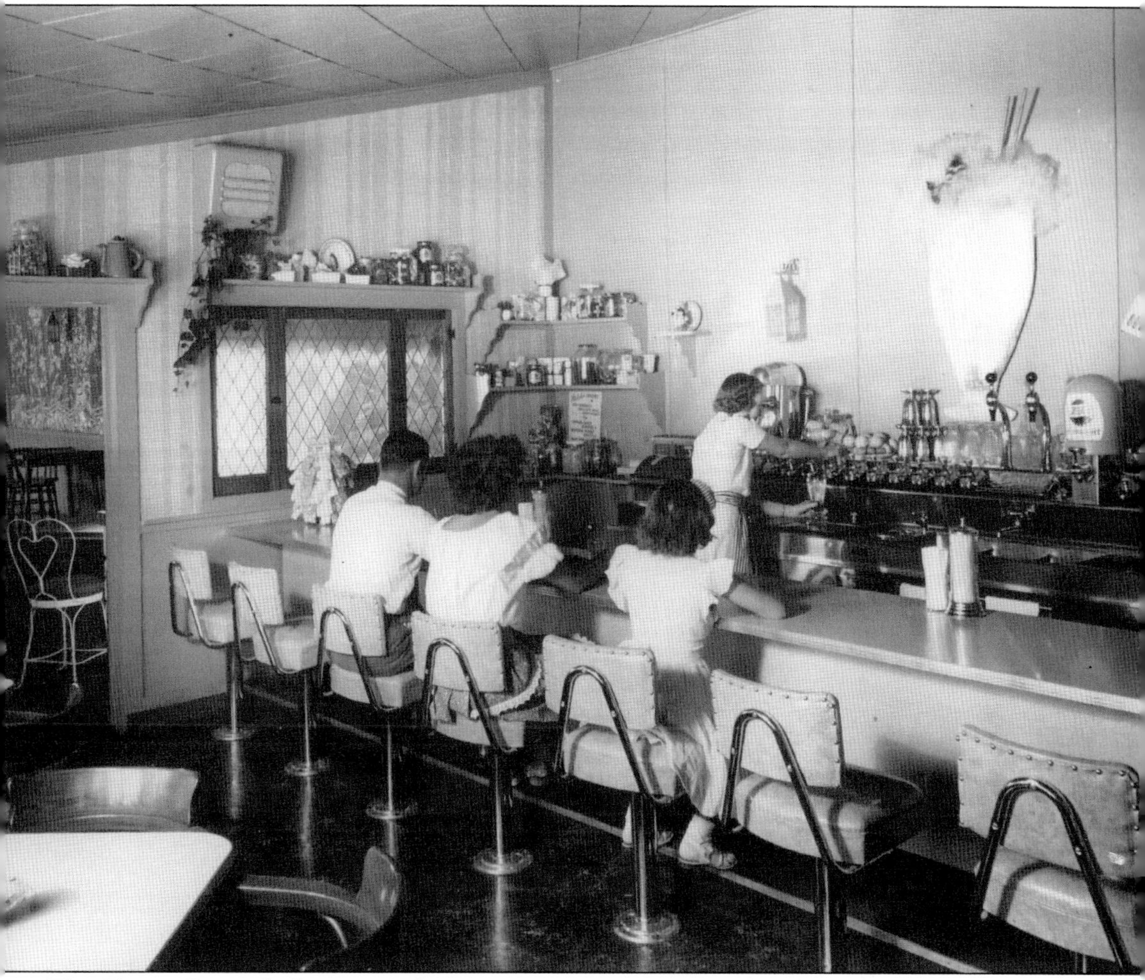

The Chatter Box soda fountain, "where ice cream concoctions and cool drinks of all kinds are served in a cottage setting," is shown is this photograph. It occupied the area that was formerly a small dining room and eventually became a hallway connecting the Ortega and Palomar Rooms with the reception area of the lodge. The original kitchen was converted to housekeeping. The Furze granddaughters recall an employee dining room and children's dining room with a mural portraying children at the ranch behind the kitchen. Promotional materials from this time state that Warner's is the "place where you'll spend some of the greatest hours of your life! If it's quiet time that'll make your vacation fine, we'll see that you get it. If you want action, you can have that too . . . and plenty of it, in many forms of real fun." Reservations in those days were made by calling TRinty 5951, the Los Angeles office of the Riverside Cement Company on Hope Street, owned by William Henshaw. There were no telephones or televisions in the rooms. A switchboard took phone calls, and a note was sent to the guest's casita. There were two pay phones in booths in the lobby to the left of the fireplace for outgoing calls. An annual rodeo fundraiser for the school was held on ranch grounds about where the arena is today. Guests visiting at Christmastime were encouraged to bring gifts for needy children at the school.

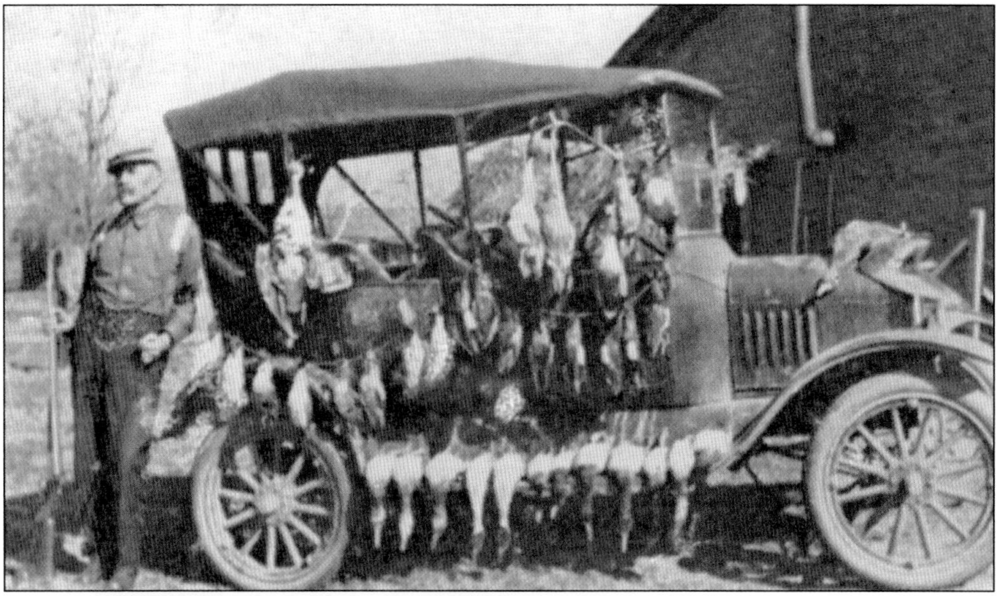

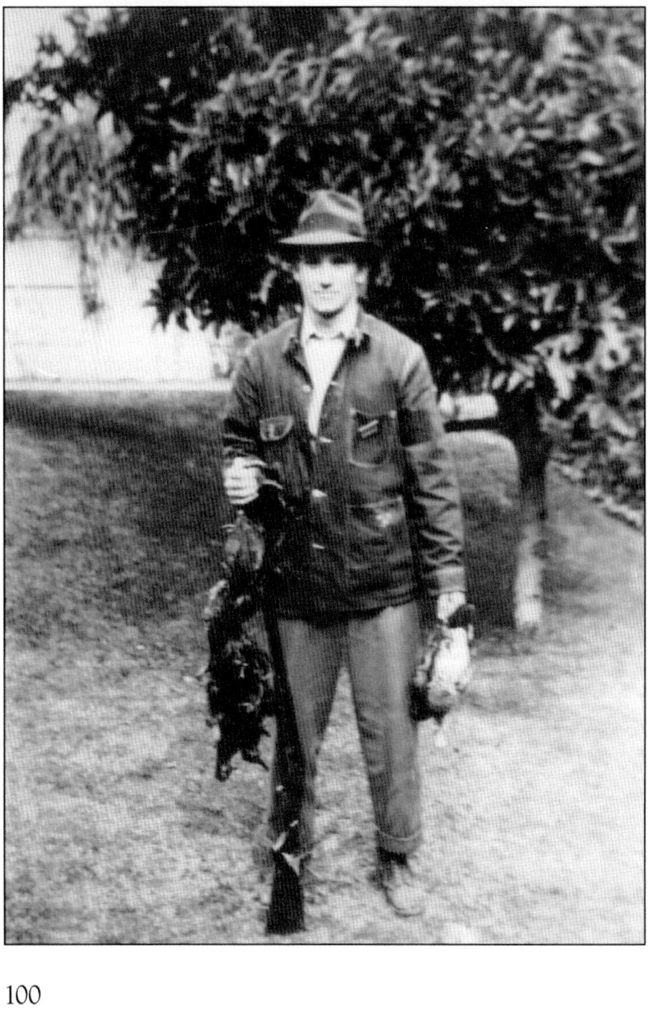

The Warner Valley was a popular hunting area for decades, as seen in this 1920s photograph. When there was plenty of water, a number of small lakes called the "chain lakes" of Big Lake, Chimney Lake, Tules Lake, Canvasback Lake, and Oak Lake existed. Later, some of the names were changed to Big Laguna, Little Laguna, and Swan Lake. Chimney Lake is being restored.

Howard C. Fletcher Jr. is pictured here after a successful day of hunting on the ranch. Permits were granted by reservation only and the number restricted each day to avoid overcrowding. The permits included duck blinds, decoys, and retrieving boats. There was also hunting for pheasant, chukkar, dove, quail, and rabbit from October through the end of March. (Courtesy H.C. Fletcher family.)

Nine

Fun and Games

Swimming, horseback riding, hiking, tennis, badminton, billiards, shuffleboard, lighted volleyball, croquet, Ping-Pong, and a children's playground were all part of the fun at Warner Hot Springs. There were trips to Lake Henshaw, Mount Palomar Observatory, old stage stops, gold mines, Julian, Mission Santa Ysabel, and desert wildflowers. Dancing was on Friday and Saturday from 6:30 p.m., and movies were shown at 7:30 p.m. during busy summer months and holiday weekends.

In the 1940s, a nine-hole, par-3 golf course was put in, advertised as "a favorite of husbands wives and kids." In 1965, an 18-hole, 6,500-yard golf course was completed, eventually followed by a clubhouse, pro shop, and grill. A 5,000-foot dirt airstrip "in the clear, with no obstructions" was available for private planes and, later, sailplanes. Transportation was available in the early days by calling the main lodge from the telephone on the windsock.

Helen Hunt Jackson and F. Scott Fitzgerald visited, and it is rumored that some of her famous 1884 book *Ramona* was written at the springs, as were parts of Fitzgerald's *The Great Gatsby*, while he was "drying out." A film version of *Ramona* with Don Ameche and Loretta Young was filmed at Warner Hot Springs, and many local residents were extras, including Chet Taylor and Indians from Los Coyotes. Mary Pickford, Douglas Fairbanks, Charlie Chaplin, Clark Gable, Jean Harlow, Cary Grant, and Gary Cooper were guests, and Lon Chaney Sr. and Jr. had a ranch nearby. Walt Disney came, and Art Linkletter celebrated his 68th wedding anniversary at the springs at age 91. Bing Crosby owned a five percent share during the Rossi years, and a casita was built for him within the original Cupa village. Will Rogers and other celebrities frequented the Warner ranch house, spending time with the Sawday cowboys in the 1930s. John Wayne was the most frequent visitor in the 1940s and exchanged hats with George Sawday, with Wayne wearing Sawday's hat in *She Wore a Yellow Ribbon*. Alan Hale and James Cagney filmed *The Fighting 69th* here, and later Dean Martin and Joey Bishop made a Western called *Texas Across the River*.

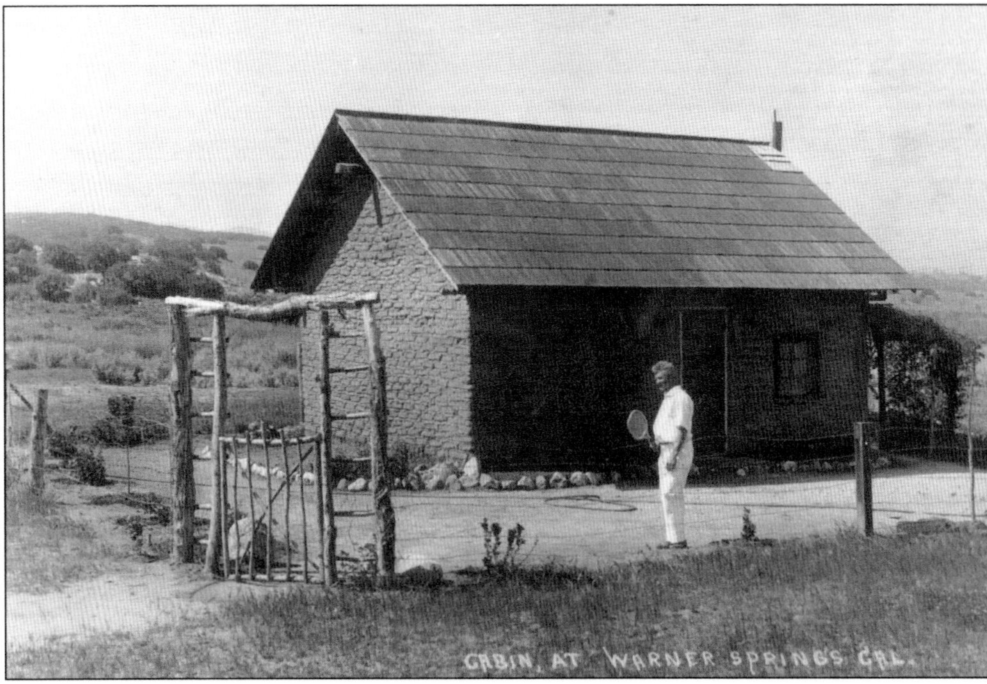

In the earliest days of the ranch, tennis was played on a dirt court. This photograph is of a tennis player in the early 1900s, and the court was near the bathhouse in the background.

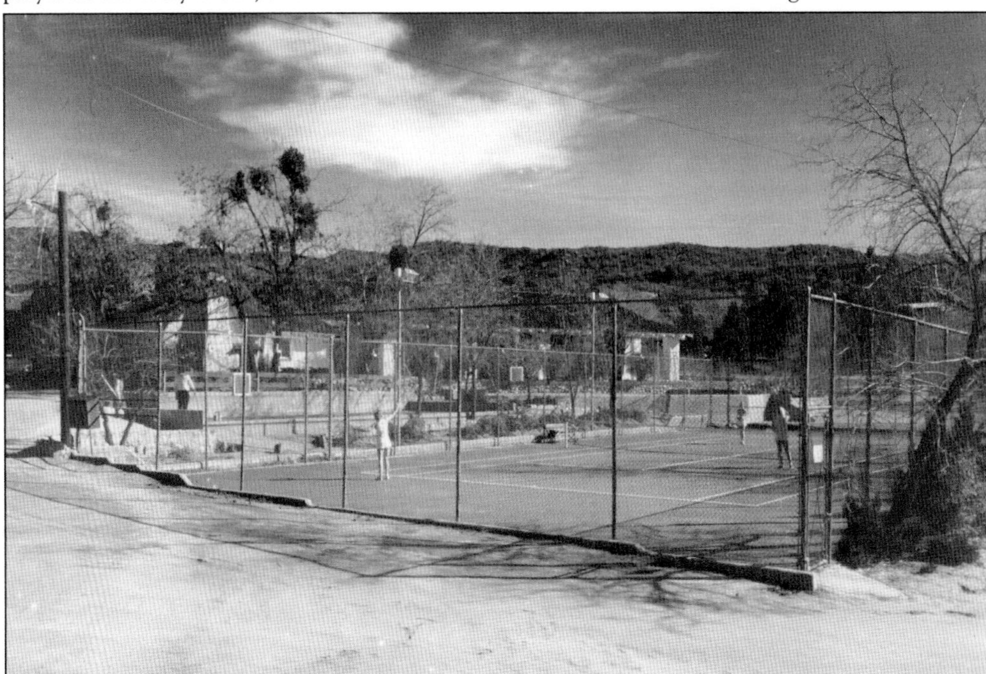

During renovations of the 1940s, a tennis court, shuffleboard courts, and a badminton court were added just west of the main lodge. Later, eight more courts were added where the swimming pool parking lot was, and an additional group of courts was added near the golf course clubhouse. The ranch owner association removed them in the 2000s, as they were rarely being used.

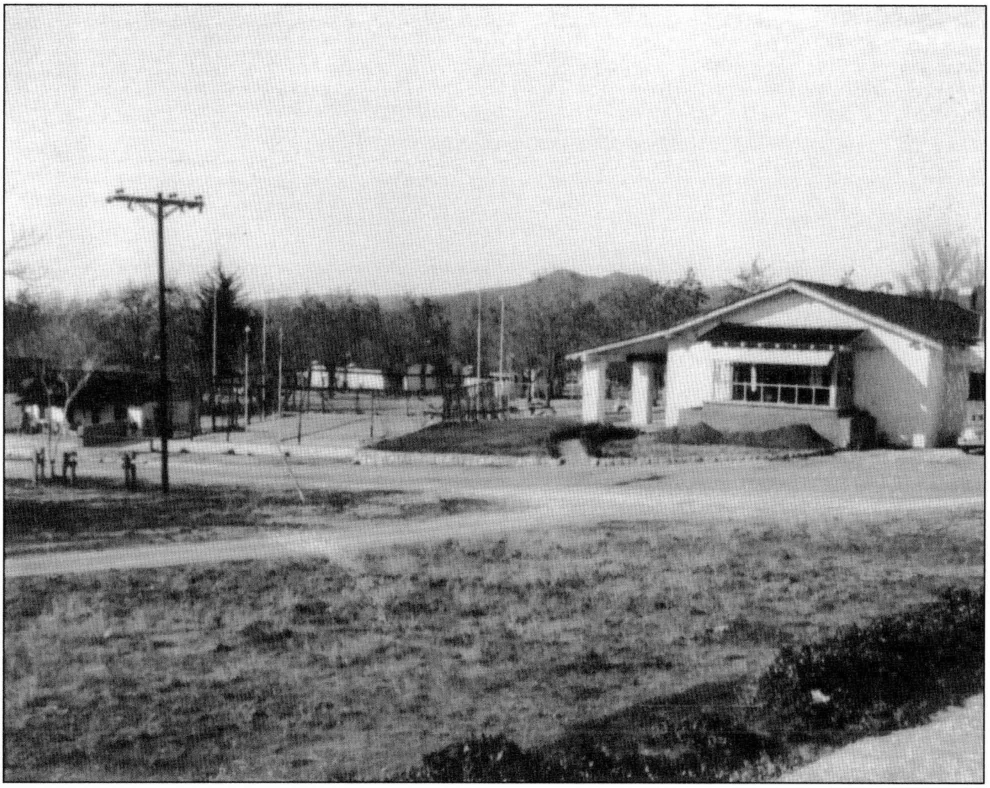

This photograph shows the single tennis court as seen from the area that would become the pitch-and-putt course. The building on the right is the Anza Dining Room.

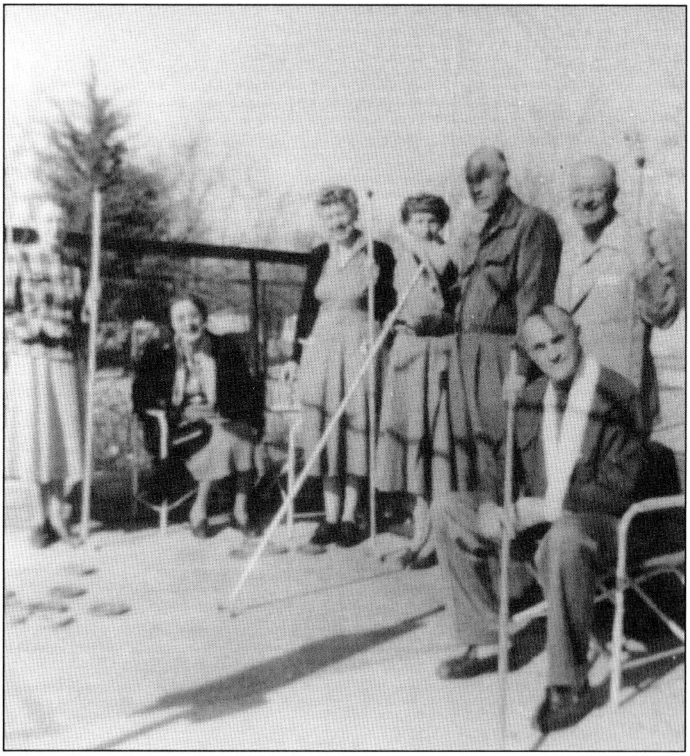

A group of guests pauses during a game of shuffleboard. The courts, although showing wear and tear, are still there.

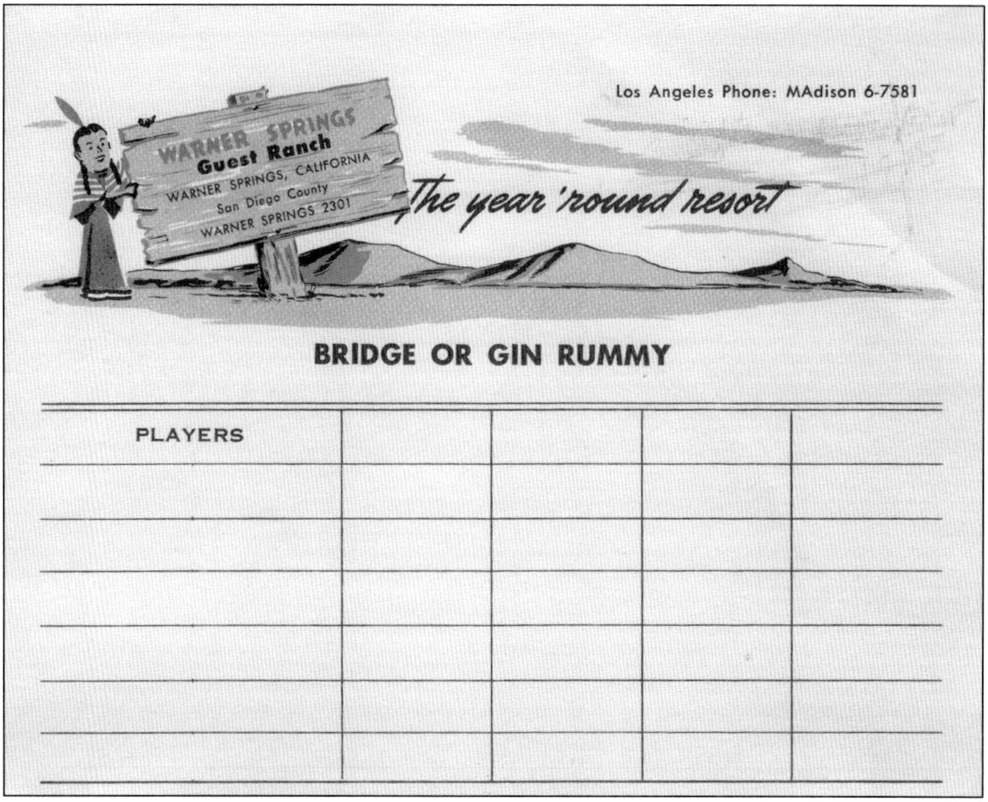

Bridge and gin rummy were popular card games, especially in the years after World War II. A scorecard from that time shows the "War-ner Ranch-A" logo and a new Los Angeles number for reservations, MAdison 6-7581. Later, Warner Springs would be part of the 714 area code before being transferred to the 760 area code.

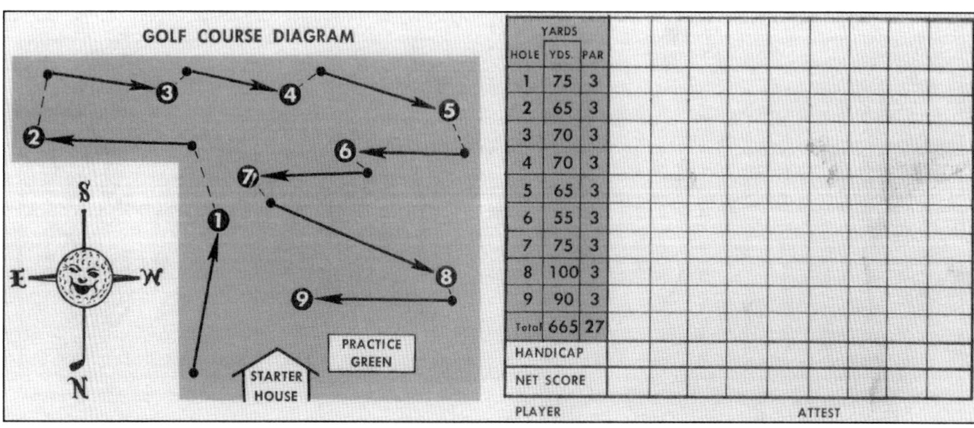

This is a scorecard and diagram of the pitch-and-putt par-3 golf course. It was removed by the Rossi development and new casitas built in its place.

An early golfer getting ready for a round is shown in front of Honey Moon Row.

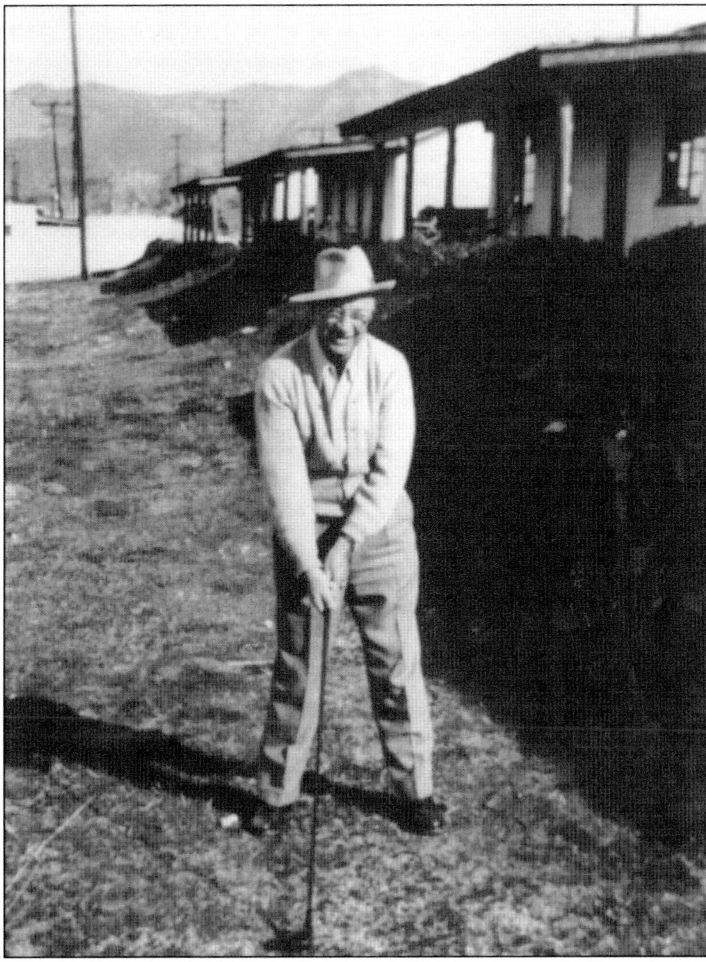

This postcard shows the pitch-and-putt course with Cottage Row and the mountains in the background.

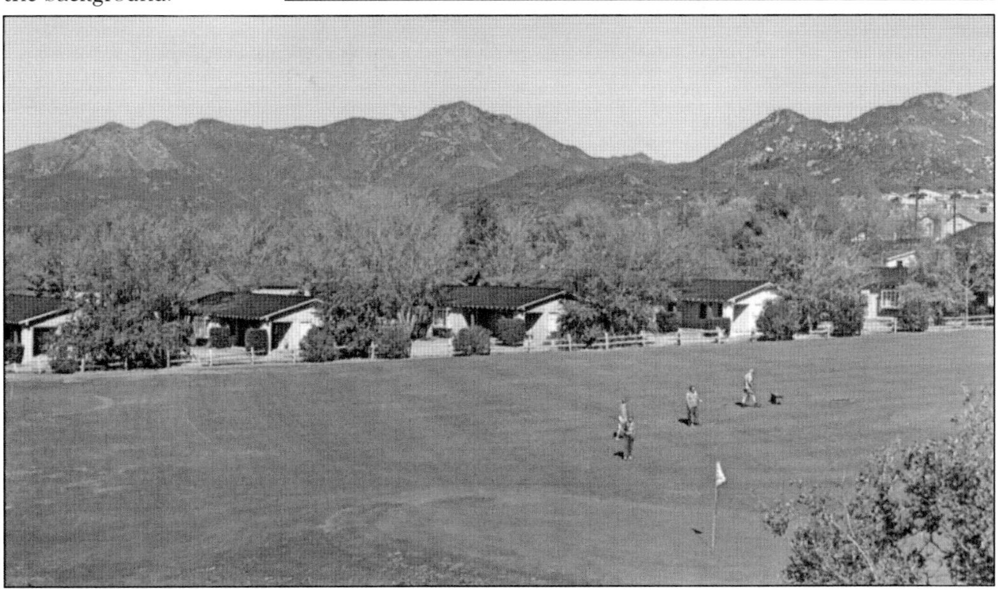

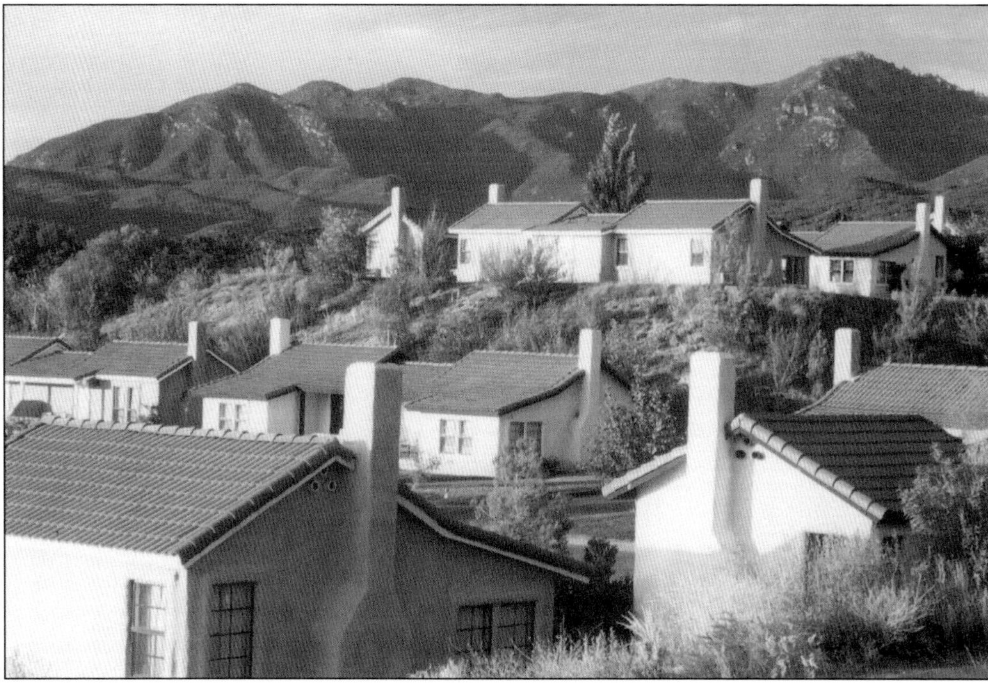

A later photograph of the same area shows the modern-day casitas built by Cal Rossi that replaced the pitch-and-putt area, expanding the number of cabins to about 250.

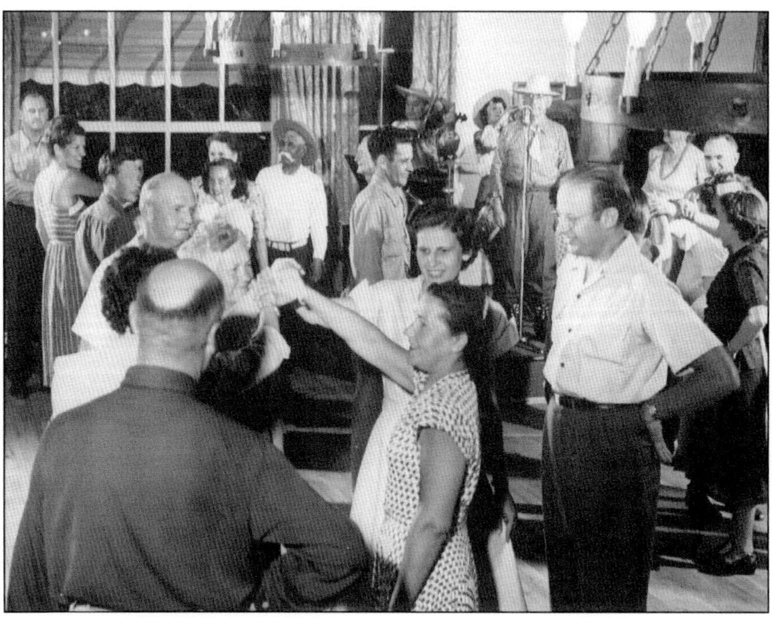

Square dancing was very popular in the 1940s, as were singalongs and board games. Julio Ortega can be seen in this photograph (directly under the chandelier in a long-sleeved white shirt and cowboy hat with his signature white mustache) along with musicians Jay Hutton on violin and his wife Eleanor on piano.

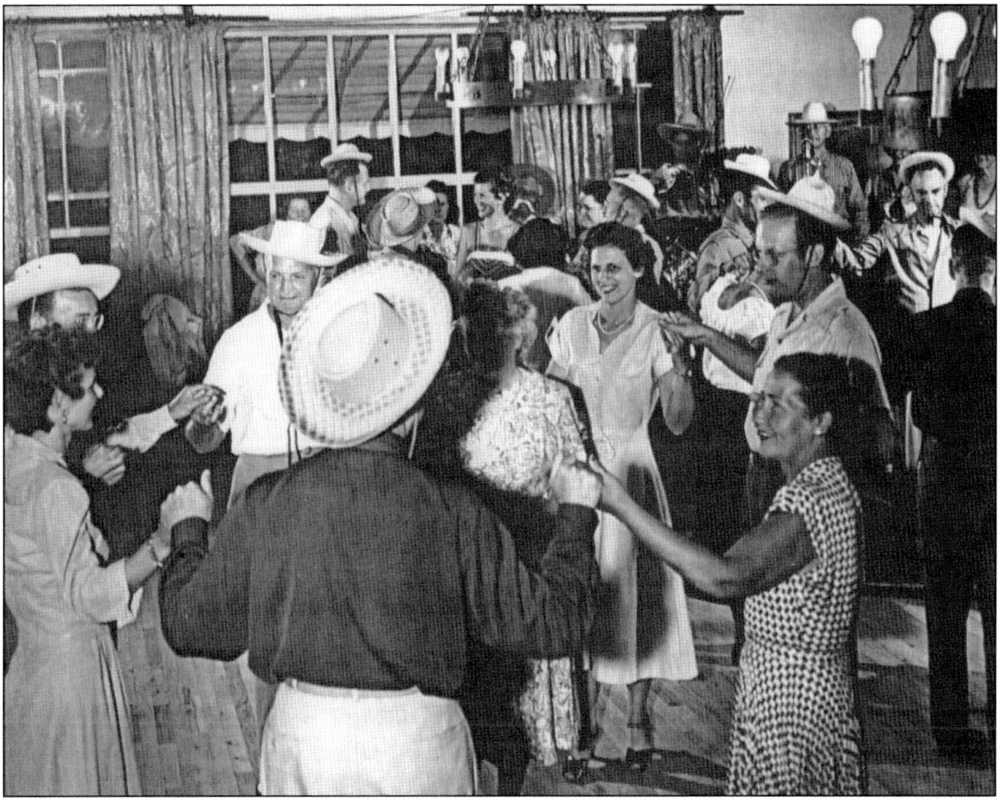

Two other photographs of square dancers show guests enjoying the festivities and wearing silly hats. These pictures show the dance taking place in the Palomar Room with the original wood floor and handmade iron light fixtures. A raised platform for a band and a wood dance floor were placed in the Anza Dining Room for special holidays like New Year's Eve. Reservations needed to be made well in advance for holiday weekends at Warner Hot Springs, with many families making a tradition of returning year after year.

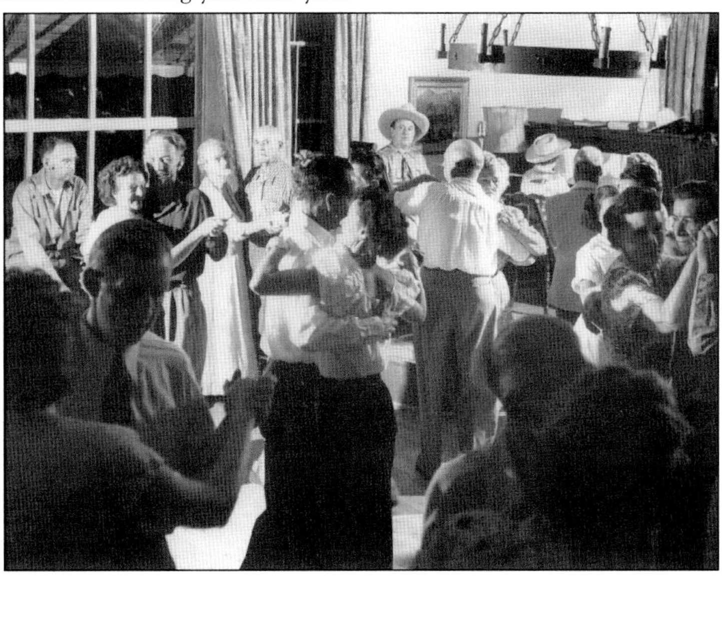

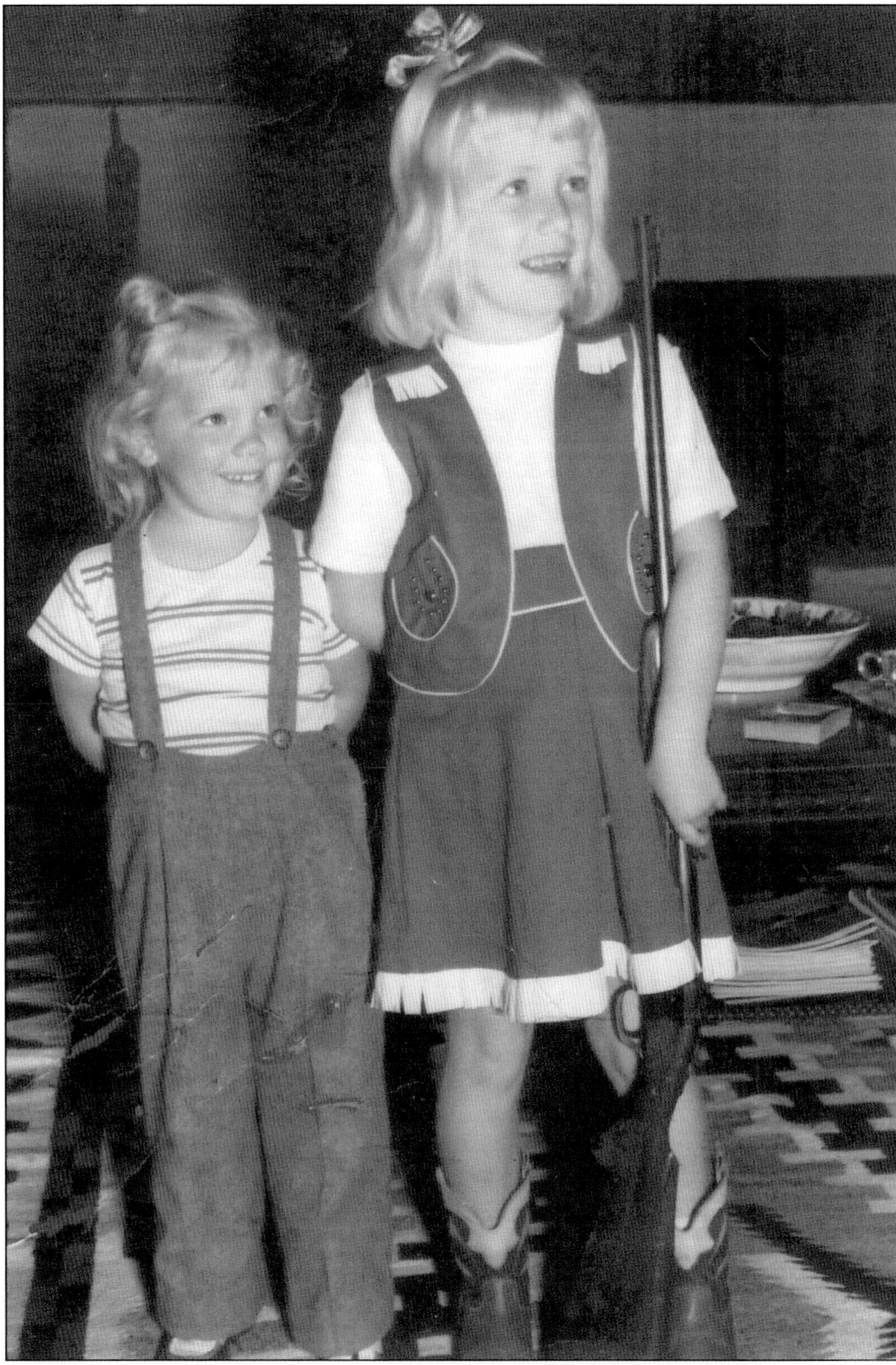

Perhaps the guests who had the best time at the ranch were children, "who take to this place like ducks to water," states the 1940s *Warner Hot Springs Guest Ranch* handout. Beth Karelius, dressed in new Western wear from the Trading Post, and her little sister Karen show their delight at being at the ranch. During the summer months, children could stay for no extra charge in their parents' room, and special activities for children were planned. (Courtesy H.C. Fletcher family.)

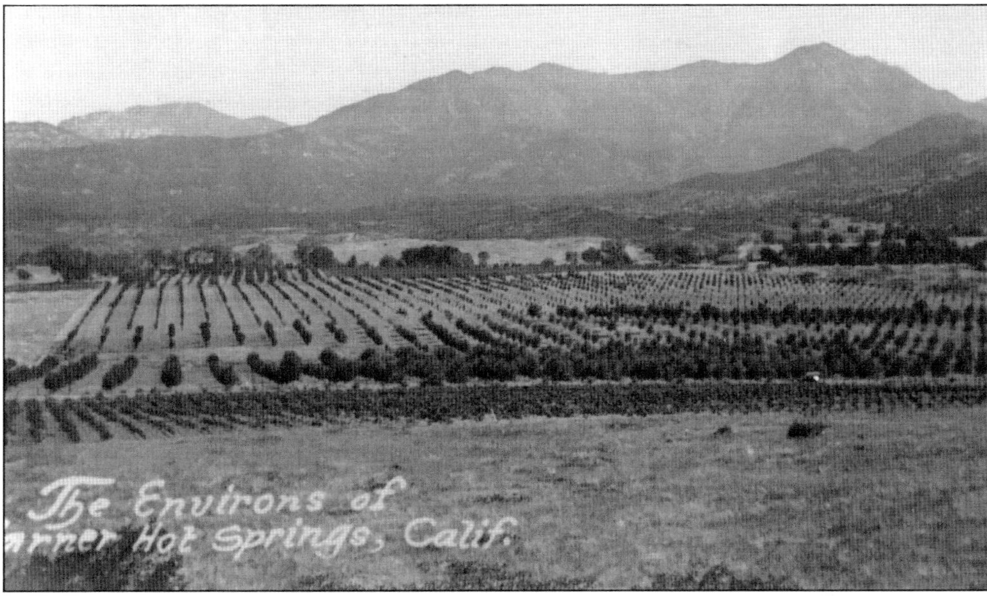

This early photograph of the ranch shows the orchard where the 18-hole golf course is today. The orchards were under the supervision of agricultural manager Jay Ream. His wife, Elsie, had a sister Louise, who was a teacher at the school. Henry Dart Greene of the Greene and Greene Architects family recuperated from the Spanish flu by working for Ream at Warner Hot Springs in the summers of 1918 and 1919.

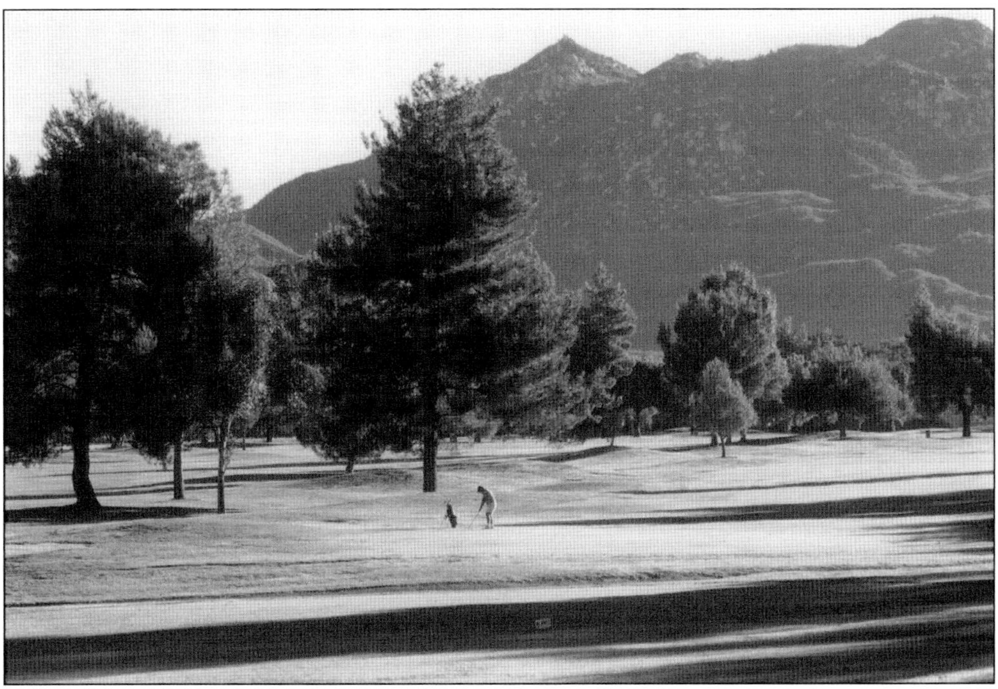

The golf course was designed by Harry Rainville. Henshaw wrote "you can never throw enough money at a course to make golfers happy," but many happy rounds of golf have been played at Warner Hot Springs. The original order of the holes was reversed at some point, and water in the ponds is from a combination of well water and reclaimed sulfur water.

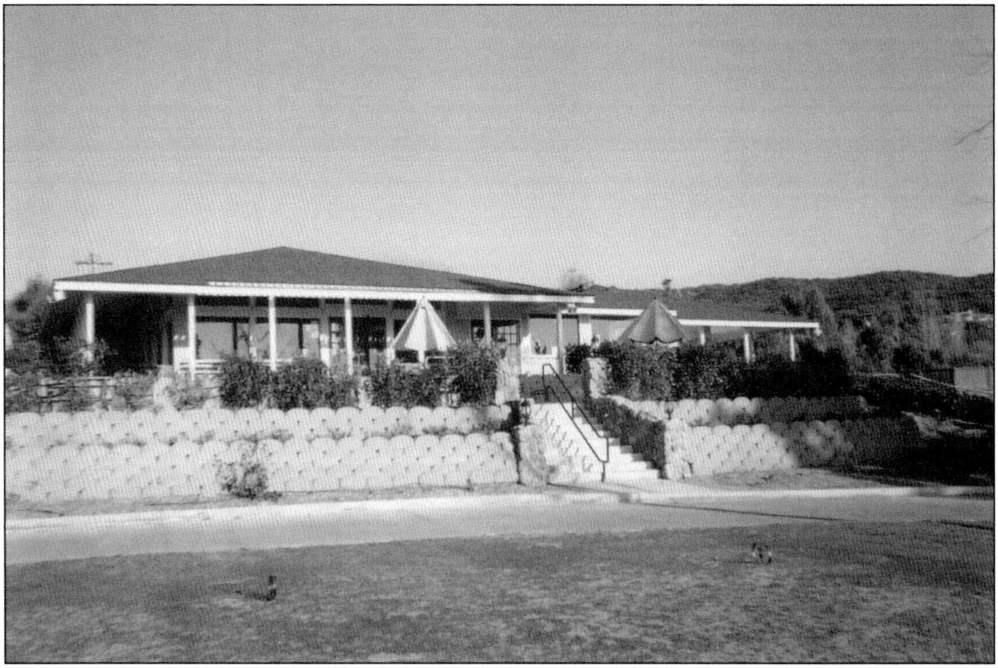

In this picture, the clubhouse built during the Cal Rossi development in the 1980s is shown from the west side.

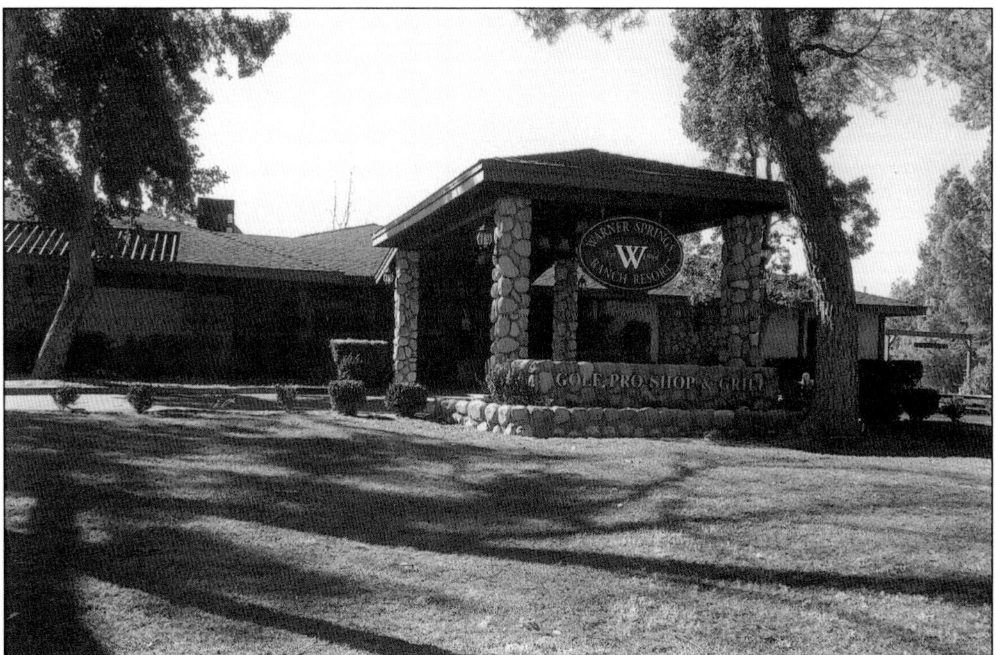

The entry to the clubhouse on the east side and 2015 improvements by the Warner Springs Ranch Resort ownership are shown in this picture. The parent company is Pacific Hospitality Group of San Diego, which owns Salt Creek Golf Course and hotels in San Diego and Palm Springs. Company president Fred Grand is from a longtime Julian family related to cowboy Ed Grand.

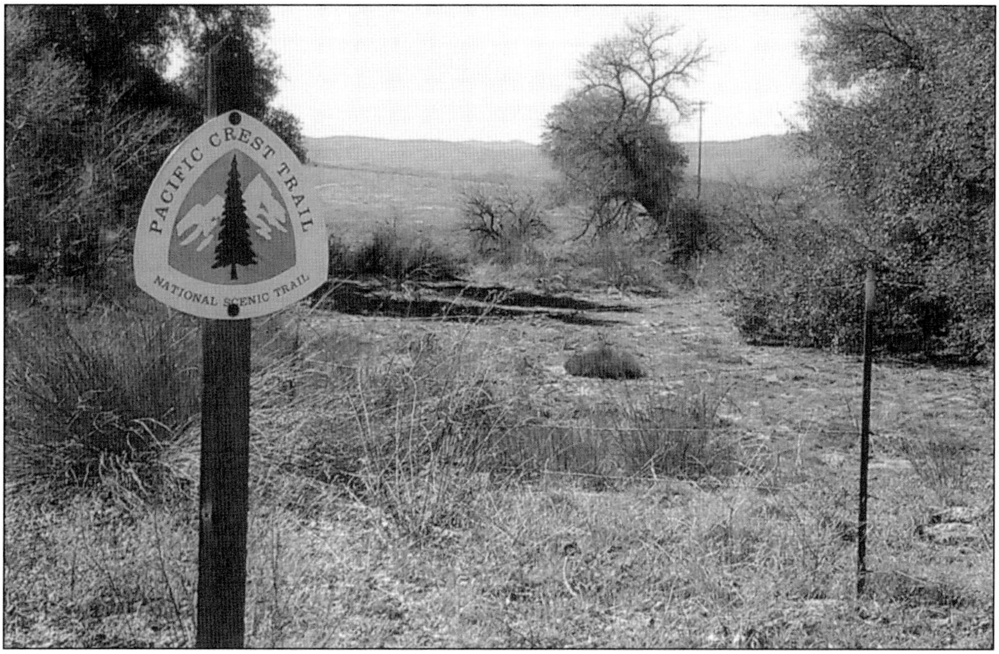

The Pacific Crest Trail (PCT), which goes from the Mexican border to Canada, crosses the Warner Valley after 109 miles going north. Warner Springs has long been a popular stop on the trail, and hikers relish a chance to have a margarita in the cantina, soak in the hot springwaters, and do their laundry. It is also an opportunity to pick up mail and supplies.

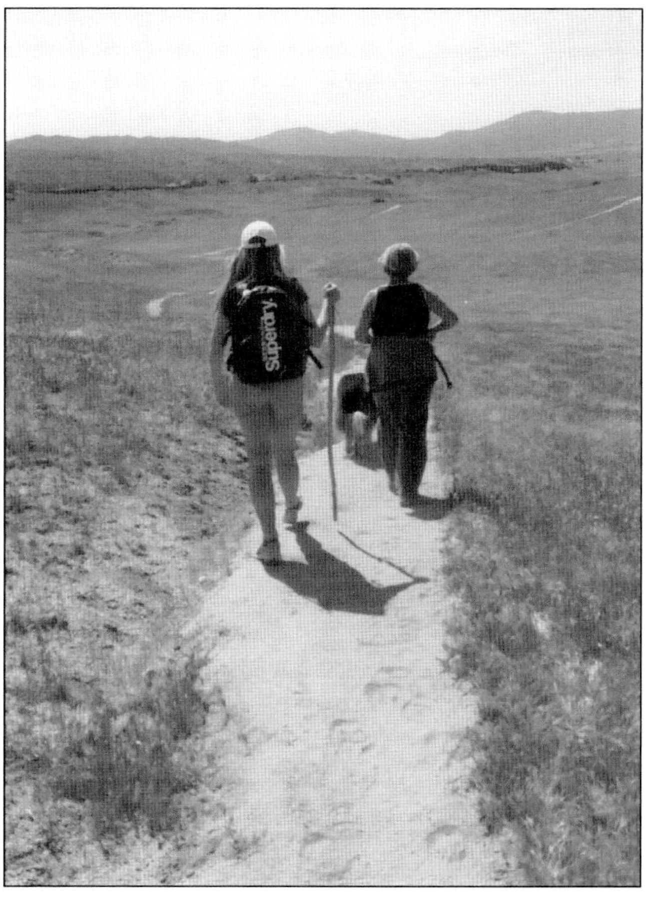

The PCT is also popular with day hikers enjoying the Barrel Springs, Eagle Rock, and Agua Caliente Creek sections of the trail. The Pacific Crest Trail Association maintains the trail, and there are caches of water hidden at certain points along the route. Activity on the trail peaks in April, with some hikers doing sections of the trail and other through-hikers doing the entire route.

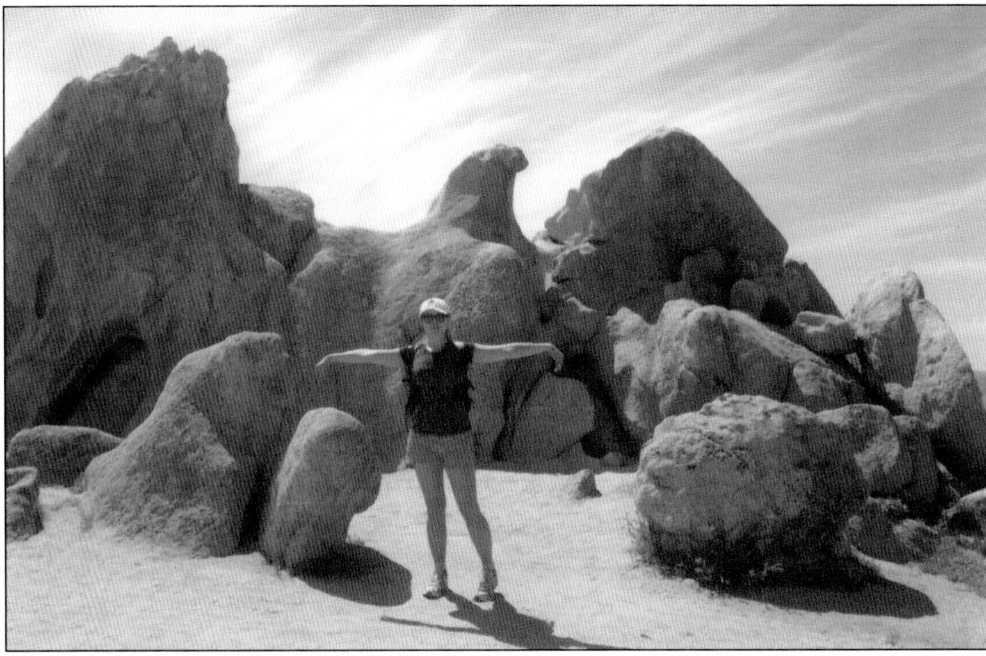

Happy hiker Lauren Saginaw stands in front of the famous Eagle Rock, a formation on the trail between Barrel Springs and Warner Springs that is a remarkable symbol of an eagle. Eagles, red-tailed hawks, owls, and many other bird species thrive in the Warner Valley, and the resort is a sanctioned bird sanctuary. (Courtesy H.C. Fletcher family.)

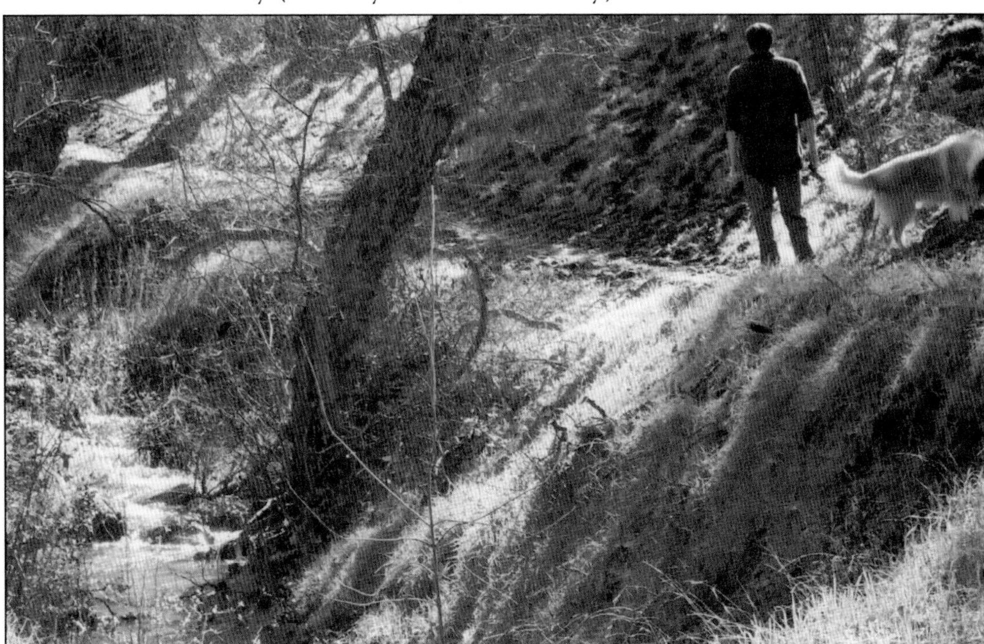

Shade and water make for pleasant hiking for man and dog. Kurt Kalanz is shown hiking the Warner Springs–to–Eagle Rock portion, which begins next to the fire station and school on Highway 79. In good years, this section and Agua Caliente Creek have flowing waters, but recent drought years have made the streams go underground.

This photograph shows John Wayne and his second wife, Jachta (third from right), with members of Fred Halleman's family, including his wife, Lorraine (second from right), and aunt Phyllis (far right). Fred, a wrangler and lifeguard at the ranch, married the daughter of Sidney Furze. In 1952, he would take his growing family to La Jolla, where he would establish the Cotton Patch and later five Boll Weevil restaurants, which he franchised.

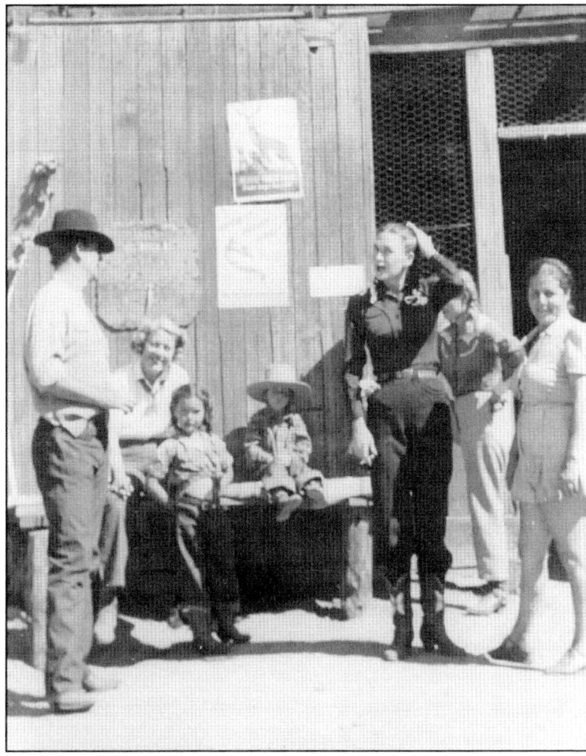

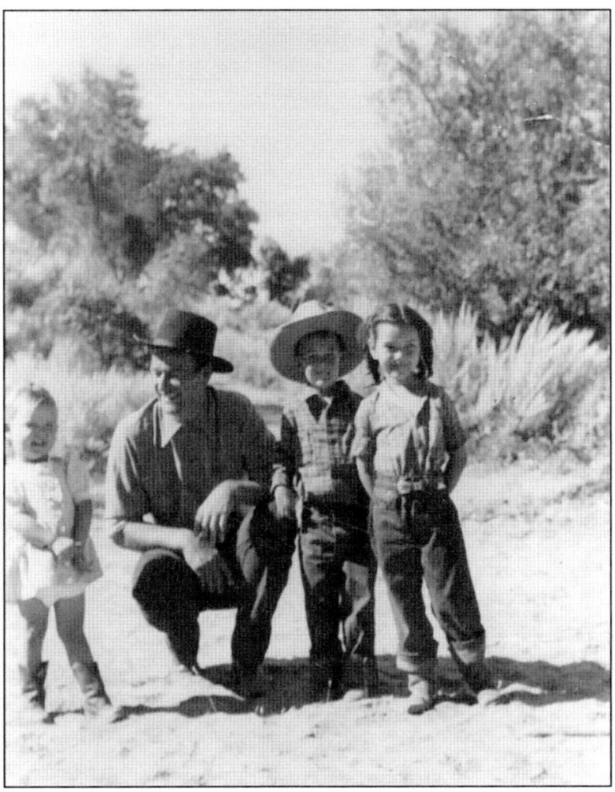

John Wayne enjoys the company of Brenda Halleman Richardson (left) and Melinda Halleman Baker (right) along with Johnny Coop. The Furze granddaughters recall that their father gave Wayne horseback riding lessons to prepare him for his Western movies. Wayne also visited the "real cowboys" at the Warner ranch house. Movie stars visiting the ranch were given the respect of privacy.

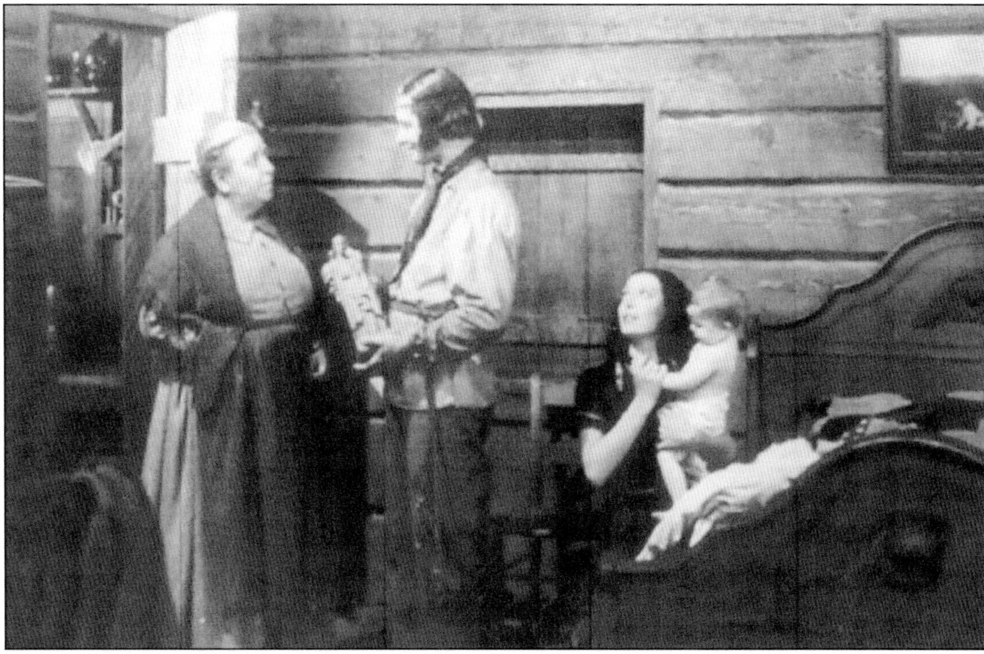

Ramona was filmed at Warner Hot Springs in 1936, and many sets built for the movie remained until the 1950s. Loretta Young (second from right) and Don Ameche star in this version. Film was flown from the airport to Hollywood for editing. The daughter of Arthur and Theresa Taylor, Marian "Tiny" Taylor (McGill) is the baby in the picture. Her toes would be pinched to make her cry for certain scenes. Also pictured in this scene is actress Jane Darwell (left).

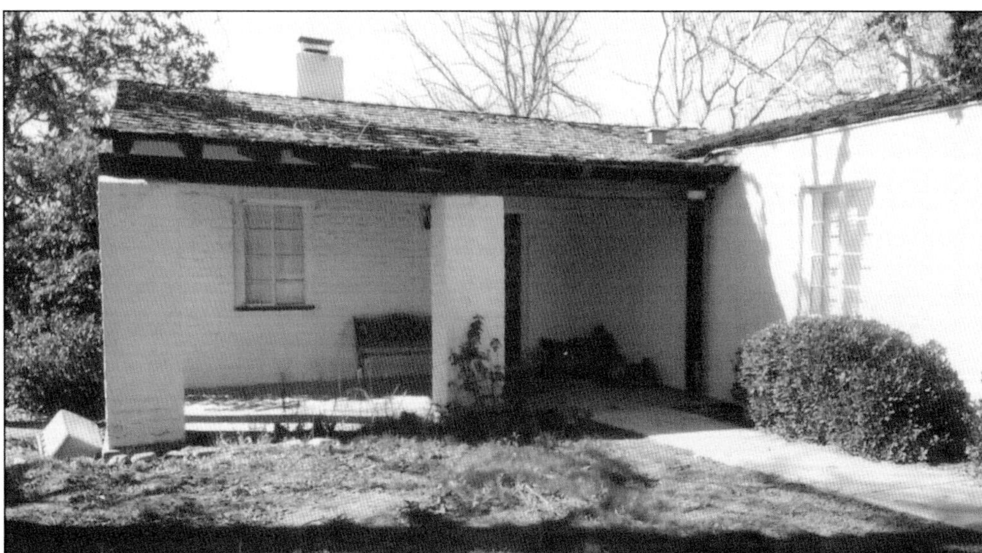

Shown here is the Loretta Young Adobe on the west side of Highway 79, next door to the present post office. It was built specifically for Loretta Young during the filming of *Ramona*. For many years, it was the office of Warner Springs Realty and longtime Los Tules resident Paul Newell, author of the recent best-selling book *Empty Mansions*.

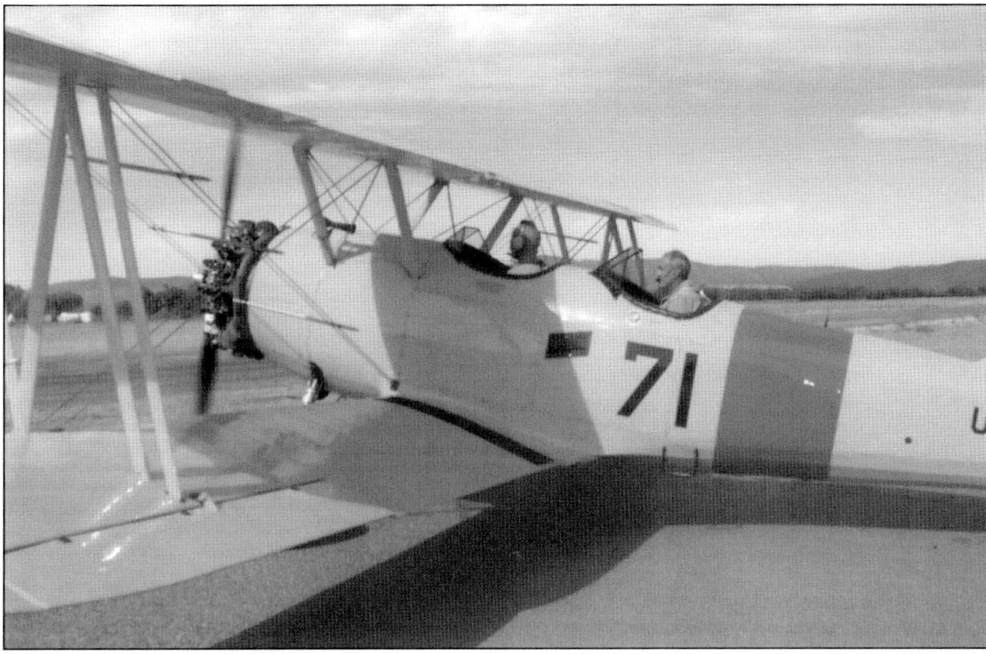

The Warner Springs Airport has been part of the resort for many years. During World War II, pilots in training conducted touch-and-go landings here. Los Tules resident Jon Goldenbaum, a jet pilot in Vietnam, is shown here in his restored biplane, a Navy version of a Stearman training plane. (Courtesy Kathryn Fletcher.)

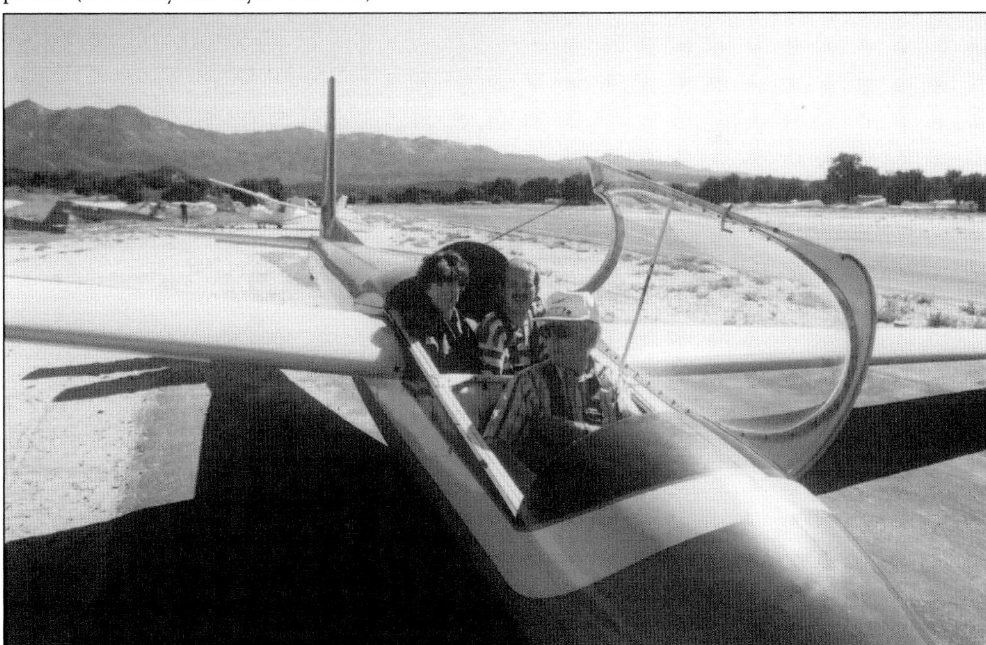

Sky sailing, or glider rides, is popular at Warner Springs and a great way to see the Warner Valley. Piloted rides and lessons are available from the longtime operators of the airport, the Willat family. Both sons are world-class sailplane pilots, and Warner Springs attracts enthusiasts from around the world due to its ideal location and wonderful thermal drafts.

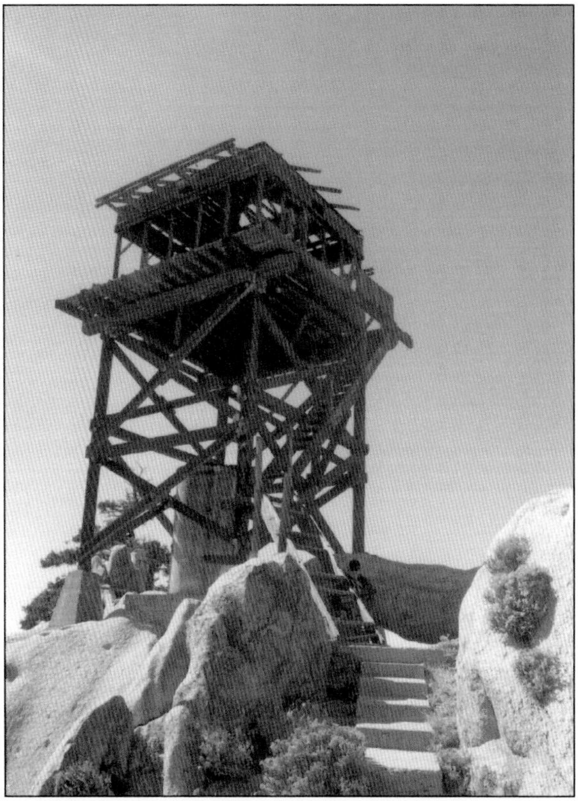

Seen by sailplane passengers is the smoke tower on the peak of Hot Springs Mountain. It may be restored, as have the Mount Palomar towers, and staffed with volunteers. From here, there is fabulous view of the Warner Valley, the Anza Borrego Desert, and on a clear day, the Pacific Ocean. On the land of the Los Coyotes Indian Reservation, the tower can only be reached with their permission and in a high-clearance, four-wheel-drive vehicle.

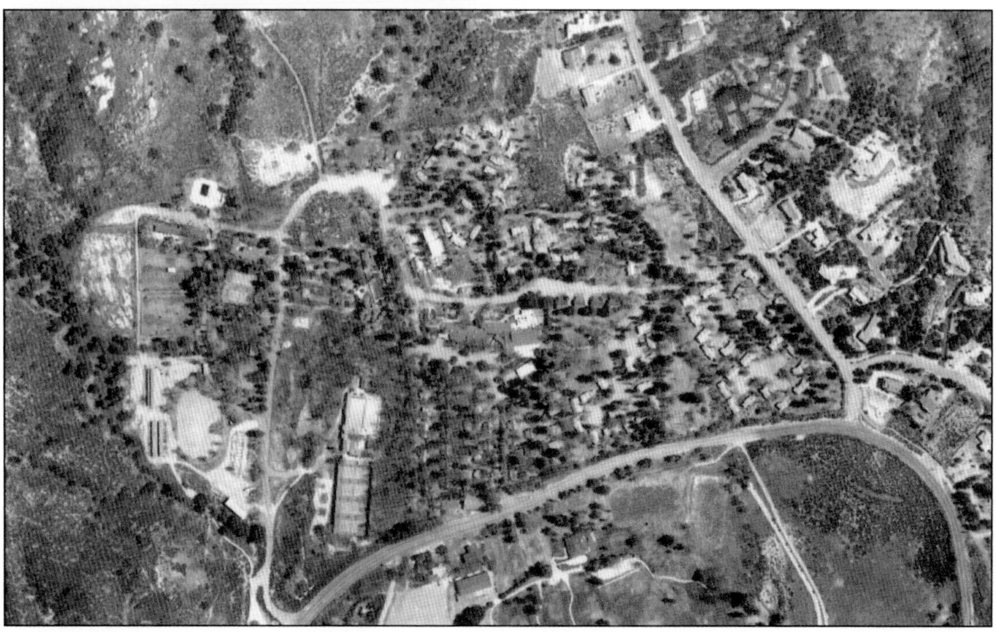

This aerial photograph shows Warner Hot Springs Ranch as it is today. The equestrian facility, hot springs, pools, lodge, casitas, and other resort buildings are east of the highway at the top of the picture, the golf course to the west, and portions of the residential community of Los Tules to the south.

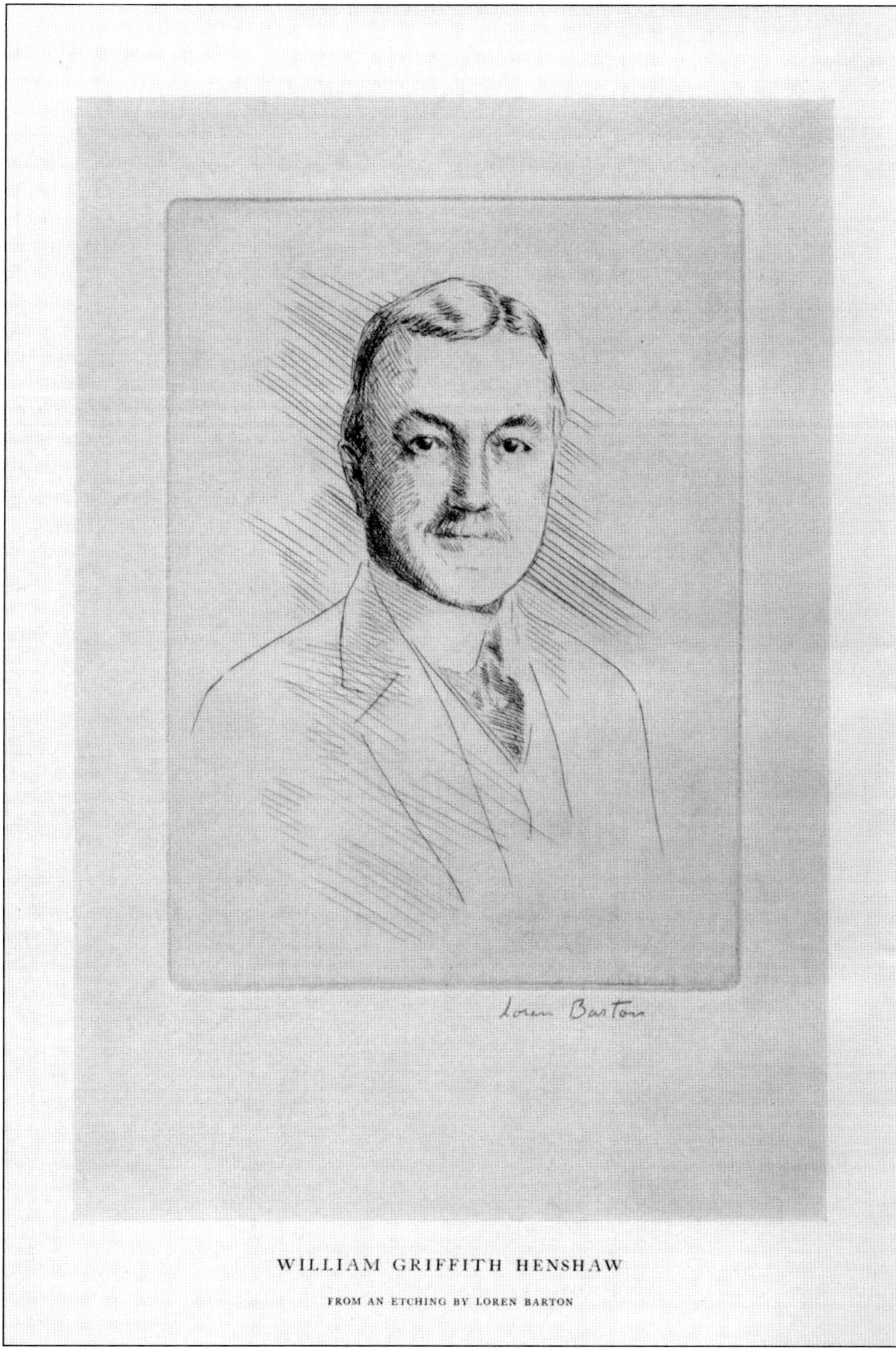

William Griffith Henshaw, a pioneer, entrepreneur, developer, visionary, and one of the most important people in the history of San Diego County, was born in 1860 and died in 1924.

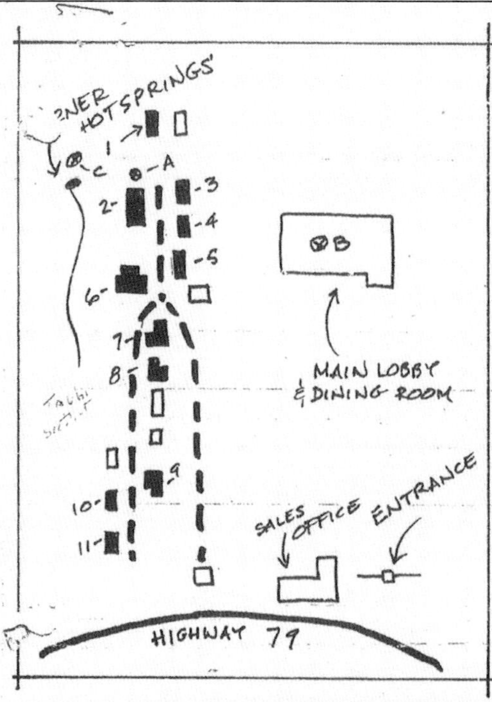

WARNER SPRINGS (CUPA VILLAGE)

There are at least 17 adobes remaining from the Cupeño Indian village of Cupa, just to the east of the hot springs. All were built between about 1830 & 1903, when the Cupeño were "removed" to the reservation at Pala. Roscinda Nolasquez (1892-1987) was the last surviving native of Cupa & identified the owners of some of these adobes for me.

1- Andreas Moro

2- Adolfo Moro (1836-1925). Moro was a northern California Indian ~~who came~~ here in the early days & married into a very prominent family. This adobe was built by the Mission San Luis Rey around 1830 as a granary, I presume. Moro's father-in-law, Jose Maria Moro, who was "Captain" (chief) of the tribe for many years lived here before him. Before that this may have been the home of Jose Nocá, who the missionaries appointed as Captain.

3- This was the Nolasquez family home, where Roscinda grew up. The family also had a second home (now gone) closer to Los Tules to the east.

4 -Juan Maria Cibimoat. Cibimoat (or Blacktooth, an English rendition of his clan name) was Captain at the time of the Removal in '03 — mostly because no one else wanted the job.

5- Valentine LaChappa

6- Gabriel Cibimoat. A nephew of Juan Maria?

7- Leonardo Owlinguish (ca 1813-1905). Owlinguish was one of the patriarchs of the tribe, whose memories extended back to the days of the Missions & the coming of the Americans. He was also Roscinda's godfather, I believe. Several photos of him survive.

The hand-drawn map and notes on this page and the next were done by historian Phil Brigandi, who had the opportunity in 1983 to interview Roscinda Nolasquez. Brigandi has also written extensively on Losy Valley and the Boy Scout camp there. He has been a wonderful speaker at the ranch about the removal of the Cupa and a contributor to the historical society.

2

8- JUAN OWLINGUISH. Leonardo's son. He was still living in 1919 at the age of 75.

9- Manuella Cibimoat (1852-1927). She and her daughter, Salvadora, were important "informants" for several early-day anthropologists.

10 - F. Lyons. This is one of several Cupa families who acquired anglo names through intermarriage in the 19th Century.

11- "Pancho" Chutnicut.

Other points of Interest...

A- Just below the Moro adobe, on the trail to the spring, is a flat rock that was once a powerful lady doctor. One day, she lay down here & became a rock, but the people still came to see her with their ailments — even Roscinda stopped to rub her arthritic hands on her when we visited here in August, 1988.

B- The main lobby & dining room are built on the site of the old ceremonial grounds, where funeral rites & other important activities took place.

C- Above the spring is the 'Rock where the fleas came out' ("Mekwashma" ?), one of the many spots associated with Cupeño mythology.

And, of course, there is the spring itself ("Palatingua"), the center of Cupeño life for centuries.

Though I have some questions about its history (I suspect it was built more like 1893 than 1831) you may also want to visit the old chapel . . . and you really should visit the cemetery behind it, where Roscinda and an untold number of her people are buried.

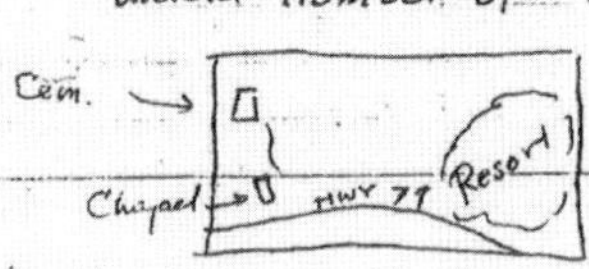

Phil Brigandi
10-7-88

Phil Brigandi

A continuation of the interview with Roscinda Nolasquez, this page further delineates the original owners of the Cupeño adobes, many of whom intermarried in the 19th century and assumed Anglo names. It also has several points of interest from his interview, including descriptions of the Mother Rock and Flea Rock.

CUPENO ADOBES AT WARNER HOT SPRINGS

Rosalinda Nolasquez (1892 - 1987) was the last of the Cupenos to have lived at Cupa and is buried in the graveyard behind the chapel. In August of 1983 she provided the names of several of the owners of the old adobes, and pointed out a number of other spots around the springs. Until the last remodel the adobes all bore names instead of numbers. This guide is intended to help visitors match up the present day numbers with the old photos and original names. Julio Oretga, an early pioneer, wrangler and long time resident is said to have done some of the naming of the adobes.

70/71	"Ramona" this was the adobe used in the filming of Ramona. Star Loretta Lynn stayed in the Real estate office adobe which was built for her.
72	"Tacupin" was the home of "Pancho" or Francisco Chutnicut (1872-1941), a member of a prominent family at the turn of the century.
73/74	"Ticanu" was the home of Florence and Amy Lyons.
75/76	"Mataguay " and "Manzanita" were the homes of Manuella Cibimoat Griffith (1852-1927)
77	"Tumca"
78/79	"Curilla"
80	"Wilikil"
81	"Tauhi" was the home of Juan Aulinguish
82	"Tomiki" was the site of the Leonardo Aulingish home (1813-1905)
83/84	"Capatay" was the home of Gabriel Cibimoat
85/86	"Tucomac"
87	"Kupa" was the home of Valentine La Chappa
88	"Pamo" was the home of Juan Maria Cibimoat who was the Captain at the time of the 1903 removal.
89/90	This is the best candidate for a mission-era adobe at the springs. It was the home of Adolpho Moro (1836-1925) in Roscinda's day and Juan Maria Moro before that. Perhaps also Jose Noca and even Antonia Garra (leader of the Garra raid on John Warner).
91/92	"Awanga" and "Pala" Home of Salvador Nolasquez (1861-1933). Roscinda was born here in 1892.
A	Andres Moro lived up here on the rise and parts of his adobe may survive in the building on the right.
B	Home of Judge Vicente Cabimas - shown in the oft reproduced Lummis "junta" photo taken in 1902.
C	Unidentified adobe
D the	The walls of the cantina reportedly contain part of an old adobe, The left portion of the lodge covers the rocks where "first people" slept when they came to Cupa. Image burning ceremonies and other important ceremonies happened here.

The first "Tourist cabins" at the springs were those numbered 54-69 and perhaps in the 40's as well. The building south of the cantina marked "Tienda" across from the old tennis courts was a store or market in Roscinda's day.

This page was produced from the Brigandi interview and is a legend intended to help present-day historians identify the current adobe building names and numbers with their original Cupeño owners. It is said that longtime wrangler and tourist guide Julio Ortega helped to give the buildings their names.

Ramona

Filmed on or near Warner Springs Ranch in 1935

The house that presently stands next to the Post Office is said to have been built for Loretta Young to live in while starring in the movie.

The Airport runway is said to have been built for the director, Mr. King, to use to fly to Hollywood to edit the film and fly back.

The movie took place in the 1870's and the town of Temecula is mentioned in it.

Recognizable Scenery

Opening scene	- "North Pasture" near cemetery.
Following scene	- Orchard that is now the Golf Course.
Exterior view through Hacienda Gate	- Appears to be toward Palomar.
Ramona initially meets Padre	- "North Pasture" south of new wells (old Navy training area).
Indians ride in	- Possibly near Chimney Lakes (south of airport). View looks south toward Lake Henshaw (not in view).
Alessandro rescues Ramona from Apple Tree	- Orchard in area before Golf course was built.
Match races	- Appear to be in Old Warner Ranch north of S-2. Mountains in background appear to be Los Coyotes Reservation, including Hot Springs Mountain.
Marriage breakfast	- Orchard before Golf Course
Leaving Chapel after marriage	– Mesa Grande Chapel
Crying Baby	- Two babies were used. One was Tammy McGill's mother. It is said that her toes were pinched so she'd cry.
Alessandro drives sheep	- Meadow near Chimney Lake. Hot Springs Mountain to right in background.
Burning homes	- "North pasture" north of cemetery. View is from west. Alessandro gallops in from north.
In cart going somewhere else	- Turn off of Hwy 76 on Mesa Grande Road then up hill on Mesa Grande Ridge
Ride to Dr. in San Bernardino	- Through Chaney Ranch.
Alessandro stole horse	- May be Old Warner Ranch.
Funeral walk	- Appears to be in campground.

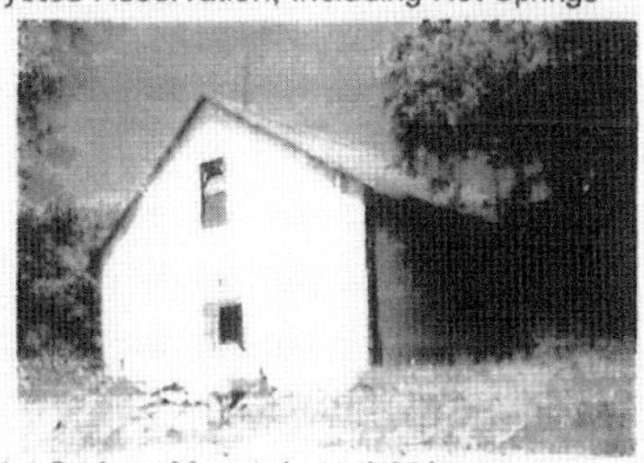

Found on this page are the locations on the Warner Springs Ranch used in 1935 for the filming of *Ramona*, which was released in 1936. The story, by Helen Hunt Jackson, was based on the true story of a Cahuilla Indian. The *Uncle Tom's Cabin* of its day, it focused attention on the plight of Native Americans. The film is still available for viewing, and the book became the basis for the famous annual outdoor Ramona Pageant, held in Hemet, California.

OWNERS AND GENERAL MANAGERS AT WARNER HOT SPRINGS ALSO KNOWN AS WARNER SPRINGS RANCH

1868 - 1908 GOVERNOR JOHN DOWNEY AND HEIRS

1908-1975 WILLIAM HENSHAW/WARNER RESORT COMPANY

1914 Eugene Batchelder and Ed Fletcher
1920's Guy Woodward and Ralph Jasper
1930-1939 E.B. Hewlett,
1939-1952 Sid Furze
1952-1965 Thomas O'Hara and John Koop
After 1965 Glen Faucett
1968-1971 Ed Maler and Mr. Gray
1972 Dan Miles

1975-1979 CAL ROSSI FIRST PHASE

1976 Dan Varner (West German lease period)
1979 Claude Banner
1981 EST Private Education Organization rented from Rossi

1981 - 1990 CAL ROSSI SECOND PHASE

1983 Coleen Griswold
1984 Bob Phillips
1985 Erialios , Enteman and Carol Bleck
1987 Fred Mayo
1989 Jim Kennedy and Harry Rayfield (interim)

1990 - 1991 SANTA FE MANAGEMENT ERA

1990 Alpheus Bruton, 1991 Biggs, Brian Mau

1991 - 2010 WARNER SPRINGS RANCH OWNERS ASSOCIATION ERA

1991 Don Davis
1995 Vernita Loveridge and David Waymire
1998 John Schmidt
2001 John Girsdorf
2004 Lori Schwank
2004-2005 David Lowe (Interim)
2005 Luis Izurieta
2006 - 2007 David Lowe (Interim)
2007 - 2010 Jim Stilwell

2013 WARNER SPRINGS RANCH RESORT

Fred Grand President, Bill Mc Whethy CEO

This page is a guide to the owners and general managers of Warner Hot Springs from 1868 to the present.

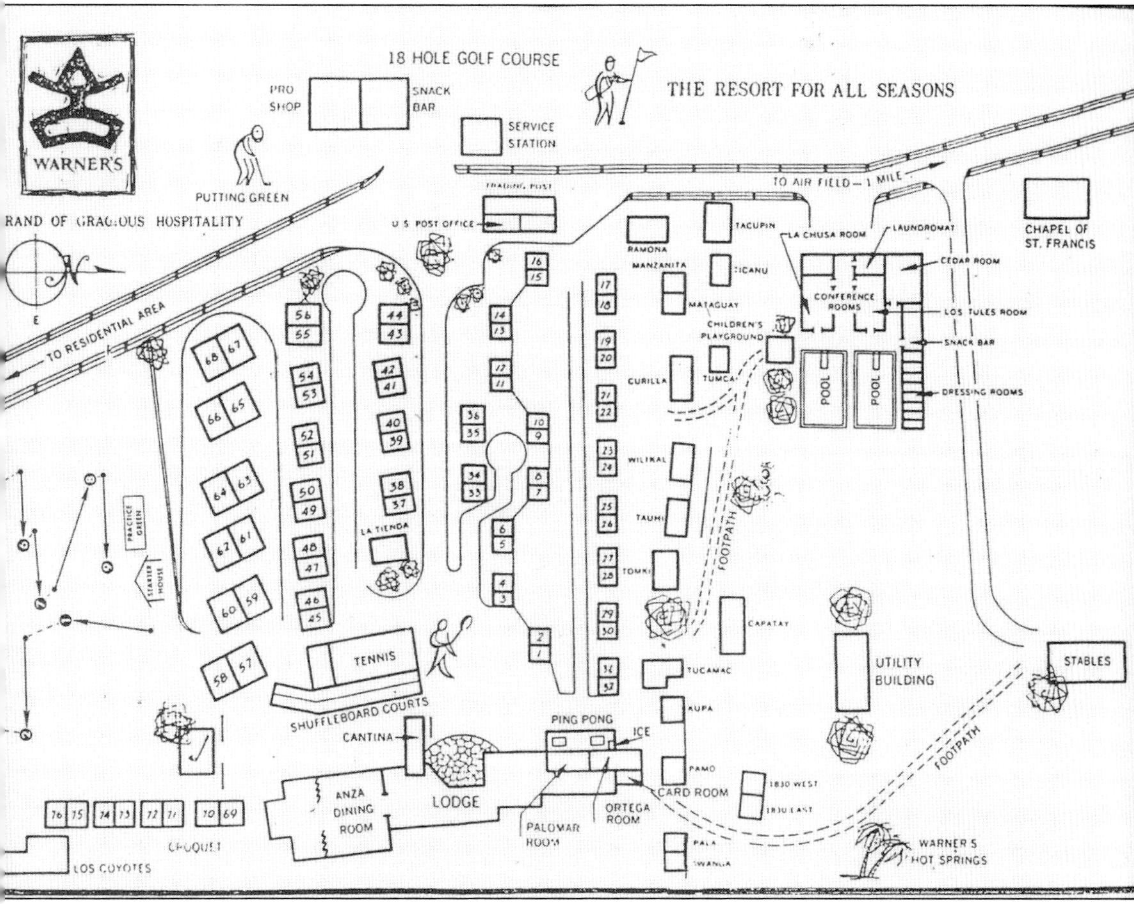

This page is a schematic representation of Warner Hot Springs as it was during the Henshaw days. It was handed out to guests as a guide to the ranch. Information obtainable at the history room at the main lodge and historical signs and plaques made learning the history of the area interesting for visitors and hopefully will again in the future.

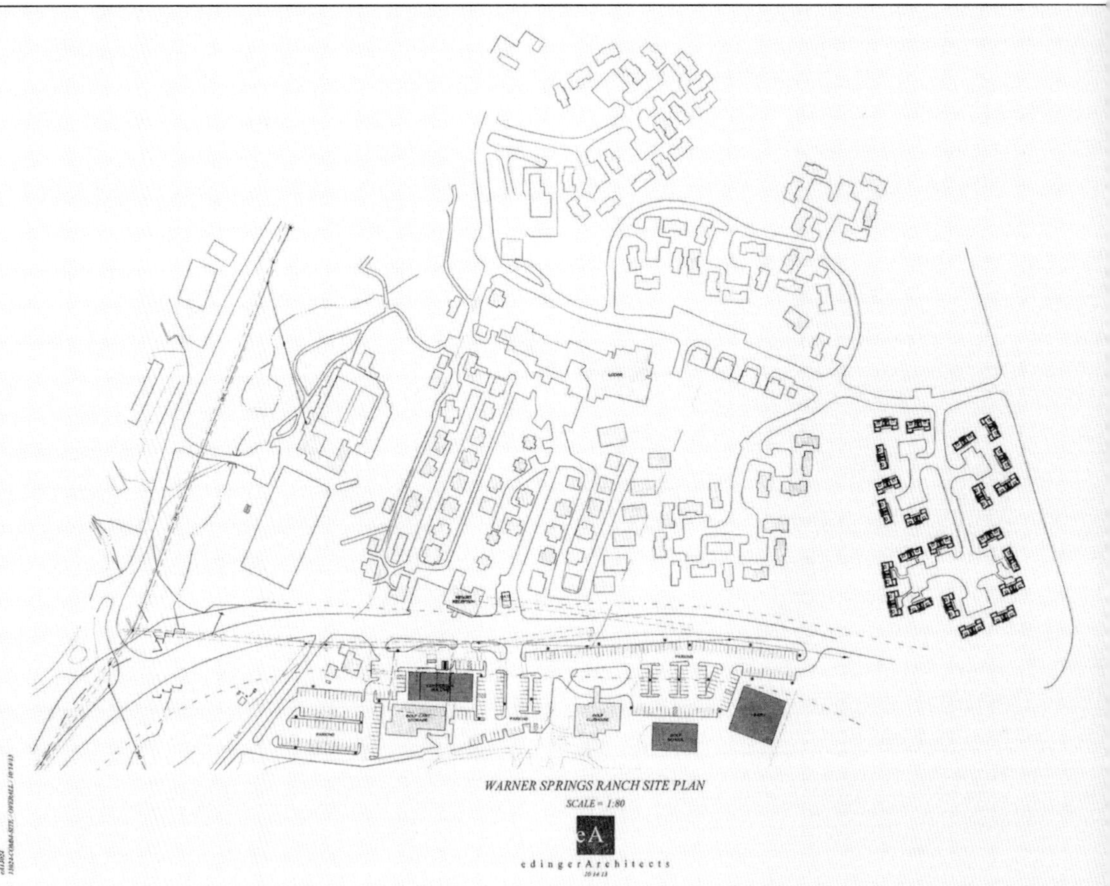

This page is the site plan for the future development of Warner Hot Springs as Warner Springs Ranch Resort. Extensive research and an environmental impact report on this historic property must be completed before renovation and new development can take place. It is hoped that with new plans for renovation and development, the historic Warner Springs Ranch will be preserved and can be returned to its glory days and enjoyed by new generations of families.

About the Warner Springs Historical Society

After 1975, the ranch was sold by the Henshaw family to A. Cal Rossi, Bing Crosby, and the Dennis Development Company for $2.8 million, and a new concept of offering memberships as proprietary undivided interests in the 2,512 acres was developed. The listed charter membership price was $17,500, after opening at $25,000 or more. Frustrated with his inability to raise capital, Rossi sold out in 1986 for $10 million to American Ranch Ferien GmbH & Co. Problems before that time and since saw a series of lessees, owners, and bankruptcies, with the property returning to Rossi. Finally, the Warner Springs Ranch Owners Association was formed to hold it as a private/semipublic time-share resort for many years until the ranch went into bankruptcy and was bought by Pacific Hospitality Group of San Diego in 2013.

Under the Warner Springs Ranch Owners Association, Terry Chambers, historian at the Sherman Foundation Library and Gardens in Corona del Mar, California, founded the Warner Springs Historical Committee in 1990 and the Warner Springs History Center in the lodge in 1992. In order to explore and preserve the history of the area and share it with visitors, Terry put together information in dated files of various eras of ownership of the ranch with photographs. This includes invaluable legal papers and surveys, oral interviews, and personal diaries. He also wrote many guides for the enjoyment of visitors, including the *History of Warner Springs Country* pamphlets, which were sold for income for the historical committee.

Terry and a committee of interested ranch membership owners and local amateur historians also welcomed materials and photographs from visitors, and some of these are included in this publication.

Betty Rayfield, former teacher and Los Tules resident, took over from Terry in the later 1990s and was a driving force in preserving the history. She was instrumental in continuing to gather materials and put together popular programs like newsletters, history articles, and quarterly speakers. She also conducted tours for groups like Elderhostel, JPL scientists, educational groups, and others. In 2008, Betty and the author held a very successful 150th Anniversary Celebration of the Butterfield Stage Route at Warner Springs Ranch. The Copley family kindly agreed to loan the famous Marjorie Reed paintings of the route from their collection, and author Gary Fillmore conducted a lecture and book signing on his recently released book *All Aboard: The Life and Work of Marjorie Reed*. A portion of the proceeds raised went to the restoration of the Warner-Carrillo Ranch House.

When Betty's health was failing and it was apparent that the Warner Springs Ranch Owners Association would be putting the resort up for sale, she asked her neighbor, committee member and author of this book Kathryn Fletcher to take over her position, which I did in 2010. Most important to Betty was the preservation of the historical committee's archives and photographs and the collection of pottery, baskets, grinding stones, mud wagon, mining cart, and other historical items for the public good. The first order of business for me was to photograph and inventory everything. The second in 2001 was to get the board of directors of the Warner Springs Ranch Owners Association to declare that the collection and archives were gathered for the public good and were not assets of the ranch to be sold.

With the sale of the ranch approaching, an online auction was held to sell duplicate items and memorabilia from the ranch to former ranch owners and raise money to preserve and protect the collection for the future. This sadly included a Marjorie Reed painting, but the funds raised made preserving and moving the collection possible. The committee then became the Warner Springs Historical Society. Various members of the committee gathered the collection together and moved it into storage, then to the Warner Resource Center, until it could be moved to its present home at the Warner Carrillo Ranch House under the umbrella of Save Our Heritage Organisation. After the collection's initial move, Betty passed away, content in knowing that the collection and her years of work would be preserved.

The work of preserving and sharing the history of Warner Hot Springs and the Warner Ranch are ongoing, and volunteers are welcome to become members of the society. They may also wish to visit the Warner-Carrillo Ranch House Museum and restored Santa Ysabel Mercantile Store, both preservation projects of Save Our Heritage Organisation. Visit the website at www.SOHOsandiego.org for more information.

Bibliography

Fletcher, Ed. *Memoirs*. San Diego: Pioneer Printers, 1952.

———. Papers. Special Collections & Archives, University of California at San Diego Library.

Greene, Henry Dart. *The Memoirs of Henry Dart Green and Ruth Elizabeth Haight Greene*. La Jolla, CA: Virginia Dart Greene Hales Publisher, 1996.

Hayes, Benjamin. "Journey Overland Diary 1850." In *History of California*, vol. 18, by Hubert Howe Bancroft. San Francisco: History Company, 1884.

Henshaw, Griffith. Letters to Terry Chambers, founder of the Warner Springs Historical Committee. Warner Springs Historical Society Collection.

Hill, Joseph J. *History of Warner Springs and Its Environs*. Los Angeles: Privately printed by John Treanor, 1927.

Julian Sentinel. Various issues, 1903–1908.

Long, Helen O. and Robert W. *Diary of the One Room School at Warner's Ranch 1937–1939*. San Diego: Privately published, 1983.

Morrison, Lorin L. *Warner: The Man and the Ranch*. Los Angeles: self-published, 1962.

Murphy, Garth. *The Indian Lover*. New York: Simon & Schuster, 2002.

Pourade, Richard F. *The History of San Diego: The Glory Years*. Vol. 4. San Diego: Copley Press, 1964.

Reed, Lester. *Old Timers of Southeastern California*. Redlands, CA: Citrograph Printing Co., 1967.

San Diego Historical Society Archives.

Schairer, Mary Treanor. *May the Circle Be Unbroken*. San Diego: Printed privately for the family of John and Elizabeth Treanor, 2006.

Sherman Foundation Library Archives, Corona del Mar, CA.

Vail, Edward. "Diary of a Desert Trail." *Arizona Daily Star*, February 22, 1922.

Discover Thousands of Local History Books Featuring Millions of Vintage Images

Arcadia Publishing, the leading local history publisher in the United States, is committed to making history accessible and meaningful through publishing books that celebrate and preserve the heritage of America's people and places.

Find more books like this at
www.arcadiapublishing.com

Search for your hometown history, your old stomping grounds, and even your favorite sports team.

Consistent with our mission to preserve history on a local level, this book was printed in South Carolina on American-made paper and manufactured entirely in the United States. Products carrying the accredited Forest Stewardship Council (FSC) label are printed on 100 percent FSC-certified paper.

MADE IN THE USA